ARCTIC OCEAN

RUSSIA

ST. MATTHEW IS.

BERING SEA

ST. PAUL IS.

PRIBILOF
ISLANDS

ST. GEORGE IS.

KAMCHATKA
PENINSULA

KOMANDORSKIYE IS.
(COMMANDER IS.)

ATTU IS.

ONALASI

PACIFIC OCEAN

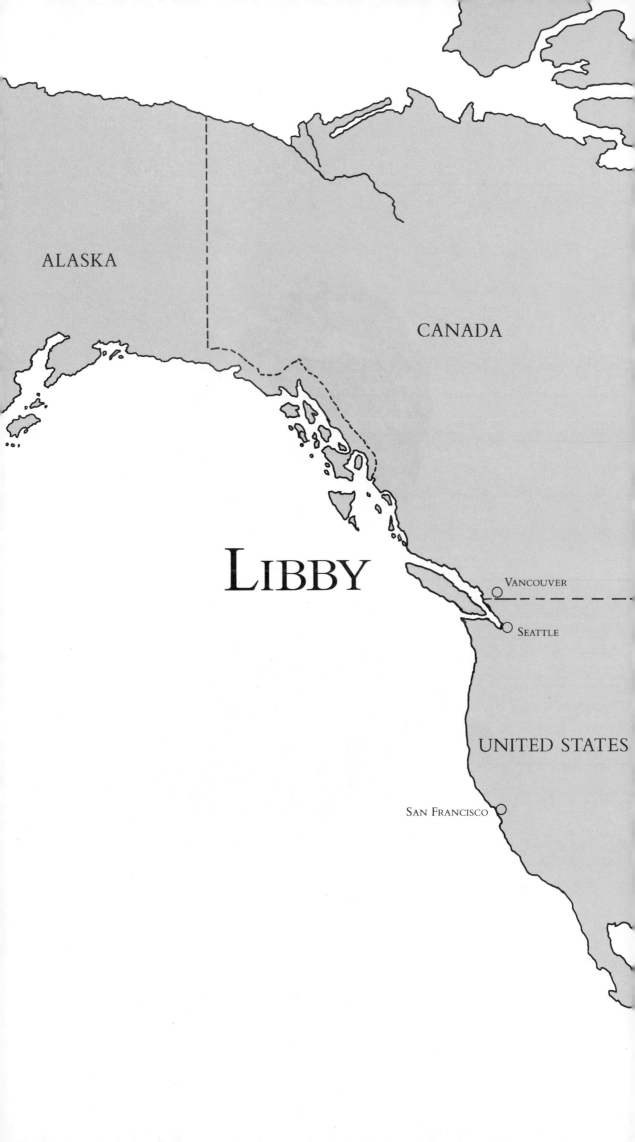

Elizabeth Beaman

LIBBY

The Sketches, Letters & Journal
of LIBBY BEAMAN,
Recorded in the Pribilof Islands
1 8 7 9 · 1 8 8 0

as Presented by her Granddaughter
BETTY JOHN

Published by Council Oak Books · Tulsa, Oklahoma

COUNCIL OAK BOOKS
1428 SOUTH ST. LOUIS
TULSA, OKLAHOMA 74120
800/247-8850
918/587-6454 in Oklahoma

DISTRIBUTED BY
INDEPENDENT PUBLISHERS GROUP
814 NORTH FRANKLIN
CHICAGO, ILLINOIS 60610
312/337-0747

ISBN 0-933031-09-2

Library of Congress Catalogue Card Number 87-071438

Manufactured in the United States of America

BOOK AND COVER DESIGN BY CAROL HARALSON.

Editor's Note: Libby's drawings are those which do not bear an artist's name but are identified by captions only.

AW

*To Charlotte Denise and Mary Caroline
and to the memory of Gertrude Susan,
my sisters
and
Libby's granddaughters*

BJ

FOREWORD

Today there's a landing strip on St. Paul Island, the Pribilofs. Though socked in most of the time by the same sort of dense fogs that have always shrouded these Seal Islands from the world, they can be reached in minutes by plane from Alaska or the Aleutians. There now is also radio and telecommunication. But the sea around the islands remains just as turbulent as in Libby's time. The roiling waters, the fogs, the storms, and the strange tides combine to make the islands as remote and isolated as they were in the 1870s when my grandmother, Elizabeth DuBois Beaman, sailed there with my grandfather, John Warren Beaman, to become the first non-native American woman to set foot on the Pribilofs.

During Libby's long life, she was extremely reticent about her personal experiences there. She told us about the Aleuts who lived there, about the animals and the flowers, and about the weather — little about herself. She permitted her grandchildren to look over her shoulder as she turned the pages of her sketchbook or her journal. We never could touch them.

The first time I actually held her sketches and read her journal was many years later when I found them in an old trunk in my father's office. I had several of these items photographed. However, my father refused to let me keep the originals, and when I finally inherited her sketches and journal, many of Libby's sketches and even some pages of her journal had disappeared.

In Libby's book, therefore, I've had to fill in some gaps by conjuring up memories of the stories she told me and by doing research into her times. Her story, nonetheless, is the true tale of a very real woman who braved the hazards of the Bering Sea and life on our country's most remote outpost.

The United States government has supplanted the Alaska Commercial Company and now operates the fur seal industry exclusively. The pelts no longer are sent to England in sailing vessels to be processed but are brought to a Pacific port in navy ships, then are transshipped to South Carolina, where a single firm processes the pelts.

The adventure, the drama, and the romance of America's early presence in the Pribilofs is preserved in the brief pages in which Libby recorded not only her own intense and private experiences but also the history through which she lived.

BETTY JOHN
Summer 1987

I BEGIN THIS JOURNAL WITH MANY MISGIVINGS. My brother Charles gave me this diary at the moment of parting from my family in Washington, D.C. I can hear his voice even now, husky for Charles, as he handed it to me. "Keep a record, Libby, everything as it happens to you. Promise me you will. What you will be doing will be so strange to us, so foreign, so unusual. Where you are going lies far beyond our comprehension. Write it all down. One forgets too quickly."

Forget?

How can I forget a single moment of this?

I could not write the first night, nor could I yesterday. I do not know how to weep in words. Pribilov. Pribylov. Pribylof. Prybilof. Pribyloff. Prybiloff. Pribilof —

ABOARD THE S⟨ᵗ⟩ PAUL

1 · 8 · 7 · 9

Two tiny pin dots, the Seal Islands, the islands of St Paul and St George in the Bering Sea — 2,250 miles from San Francisco, more than 5,000 miles from home — almost, but not quite, within the Arctic Circle. My husband, John Warren Beaman, and I are aboard the *S.S. St Paul*. We are sailing there.

We boarded the *S.S. St Paul* in San Francisco late the afternoon of May 9th. This is the very latest type of sailing vessel, with an auxiliary steam engine in case the sails fail. It is the first ship of its kind on the Pacific and had to come around the Strait of Magellan from the yards in New London where it was built. Captain Erskine, who brought it from New England, has been its only captain. It has been owned by the Alaska Commercial Company for these past ten years.

Captain Erskine inspired our confidence the moment we met him, and he has been most kind to me. I am the only woman aboard. But Captain Erskine says I have a greater distinction. I am the first white woman, the first American woman, to sail to the Aleutians and to the Pribilofs!

Should I be proud of another first?

SAN FRANCISCO BAY

San Francisco Bay,
1879 — That is the
St Paul riding at
anchor in the bay
called the Golden
Gate.

Any enthusiasm I may have had when he said that was quickly dispelled the very first evening aboard ship as we entered the dining saloon. All eyes turned toward us, some indifferent and some unfriendly. There was a sudden silence. Captain Erskine broke away from one small group of men and hurried toward us, greeting us cordially and reminding us that he had asked us to sit at his table for the voyage. His was the only friendly gesture. Most of the men he introduced us to left the ship immediately after eating. They were Alaska Commercial Company officials who had been aboard only to discuss business with the captain during dinner. From time to time, the ship's officers tried to make conversation with us, but that too seemed difficult.

Just as we were rising from the table, a new man entered the saloon. He was almost as tall as John — who is six feet — and though in civilian clothes, he had a military air about him. He commanded attention, though he was unaware of it. I sensed, rather than saw, John stiffen slightly. Captain Erskine rose to greet the new man. The two shook hands in a warm, friendly handclasp and exchanged a few words. Then the newcomer came directly to John.

"Well, Beaman," he said gruffly, and there was no longer the pleasure of seeing Captain Erskine in his eyes, "you did bring your wife after all. I should like to meet her."

I could scarcely believe John when he introduced me to his immediate superior officer, the Treasury Department senior agent, the man to whom John will be junior agent on the Seal Islands, the man with whom we have to share our lives for the next two years. Though John introduced him by name, I never shall name him. He will remain the Senior Agent, SA, no matter what happens.

"I never believed for one moment that you would actually be going up there," he said to me in a crisp, businesslike voice that had no warmth in it. "I still cannot believe it."

"But as you can see, I am," I assured him with a faint smile. I was uncertain just how I should talk to him. He had unnerved me by his brusque manner and obvious disapproval. And I never had heard anyone address my husband by his last name only. In fact, in all my life, I never had heard a gentleman addressed in such a way. I wanted to show my anger at this rudeness. I wanted to put him in his place. But I dared not. This was John's superior officer.

"The most unwise and foolhardy thing I've ever heard of," he said to me. To John he said, "I thought I told you, in our very first interview, the reasons your wife should not accompany you, Beaman."

"*Mister* Beaman," John said, knowing, as I knew the moment he said it, that he'd gotten off on the wrong foot with the SA. I was proud of John, however, for standing up for a principle in a black

moment, our blackest since coming aboard. The "mister" is a
small thing in itself, but no one in our household, or in John's for
that matter, ever had used any other form of address. First names
always have been reserved for the most intimate relationships, and
last names without the "mister" only for those unworthy to be
addressed with the "mister."

If we can keep small courtesies between us, perhaps we can
weather this unusual relationship with the SA. Thinking
back, I remember John making a point of what a
gentleman the Senior Agent was, after his first
interview with him in San Francisco.

Captain Erskine, sensing conflict, came over to us
and announced that since the SA had come aboard,
there was no reason to hold the ship in port longer
and that we'd be setting sail before midnight rather
than before dawn as planned. Onalaska (Unalaska?
Oonalaska?) would be our first port of call, and St Paul,
the Pribilofs, the next. This is the earliest possible date the
ship can sail because of the icebergs and the treacherous seasonal
storms. The captain said, too, that most of the company men
aboard were anxious to get to the Pribilofs as soon as possible.
They wanted to get there before the female seals hauled up
to have their pups and before the breeding season began. I
colored at this last statement. I think I shall have much to
learn.

SAN FRANCISCO BAY

13

John suggested we retire early rather than prolong an awkward situation. I was tired and upset, so I agreed. We excused ourselves politely and returned to this stateroom, where the ship's one steward had lit the seal-oil lamps and turned down our bunks — a service I had not expected, but which seemed a warming note after the chill of the evening's experience. I could not bring myself to ask John what he thought of all that had taken place. He offered no explanation on his own and busied himself about the cabin so obviously I knew he did not wish to talk. I could see that he was upset. His only comment came unsolicited. "He's a gruff man, Libby. We'll just have to take him as he is."

I kept thinking, as we silently unpacked and puttered about our stateroom, that I really should have been packing my own things so I could leave the ship before it sailed. The Senior Agent had shown his displeasure in such a way that going on took on the quality of a nightmare just begun. Obviously, he had wanted John to make me go ashore. The thoughts kept racing through my mind — *Should I? Should I? But what of John alone? Would my staying behind make matters any easier for him since the two men already had established their personal antagonism? Or do men just forgive and forget when one has gotten his way?*

I hadn't paused to speculate about myself left alone in the dark on a wharf in San Francisco or about where I would stay another two years away from John. Had I, there never would have been this turmoil. I had elected to go with him, and that I would.

Shouting came from the wharf and from above in the sails. We could hear commands and answering shouts, the padding of bare feet on the wooden deck, and voices outside our door. Suddenly the full realization of what was happening swept over me. We had cast anchor. We were going away from those few lights on shore — away from the solid earth that was the United States — going out into a black, black night, into the unknown, into an Arctic adventure for which we were scarcely prepared.

And whose fault was this journey? Mine.

We watched the lights falling away from us, as we stood silent, too full to speak. John's arm grew so tight about my shoulders that his grip hurt, though I dared not let him know. The hurt was so much ours together.

The air grew cooler as the ship began to move. I could not sleep for thinking.

Night silence on vast, calm waters is a stillness I've never known. I listened for sounds of shore, of land. But there were none, only the soft creaking and crunching of well-weathered planks as we rose and fell on broad swells. We heard the occasional call of the watch — all else was silence and no more light. The last beams from the shore had filtered through the lattice slats of our window shutters. I arose and peeked out, looking for the stars. Only the ship's lantern, far above in the crow's nest, gleamed in the mist like a guiding star. I went back to bed but not to sleep.

Sometime after midnight, I felt, rather than heard, the ship thud against a solid mass, heard the splash and suck of water between a ship and a solid object — the same sound it had made alongside the dock when we were in port. I heard the soft shouts of men — commands, answers, swearings — all muffled as sounds are muffled by night and fog. Faint light again filtered through our shutters briefly. Then all grew dark and quiet except for the slapping of the water and the soft groaning of the ship as it rose and fell at anchor.

Had we gone back to port? Had the Senior Agent commanded the return of the ship to put me off? Could he do such a thing? Would not the Treasury Department, with whom John had signed a contract, have told him way back in Washington that I could not go with him? I know he informed them that I would be going with him. Even President Hayes knew and had not forbade me. These thoughts had swirled around in my mind all night, and they always came back to the fact that we were in dock. We had docked for some reason, and all I could believe, in the black hours of the predawn, was that we had returned because of me.

No — the SA had not commandeered the ship.

At dawn the shouting and the noise began again. I heard loading noises and great thumpings deep in the hold. I dressed quietly so as not to disturb John, whose restlessness all night betrayed his own sleeplessness. His even breathing told me that at last he had found sleep. I slipped out on deck just as the sun burst over the mountains and down upon the misty waters. We were not back in the San Francisco harbor, but at a tiny island far out in the bay, a beautiful little island with a conical peak and wisps of mist in layers reflecting the early morning sun, then dissipating in its warmth. Below, I could see a small wooden wharf where our sailors and the dockhands were busily loading more cargo.

"So ye're still a superstitious lot?" I heard a foreman ask one of the crewmen as he checked a bill of lading in his hand. "Had to set sail afore midnight last night lest ye be setting sail on a Friday."

"Ye're damn right, Mr. McTraver. There's no good temptin' fate. We're doubly cursed this trip." The sailor leaned close to McTraver. "There's a woman aboard."

"Naw! An' ye doan't say!" McTraver exclaimed and drew back, feigning shock. "But I dare say it's not the first time. Ye've taken womenfolk to Alaska afore this."

SAN FRANCISCO BAY

"Aye — to Alaska — and every trip's been the devil's own holiday, too, when they're along. We've got used to that. This female's goin' beyond. She's goin' into the Bering."

"Well, ye're no longer doobly cursed. Ye did set sail afore Friday, even though ye weren't properly battened down so ye had to stop here to lash down the cargo. Is that the last of those cases, man?"

"Aye, sir," our crewman said as he carted something aboard ship.

So! That explains the unfriendly glances. The men are superstitious about having a woman aboard. It's an old superstition I had thought long dead. But here it is. I heard it spoken. If the sea gets rough, if anything happens to this ship, I shall be blamed.

"A cutter will be going back to San Francisco within the hour, Mrs. Beaman."

I jumped and swung from the rail to face the Senior Agent towering directly over me. He raised his hat slightly, bowed ever so slightly, and smiled still less slightly. Then his eyes grew hard as steel again, as hard and cold as they'd been last evening when John and I boarded the St Paul, when I met him for the first time.

"Oh," I said. "Good morning."

"I am sending dispatches back with the cutter. If you wish to send a last message to your family, I can arrange for it to be taken. It will be a long time, you know, before anyone can possibly hear from you again — August, perhaps even later."

You don't want me aboard this ship, I thought. *You are deliberately trying to make me homesick. You want me — not a letter, but me — to go back to the mainland on that cutter. Is that not what you want, Mr. Senior Agent? But why?* Aloud I asked, "But where are we? And why have we stopped?"

"This is Angel Island, near Sausalito."

"Sausalito." I repeated it slowly, trying to think beyond the words of our conversation. "Sausalito — what a lovely name — under the sky."

"The St Paul often stops here to check the lashings of its cargo against the rough voyage. That is, if she sets out too soon, as she did last night."

Yes. I just heard why, down there on the wharf, I thought. Aloud I said, "How long did you say I have?"

"About an hour."

"Thank you, sir. You are indeed kind to suggest a letter home. I shall have it ready before the cutter departs." I turned abruptly from him and hastened to our stateroom. I did not want him to see the tears that had sprung to my eyes. He must never see my tears or any sign of weakness.

John was still asleep. I stood there against the door I'd closed upon the deck, upon those hard and steely eyes. For one long, heartsick moment, the impulse was again strong within me to pack swiftly and to slip away to the cutter without letting John know what I'd done until after the boat was under full sail. I raced across the room to gather my toilet articles into my travel case. I turned then and looked at John, looked long and hard at the dear, dear face of my husband, relaxed and so helpless in sleep, and I knew I never could part from him again. There have been too many partings. No matter how difficult our time will be in the Pribilofs, I shall have to share it with him. This venture is all my doing. I am responsible.

If I'd not taken matters so boldly into my own hands back in February and gone to see President Hayes, we'd not be in this peculiar situation today. That is why, no matter how much the Senior Agent hates me, I have to stay at John's side and see him through.

I wrote the letter to my parents, so far away from us in Washington. It was a second farewell letter, rather light, since I do not want them to worry more than they do. But when I sealed the letter, I had that ominous feeling that I was also sealing my fate.

I write this as I watch the cutter breaking the sun's path back to the mainland while we cut cleanly through the great swells. We are headed out the Golden Gate, and I am going on, not back, but on into my own vast unknown.

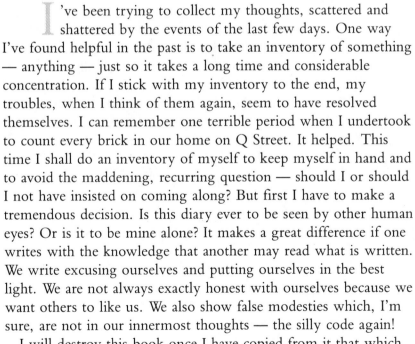

I've been trying to collect my thoughts, scattered and shattered by the events of the last few days. One way I've found helpful in the past is to take an inventory of something — anything — just so it takes a long time and considerable concentration. If I stick with my inventory to the end, my troubles, when I think of them again, seem to have resolved themselves. I can remember one terrible period when I undertook to count every brick in our home on Q Street. It helped. This time I shall do an inventory of myself to keep myself in hand and to avoid the maddening, recurring question — should I or should I not have insisted on coming along? But first I have to make a tremendous decision. Is this diary ever to be seen by other human eyes? Or is it to be mine alone? It makes a great difference if one writes with the knowledge that another may read what is written. We write excusing ourselves and putting ourselves in the best light. We are not always exactly honest with ourselves because we want others to like us. We also show false modesties which, I'm sure, are not in our innermost thoughts — the silly code again!

I will destroy this book once I have copied from it that which

MAY 11th

the family and friends may wish to know of our experiences. The rest is for me and for my eyes alone.

There, it is said.

I was born Elizabeth Gertrude DuBois, 1844, in Washington, D.C. I am tall and slim with an eighteen-inch waist sans stays. Everything else is proportionate except the need for shams. I have an unusually white, white complexion and long black hair, so long I can sit on it. I wear it in two braids like a crown on my head. I've large, blue-gray eyes, set wide apart, not beautiful. In fact I am no beauty. This I should know because I studied true classic beauty among the statues at Corcoran. In spite of what I always say, my parents think I am beautiful. I am vain of what looks I have, vain especially of my abundant hair that makes up for other inadequacies. My sister, Carrie, was truly beautiful; I, by comparison, am only good looking. Carrie was too beautiful to live.

I wear clothes well — always the latest fashion — not out of vanity, but because I am comfortable only when well dressed. Though I've been the rebel of our set about so many feminine restrictions — about the silly, outmoded customs and manners we have to keep — I've not gone mannish like Cousin Fanny Chase. I prefer to win my rebellion while remaining entirely feminine. I've brought along only a few complete outfits. But they would do John credit in any foreign court or legation. He says they will be wasted on the natives. They will be, of course, but I shall be comfortable and not eternally preoccupied with thoughts of clothes. I've other plans. I want to explore the islands and to learn.

I think I've a good mind, my own, not easily swayed. I think I think like a man. My talents are a man's: careful, meticulous, exacting in detail. I've a scientific curiosity about natural phenomena, more intense zoologically than botanically (the latter being the only ladylike field). God gave me these talents and interests. Why, because I am a woman, must I hide them? I am, withal, not brilliant as Carrie was brilliant. I am not intent on outdoing men. I am only trying to prove that women can do the things they can do and should be permitted to do them. I think in this I am a rational creature. I usually see both sides of an issue. I seldom let emotion control the choice — seldom — there are occasions. I carefully anticipate, rarely plunge headlong into action — though I admit, in this adventure, I did not anticipate everything. I am not a genius. Some think I am headstrong. Perhaps I am: a part of my rebellion. I had a good education as far as it went. I should have liked to go on to college. But the war years made that well-nigh impossible. Lovely Carrie went to college and died there of diphtheria. If I had gone to college, I would not have met John. Wasn't I destined to meet him by leading the life I did? My college was the war itself, art classes at Corcoran, our own library, music lessons I did not like (but that every well-brought-up young lady had to take), my father's experience, my mother's love, my close family circle, and the salons of the diplomatic corps up and down Massachusetts Avenue. Should I have had more? After yesterday I feel certain lacks. Would I have learned in college how to cope with the SA?

Is it mind or spirit that learns to deal with our fellowman? I've been brought up a Presbyterian out of a long line of French Huguenots who came to this country because of their faith. They braved the wilderness to settle at New Paltz, New York, and DuBois, Pennsylvania, because of their faith. I've inherited their faith. I'll need much of it to get me through these trying days. Most people confuse morals and religion. They are not the same. But they involve each other. I believe I am an essentially moral being. It is inherent in me to try to obey the Ten Commandments and our Lord's supreme command. I hope this keeps me fortified under extreme trials. Only then will I be able to measure my moral strength. I have many weaknesses. Though I never have been given to subterfuge, my entire long courtship with John was one huge subterfuge. I've never been given to intrigue, secrecy. Yet we would not be here upon the high seas if I had not had that secret interview with the president.

I've been accused of being haughty. I don't want to be. But how does one reveal one's true nature without letting down the bars too far? Because of my unique position among men, I built an external armor, the only way of preserving my personal integrity. I think I shall be needing more, not less, of this armor where we are going. I would prefer to seem warm and human instead of coldly repelling. John's devoted love has not melted the cold, exterior wall, but he knows that my heart is wax in his hand.

John was born John Warren Beaman, 1845, to Elizabeth Worcester and Warren Harrison Beaman at North Hadley, Massachusetts, where his father and his grandfather before him were farmers. His mother's father was a Congregational minister who taught at Harvard College, the famous Samuel Worcester, cousin of Joseph Worcester, who wrote the *Worcester Dictionary.* John is tall — six feet — broad shouldered and truly handsome, distinguished looking by my standards and those of my friends. He has a ruddy complexion from much exposure to the elements, soft, curly, light brown hair, and sideburns. His eyes are gray, large and intelligent, more easily read than mine. He has strong, well-kept hands. In fact, the whole of him exudes strength and fineness, a man to lean upon.

John is more interested in quality than in fashion. He has an extremely good mind, not brilliant but well trained, though in engineering, a field he would not have chosen except for me. He planned to follow in his grandfather's footsteps. I never could reconcile — nor has he ever explained adequately — why he changed his mind so radically, deciding not to become a Congregational minister. At nineteen he passed third in a class of nineteen candidates for admission to West Point. Certainly he must have some inclinations to fight. He has said only that he would have gone to West Point, but he suddenly felt the call to the ministry. Has he regretted his career in engineering? He never has complained.

Family traditions are strong in him, coloring his attitudes. We've many missionaries in both our families. But neither of us has ever felt any real missionary zeal of our own. He is intellectually curious and intellectually sound but with fixed convictions. His personal integrity cannot be shaken. He has little initiative, allowing things to happen and then putting everything in God's hands. I am more inclined to make things happen. He believes that, too, is God's will. He's doggedly stubborn when he gets certain notions, and he lives by the Golden Rule, even under the greatest provocation — a truly beautiful soul, human withal, an ardent lover.

How well we know ourselves. How little we know others. Pages for me, paragraphs for John, only a sentence or two for the Senior Agent.

He is, John tells me, only forty-two. I had thought him older. He is almost as tall as John, with a commanding bearing that makes him seem as tall. He is dark with straight black hair, rather sparse, and he wears a sharp goatee. His blue-gray eyes are extremely penetrating but reveal none of his thoughts. He was, so he tells us, at Bull Run, Antietam, and before Richmond, and he acquired the rank of colonel. He served for a while in the Government Printing Office, where our paths may have crossed. He also worked for a while in the U.S. Patent Office before going to California to live.

He was appointed special agent to the Pribilofs last year. We asked ourselves why he sought this sort of assignment, whether he is married, and why he spent the winter in California instead of on the islands he is supposed to be supervising.

This is a mere bare bones of an inventory.

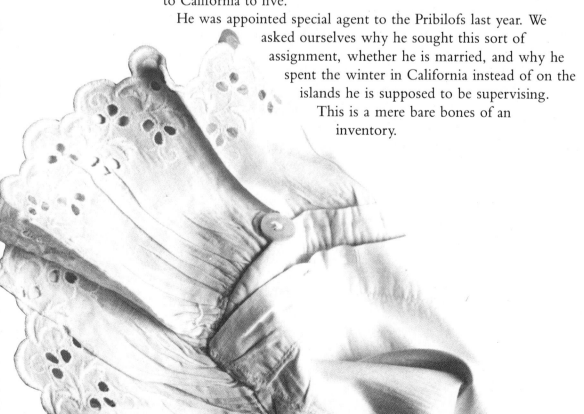

We are moving full sail into our fourth sunset on a calm ocean of wide, low swells that rock us gently. We are cutting through waters intensely blue and endless. Captain Erskine says this is unusual for this time of year. Soon, when we come into the Japan Stream, we will meet with more turbulence. The air is still balmy warm which, the captain says, is because of the Stream. It is the purest, most wonderful air I have ever breathed. It has given John and me hearty appetites, against which we've been warned because the deck is so small we can't get enough exercise. Today I feel a little less frightened of the future. Here we are aboard a ship sailing smoothly toward a destination for which we set out. Come what may, we're going to have to live through our two years.

Matters may never be simple, but for today, I am lulled into believing they may never get out of hand. That is a prayer. John says he has foreseen some of the difficulties: a lone white woman among men deprived of their own women for many months at a time, I could provoke trouble even unwittingly. It is an old argument I thought we'd settled while still in Washington. There will be no trouble as long as I conduct myself like a lady. I believe the SA recognized this intention, for he has shown me a grudging respect and a slight deference at the table. I know I could be coquettish, trying to win all these gruff men to me and have immediate friends. But what of the future? The SA seems to have accepted the fact that I am going along. But he has not accepted me.

In answer to John's query a while back — "Lib, how in the world do we find ourselves on this wild venture? Why are we here?" — there was little I could say except to remind him of how desperately in need we are. But now, writing in my diary, perhaps I had better take a historical inventory, thinking through from the very beginning just how and why we are here.

This much I do know and could not tell him: *I am responsible.*

Whatever has happened, whatever will happen, of good or of evil, I am to blame. But where did it all start? Certainly not with that impulsive interview with President Hayes! Events precipitated that, and other events precipitated other events — a long chain back into time. The interview with the president was only one link in the chain, the one I forged. But ladies do not take the initiative. Young ladies do not do this. Young ladies do not do that. Where have I heard that? Where did I begin to hear "Young ladies don't — ?"

Why, with Tissie, of course! Tissie, short for Clematis, telling me, "Young ladies doan' never do dis" and "Young ladies doan' never do dat." Tissie calling to me to be careful, or I'd fall into the Potomac, or muddy my pinafore, or — well, there were all kinds of mischiefs I could manage. Calicoed Tissie with a red kerchief on her head and a snowy white one around her neck, calling after me, minding me no matter where I tried to wander — and Ben, too, helping Tissie occasionally, though he was usually busy about the horses or polishing brass. I was Tissie's responsibility, and the rolling hills of Mount Vernon daily saw her scrawny legs galloping after me. I was free as only a tiny child can be free — to run, to explore, to laugh, and to rule a doting household. I was three years old and my brother Rhesa not yet one, when we went to Mount Vernon to live. I am the firstborn of Nicholas and Lydia (née Lydia Louisa Griffin) DuBois.

Father, a civil engineer by training but a government official by career, had been appointed by President Polk to supervise the restoration of George Washington's home the year Congress voted the appropriation for making Mount Vernon a national shrine. I remember (or rather it was so often pointed out later that I know it well) the small guest house on the estate where we lived for two whole years while the repairs were going on at the manse. Father and Mother had taken with them their newly married freed-slave couple, Tissie and Ben, to look after us. Brother Charles was born at Mount Vernon with only Tissie to help. There was no time to send to Washington for a doctor or to the village for a midwife. Transportation was as difficult in those days as it was in the first president's day — and still is — and by the same means, by horse. We were as isolated from Washington as though we lived in another country or another world. So for those two years, Mount Vernon became my whole world. Not until Father had carried out the planners' wishes and completely satisfied himself that the lovely mansion had been restored to its original beauty and character inside and out did we return to our modest row house on Q Street, near the rickety P Street footbridge that crosses into Georgetown. I'd been too young when we left to remember this home before Mount Vernon. I had a whole new world to explore. Sister Carrie arrived soon after our return.

My family, the DuBois side of it, had no great wealth. They lived comfortably on their incomes, but none had land or investments such as most of our Southern neighbors did, nor did they believe in owning slaves. Mother, a Griffin, brought to her marriage considerable wealth, inherited from the Benjamin Franklin side of the family. She, like her husband's family, did not believe in possessing slaves; in fact, she deplored the institution, considering it unchristian and barbaric, and she preferred a quiet life rather than an ostentatious life that required slaves.

Father's engineering background led him into all kinds of strange assignments. Scarcely had we returned to Q Street when President Zachary Taylor sent him to Oregon to make a full and confidential report on the "forty-niners." He was gone four years!

Lincoln's election and approaching inauguration naturally caused a great deal of excitement, at least among Washington society. Southern families had said quite flatly that they planned to ignore the uncouth Illinois lawyer who had been speaking out against slavery. They, along with most of the diplomatic corps, had planned to boycott any but the most obligatory social life his presumptuous wife might undertake.

Edouard de Stoeckl, the young Russian ambassador who had recently married Elizabeth Howard, daughter of my parents' friends, hadn't helped matters much. All Washington hung on his witty, often cruel, comments and mimicked the dashing young baron, who most undiplomatically considered Northerners social boors not worth cultivating. He probably tolerated our family because of the Howards and because he probably thought we were in sympathy with the South, which put my parents in a delicate situation.

Father had known Mr. Lincoln ever since his days in Congress when cousin Jesse DuBois, trying to establish a college in Illinois, had written Mr. Lincoln a letter of introduction to my family. Mr. Lincoln humbly presented the letter one day and won my parents' hearts. I was so very young, but even I fell under the spell of his wonderful, homely warmth whenever he stopped at our house. We all followed his career with pride. When he won the presidency against so much local hatred, we decided to stand by him, which meant tacitly taking sides in an undeclared war. Baron de Stoeckl had already made his choice.

At sixteen, one suddenly begins to take political discussions seriously. At least, I absorbed something of what was being said in the parlors on Massachusetts Avenue and around on Q Street, but frankly, I was much more interested in clothes, and an inaugural ball meant a first ball gown.

"What makes you think you'll be invited?" Mother asked. I hadn't ever doubted. Wasn't Mr. Lincoln our

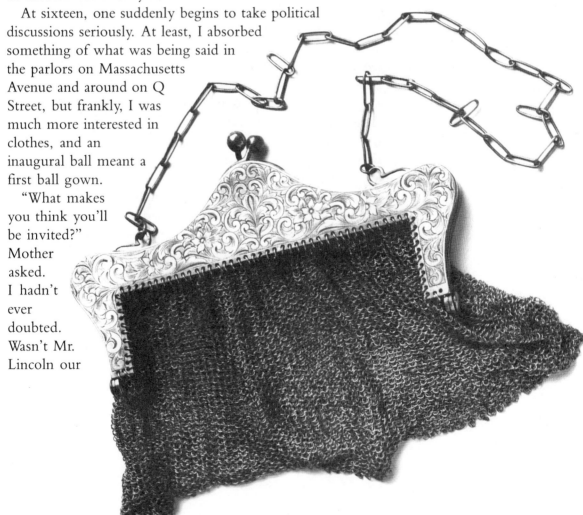

friend? My friend? He always called me "daughter" and brushed his hand over my hair caressingly, as though he really wanted a daughter. I couldn't imagine him coming back to Washington to live without including all of us, even though his new home would be the Executive Mansion.

A ball gown meant a trip to New York for material, and we would be going soon anyway. The city, with its many shops, always gave us the most wonderful excursion. Though this visit to New York tired Mother, Carrie and I, awaiting the annual trip, never could quite hide our exuberance and impatience.

"I brought this silk back from Italy just for you, Miss DuBois," the young clerk said to me at Stewart's, where we always purchased all the cloth we would need for the coming year. "I watched it being woven on a special loom. 'Luna della Mare' the weaver called it, 'Moonlight on the Water!' I thought of your black, black hair and your white, white skin even as I watched." The colors shimmered in soft grays and deep blues as he unfolded the changeable taffeta, hypnotizing both Mother and me.

"We'll have it," Mother said, aghast at the price but unable to resist the spell. Little did we dream at the time that just two years later, Rhesa would marry Mary Stewart, daughter of the store's owner, sweeping her off to far parts of the world on his diplomatic missions. (Though I was a bridesmaid, I've seldom seen my lovely sister-in-law.)

We went to New York early in January, in time to bring back all the materials for the dressmaker's annual visit. But we returned to the Capital and to discouraging gossip: Mr. Lincoln never would be inaugurated; by the time he arrived, Washington would be an armed Southern garrison; he'd need a bodyguard or even an army to protect him. Ugly rumors ran rampant. Feelings ran high. Of course, the most devastating news for me — and it was official, not gossip — was that there would be no inaugural ball at all.

The beautiful gown, the very latest and loveliest in all Washington when it was completed, hung from the rafters in our third-floor sewing room, swathed in its voluminous muslin wrappings as if in mourning.

Gloom settled over Washington. War clouds gathered. Father explained that the preponderance of Southern sympathizers in Congress would make his own position precarious, since all his appointments were subject to congressional approval. We could see the inner struggle. Was he not a Huguenot from Virginia? Should he not declare his colors to protect his family? But there loomed that question of slavery — always that question — and a deep-rooted loyalty to Mr. Lincoln, whose friendship he treasured.

We were horrified one day to learn that Mr. Lincoln had slipped into the city under cover of darkness — "like a thief in the night," Edouard had joked — to claim his rightfully elected position.

Later, a crowd witnessed his inauguration under the unfinished dome of the Capitol. Only a few cheered him along his route to the Executive Mansion. To me, it seemed more like a funeral procession than a parade.

But that same day, when we returned home damp and dispirited, we were pleasantly surprised by a messenger who handed Father a large white envelope embossed with the presidential seal, an invitation to a reception for the diplomatic corps to be held three nights later. The invitation spelled out all our names. This reception was to be the first of Mary Todd Lincoln's pathetic attempts to create a social life in the face of her enemies. I was still too young to understand the undercurrents, but I felt them.

The reception we attended was one of the most elegant and perfect affairs ever held at the Executive Mansion, thanks to Senhor de Lisboa, envoy from Portugal, doyen of the diplomatic corps by reason of his long incumbency at Washington. Though his duty may have been distasteful to him, he stood gallantly beside Mrs. Lincoln throughout the affair. Outwardly gracious himself, he made sure no one committed an ungracious act toward the First Lady. He also had seen to it that no matter how reluctant the other diplomats and their wives might be to come at the bidding of "the upstart Kentucky woman," they were all there.

The senhor seemed particularly gallant to me, though I never had met him before. But then everything seemed particularly wonderful, like a fairy tale come true, for I was wearing Luna della Mare, and I saw many an envious eye cast in my direction as each person passed me down the long reception line.

I met all the legends of Washington: Lord Lyons, the British minister, now on speaking terms with Edouard, both trying to forget the Crimea; Señor de Tassara from Spain; M. Henri Mercier of France; von Schlieden from the Hanseatic League; Edouard with Elizabeth — who looked lovelier than ever — both overlooking their prejudices toward the Lincolns out of curiosity about them; and many, many others.

"This is, you know, your real debut," Mrs. Howard said to me a little later, just as her youngest and most handsome son, later to become a rebel officer but only fifteen the night of the reception, swept me off to a cotillion just under way.

Later he escorted me to the lavish buffet where the Lincolns had joined their guests and were making the rounds, stopping to speak to each person. When Mr. Lincoln came up to me, he put his hand on my head. "You are indeed beautiful tonight, my daughter," he said. I curtsied, not knowing how to reply. He made me feel singularly blessed and beautiful and grown up all at once.

"You are, you know," Mr. Howard said, as though he had only just made the discovery himself.

The memory of that elegant affair remained the only bright memory for a long, long time. The bitter war got under way. There were other balls, other parties, for "morale" to cheer the troops. I had to follow the only pattern set for me — a silly, meaningless life of empty gestures. Naturally, I had to complete my schooling, a finishing school that nearly finished me.

I wanted to go to college.

"College!" my brothers exclaimed in one breath with my parents. "Well-brought-up young ladies do not go to college." The war settled the matter. The rebels had Washington so surrounded that I could not have gotten out to go to one of the new "female colleges" in New England I'd dreamed of attending.

"I want to attend the Corcoran School of Art," I announced one bitter winter evening. Father choked and had to leave the table. Mother stared at me, incredulous that she could have brought me into the world.

"I'll have no sister of mine making a spectacle of herself sitting in front of an easel in public," Rhesa exploded. With his marriage approaching, he was extremely sensitive to any deviation from the pattern. What he wanted to say was, "How can I ever introduce my friends to a sister who does not fit into the prescribed pattern?" Rhesa wanted me to marry one of his young friends — any one of them.

"Young ladies doan' never paint," Tissie muttered as she cleared away the dishes. "You mind you all's in fer trouble ef'n you try somethin' like dat."

"You're just annoyed because I don't spend more time in the kitchen learning how to cook like you," I remember saying. "I'm not the least bit interested in fancy food."

"The man you marry will be," Rhesa snapped.

"Then I won't marry."

"Lib, Lib," my father said, and that was all he said that night. But not long later he came to me. "Daughter," he said, clearing his throat, "I recognize your talent, and I'm afraid that, unless it is properly trained, you'll turn to china painting or some other ladylike art that will kill your talent. We wouldn't let you go to college, but I see no real harm in letting you go to Corcoran."

"What in heaven's name is Nicholas thinking of?" the collective families — both sides — asked in horror. "No *lady* ever studies painting!" Next to the theater, art was the most degrading, unladylike career a female could follow. I would disgrace the entire family. I'd be shunned by all the nice young men. I'd never find a proper husband.

But I didn't care. I was blissfully happy doing what no young lady ever had done before. I had become the first female entrant at the Corcoran. The all-male student body ignored me. My male teachers resented my presence in their men's world and set onerous tasks before me — day in, day out, I drew the human figure from casts of Discobolus, Mercury, and Juno. I hated drawing the human figure and still am not good at it. I wanted to paint, to use color. I stuck it out only because I had gained a few hours of freedom each week. Ben drove me there and delivered me home safely.

Cousin Fanny, who had just married Simeon B. Chase and was not yet involved with the W.C.T.U., really liberated me. She begged me, right in front of my family, to come with her at least two days a week to help nurse the wounded at Hallowell General Hospital across the bridge in Alexandria. I expected another session of stunned silence and protest. But Cousin Fanny, in the family's estimation, was a perfect lady and could do no wrong. She was asking me to do my humanitarian duty.

"But that's enemy territory," was Mother's only objection. "Why Hallowell?"

"Enemy or ours," Fanny said, "they need our help. There's no one to look after them except a few doctors. They were our friends before this horrible war divided us."

So every Tuesday I found myself driving with Cousin Fanny and other young friends across the bridge. We carried passes that allowed us to enter rebel territory.

Our job was to cheer the men or do little things for them that the few medical corpsmen were too busy to do. More and more often, however, we found ourselves assisting at the bedsides. We helped the doctors change dressings, held instrument trays, bathed fevered brows — that is, those of us who could stand the sight and stench of blood and pus. There were nearly as many Northern prisoners of war at Hallowell as Southern wounded.

At first we wore our prettiest dresses to cheer the men. But as we took on actual nursing care, we ruined so many of our clothes that we decided on white pinafores over our dresses. These could be laundered easily. Naturally we outdid each other with lacy frills and tuckings, even on our coveralls. But we remained serious about our work to the very end.

Money became scarce in our household, food too, because of the blockade. But I continued at Corcoran and at Hallowell. Occasionally a social event broke the gloom briefly — a wedding, a baptism, a rare official party. Parties seemed to put heart into everyone, because somehow the hosts managed to conjure up a little extra food. We had begun to feel hunger.

One party stands out vividly. At the time, I had no premonition of my own involvement in things Russian, yet the Russians touched my life even then. The Imperial Russian flagship, the *Osliaba,* tied up at Alexandria for several months while the rest of the fleet stayed in New York City Harbor. There had been almost constant entertaining aboard, and everywhere in Washington, doors opened to the handsomely uniformed and debonair officers. Edouard, who had been a part of each day's entertaining, in turn decided to entertain officially aboard the ship before its departure. We had been invited. Even the Lincolns had been invited. Though the president could not attend, Mrs. Lincoln accepted the invitation, causing no little embarrassment and a flurry of excitement since so many Southern sympathizers also had accepted.

The mazurka and a sumptuous buffet won everyone's hearts, and political differences seemed to disappear for one night. But I could not forget the war.

Fresh in my memory was the feel of one feverish brow. I had spent endless days watching at a young prisoner's bedside, trying to cool that burning forehead, and waiting, too, for his eyes to open. Somehow, among all those anguished men, the one head had become precious to me. A long time I waited for the eyes to open, and when they did, they asked for my love.

John Warren Beaman was nineteen, my own age, but oh, so much younger looking lying there so helpless, ravaged by the pneumonia following frostbite and exposure. He had been taken prisoner after General Burnside's hapless Red River expedition, and now, with care, he was recovering in the prison ward at Hallowell.

His hair was long then, soft but matted, no pleasant sight with which to fall in love. That was why I was so sure I had fallen in love. My days of care for him made it all the more certain.

John had left Amherst College at the end of his freshman year to join Burnside's brigade, much against the wishes of his family. His father and his mother did not believe in war and killing. These things I learned from John during the long slow days of his convalescence. I knew he would be a most acceptable suitor for my hand, one even my brothers could not fault. But how to ever introduce him into my home? "Young *ladies* doan' never introduce their suitors," I could hear Tissie say. I could hear my family say it in stronger words. A young lady always had to wait until a member of her family introduced her to an eligible young man.

I tried getting Cousin Fanny to entertain some of the convalescent soldiers at her home. Her family held up collective hands in horror. I tried to get Mother to go on rounds with me, but she was a squeamish woman and would have fainted at the odor before she reached the first patient. Not one subterfuge I tried worked.

"We're too young to think of marriage anyway, Libby," John pointed out to me one day when he knew he had recovered enough to be sent to Andersonville. "No one knows how long this thing will last. If I survive, I will have years of college, and then I'll have to make good before I dare ask for your hand."

"Who knows? You may be exchanged. Wounded usually are. You'd surely be discharged because you obviously cannot go back to fighting. Then I'll find a way for you to be introduced into my home." I remember how John shook his head sadly at this.

Fortunately, he did not have to go to Andersonville. He became the prisoners' executive officer and lived at Hallowell for the rest of the war, looking after prisoner exchanges, transfers to other military hospitals, notifications of deaths, and so on. Being a prisoner himself, he never could leave the compound. But we managed to see each other and exchange a few words whenever my duties took me to the prison wards. Marriage seemed a hopeless, faraway thing for us. We had pledged to keep our love secret and to allow no one ever to come between us or into our separate lives.

Something my father said one day gave me an idea. He had been put in charge of the mapmaking section of the General Land Office. He not only supervised the actual drawing of the maps for our ever expanding nation, but he sent the cartographers and engineers out to survey the land for the accurate maps. He complained one night that the war had put a terrible gap in the training of men for his department. It would take years to train new men, and in the meantime, he'd have to go on short staffed.

"John," I said hastily, next time I saw him (we always had to communicate swiftly — no frills), "I know how someday you may be introduced to me properly."

"Someday? When, Libby?"

"Oh — in the far future, I'm afraid. But I'll wait. Father needs well-trained civil engineers. Instead of studying for the ministry, study to be an engineer. Then apply to my father for a position in his department. Once an employee, you'd naturally come to his attention, a nice eligible bachelor just right for his daughter Elizabeth."

"Four years, Libby?"

"You'd need that for the ministry too."

John shrugged and laughed an uncertain little laugh. But when the war ended, he went to Rensselaer Institute in Troy, New York, instead of going back to Amherst, and I waited.

Why did I let him go so far away? Why didn't I defy my family and tell them flatly I had met the man I loved? I often wonder. So many things could have happened, could have come between our love. The fact that nothing did, that both of us, though we bided the time impatiently and with longing, weathered the long separation only proved our love.

The war ended.

Mr. Lincoln was no more.

Life had to be lived somehow.

More and more often Father brought home unfinished work from the map division. The country was growing so rapidly that his office could not keep up. The charting of our land also became more complicated as more information came in. Maps taken from the drawing board one day were obsolete the next, before they came back from the Government Printing Office. Father's department had trouble keeping abreast of the times unless he worked day and night, because he hated throwing extra burdens on an already overworked staff. He always looked so tired.

"Let me do that drawing for you," I suggested one evening when he looked particularly exhausted. "You know how much I like to letter. I think I could do a better job of it than any of your men." He was tired enough to give in. So from that time I did his homework for him, happy that I could fill the empty hours of waiting for John and feeling the resolution growing inside me to make the most preposterous request of my life.

I asked my father for a position as a mapmaker in his department.

Definitely, most definitely, no lady, no matter how poor, worked in an office. A young lady might teach, she might even become a glorified governess, but she did not, could not, work in an office where men worked. Nor could she do a man's work in competition with him even if she could approach his capabilities or — God forbid — exceed them. If she did, she was no longer a lady. I expected fireworks. I had fireworks. The whole family exploded down to the nth cousin. Even John protested in one of his rare, dear letters, secretly delivered.

I, on the other hand, had visions of the long, lean years ahead of us, even after college, before we could have enough money, a very minimum enough, to get married on. Naturally, I could not tell my family my real reason for wanting to defy custom again. I just argued that it was obvious Father needed me. That he could not deny. I argued, too, that I was doing at home what his men in the office were doing and that the caliber of my work was comparable. In fact, I could do detail wherever it was required, or why would he be bringing the finer detail work to me? I also flung out the horrendous heresy that I saw no reason why, if a lady was capable, she could not be employed on an equal basis with a man.

"Oh, never that, Libby. Our whole social system would break down," Father said. "But I might find you some subordinate position to which the men might not object. We'll see."

I never would have been employed even then if it had not been for the sudden interest in Alaska. Discussion of its possible purchase had again opened on the floor of the House. Secretary Seward had proposed the purchase on several previous occasions, but now it was in a bill up for vote. No one seemed to know much about the territory. There were no accurate maps available, except for a few in French and several in Russian. Yet suddenly every congressman wanted a map to study. Father turned to me in despair. "Please come down to the office with me and help," he said one morning. I went.

I was greeted with no enthusiasm by the men in the mapmaking office, even though everyone was scurrying around trying to translate the existing maps and comparing their accuracy against each other with only a few American notes and fixes. The men at their boards ignored me and left me to myself, considering me some queer sort of creature entirely out of place in their midst. Some few resented having me around. But I had my job and I loved it.

I can remember shivering in spite of the steam bath temperatures of those days and the many heavy petticoats I wore under my long dress — which I tucked tightly about my ankles so I did not expose them as I perched on my high stool over my drawing board, working on the details of the map of the Alaskan Purchase Territory. I had to letter in *Unexplored, Uncharted, Frozen Sea,* and *Ice Barrier* all over the area. There were some definite lines — the Seventieth Parallel, the Arctic Circle, charted islands, and Russian cities — and two minuscule dots standing for islands way out in the Bering Sea; their exact location was 57° 8' north, 170° 12' west. They were St Paul and St George islands, called the Pribilof Group or the Seal Islands. What possible concern could these tiny islands have to our legislators? Yet they were to be included in the purchase, and though I shivered, I had no premonition that they would ever be of any further concern to me!

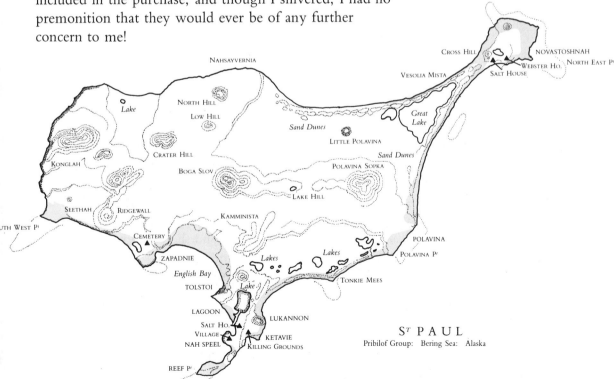

S^T PAUL

Pribilof Group: Bering Sea: Alaska

In spite of the purchase being called "Seward's Folly," our government immediately established military garrisons along the coast and on the islands; Coast Guard cutters began to patrol the waters, protecting our new possession. With them went surveyors, photographers, cartographers, naturalists, and others who brought back so much information that we continually had to revise the maps. Perhaps there was no one more familiar with the details of this part of the world than I was at the time, for the maps of the Alaskan Purchase Territory were my project. Thus I went about my work, happily oblivious of the world around me, anticipating John's all too infrequent letters.

Cousins, aunts, uncles, and my parents continued to introduce the most charming and eligible young men into our household, with obvious intent. But none made the slightest dent in my heart's armor. I pretended to prefer my independence and must have appeared to be a formidable sort of creature to many of the young men. I was bridesmaid for Rhesa when he married the sophisticated and elegant Mary Stewart of New York. I was bridesmaid for Charles when he married the lovely Rosalie Wheelock of Washington. My darling sister Carrie almost married in her freshman year at Vassar, but decided to graduate first before doing such a thing; and all the while my family became more and more exasperated with their eldest daughter. I passed from eligible maidenhood to obvious spinsterhood at twenty-four. No one could understand why. But I knew why. I kept myself for John.

Then one day I knew that John was coming to Washington, coming to apply for the job I had so long ago suggested, coming to the very building in which I worked and where I might actually see him pass my door, where — if I dared — I might brush past him in the corridor on his way to my father's office. Though I was seething with the pent-up emotions of four long years, I dared do nothing rash or foolish that would spoil our carefully laid plans. I let him pass my door. I did not know when; I dared not look up from my drawing board. The prayer in my heart was that Father would find him acceptable.

That day passed and several more before we could meet secretly as planned. Those days were terrible days. I did not know his fate. Father made no mention at home that he had taken on a new staff member or, for that matter, that he had any new applicants. Father seldom discussed routine office details at home now that I was employed there. One thing I did know. John never would be put in my office, for try as he had all through school, he could not draw well enough to become a draughtsman. He had concentrated, therefore, on surveying and the outdoor aspects of cartography. He would be put into the field.

At last one day, I sat sketching Discobolus in the school gallery as I had done as a student, and no one paid attention. There were three other young ladies and several men doing the same. Sketching? My hand shook. More than four years! But I knew him the instant he came into the hall. And in the same instant I knew that it had been right to wait.

He was filled out now, imposingly big and fine looking, with lighter, crisper hair than I had remembered. Now, his hair curled slightly at the edges, and he wore simple sideburns. He was bronzed, too, from his student work in the field with transit and line, quite in contrast to the pale, gaunt youth to whom I had said farewell at Hallowell — and a decided improvement. I could not keep my heart from showing in my eyes.

We met there many times after that, whenever I had an afternoon off. It was about the only place I could go without being questioned. I did seem to need an inordinate amount of drawing practice and criticism. Often I debated whether or not to take Tissie into my confidence, for then I might have been able to arrange another rendez-vous. But this had been a secret so well kept between John and me that I wanted no one else to share it until everyone could share it. We made our plans at Corcoran, in the coldly sterile art gallery, among the paintings and bronzes of buffalo. We talked about everything that had happened while we were apart. All we could do was talk, though our hands yearned to touch and hold each other. With our whole beings, we yearned for the marriage that we had been denying ourselves for so long. Yet neither of us regretted that we had waited for each other, though we had the hopeless prospect before us of John's finding his way to becoming a suitable suitor for my hand.

His first assignment was with Professor Hayden's Geological Survey Commission into the Northwest Territory. That meant months away. Sometimes he was years away, with little time between missions to court me in the romantic setting of Corcoran's sterile halls.

But at long last, one day John brought to my drawing board, in person, his own charts, notes, and fixes. He had insisted on doing so while he was in Father's office, discussing the charts before they would be incorporated into the map I was drawing of that particular section. I had informed him the day before that I was using his notes and that they had given me a thrill. My dry, old map had come alive. The idea of speaking with me about the map was his, and he used it for several days running until I noted a few raised eyebrows at the other boards. We had always kept cold, straight faces during our too brief discussions, though I was tempted to give John a mischievous smile. I was sure we had in no way betrayed ourselves. Yet by some subtle alchemy of mind, most everyone guessed that we had fallen in love.

Father walked into my office during the sixth or seventh superfluous interview, just before John was to leave on another assignment. He nodded to John and said quite naturally, "Oh, I see you have met. That's right, Libby, you are working on that Montana section map. Not much of the area has been explored. What seems to be complicating the drawing?"

I looked to John to answer. He looked to me to answer. Father looked at us both. "Ah, so that is how it is?" he asked. But he never asked, "For how long?" Sometime later in the day, he must have spoken to John, because John was a guest at our dinner table that very night and the next before he went away.

My family never could understand how it happened that I could change in one day from a prim and forbidding old maid to a radiantly happy and sometimes silly young woman. But I knew why. I no longer had to keep my love a secret. I could wear it out on my sleeve and in my eyes and in my smile. Our engagement was announced one wintry day in 1873, and we were married in the First Presbyterian Church the following year, when both of us were twenty-nine years old — a full ten years from the time we had met at Hallowell. That was far too long for young people to have to wait when they knew their own hearts so well right from the start.

The waiting was not over. At times, it seemed that it had only begun. Waiting took another form, naturally, after our wedding: the waiting of a young wife for her husband's return from one extended expedition after another. John continued to do the cartography for various government geological and geodetical surveys. He was gone months at a time — once, a whole year to help survey the rights-of-way for the Union Pacific Railroad (over which I have just traveled). As a married woman, I no longer could work. A genteel wife did not work, though I wanted to. The whole family, to the cousins fifth removed, put its collective foot down this time. So I lived at home, anticipating John's all too infrequent visits, trying to bear up under the family's obvious displeasure. Their darling Libby, in their eyes, had made a none too brilliant marriage.

No one should ever minimize the chaos of the postwar period or the poverty and hopelessness great sections of the country were thrown into. For my whole family, all in various branches of government service — Father at the land office, brothers Rhesa and Charles in the diplomatic corps, and John as an engineer in the field — the times had grown extremely difficult under the retrenchment program that laid off even vitally essential persons. Official surveying of our expanding western territories, being less essential, became one of the first services to be discontinued "until Congress can make new appropriations." Obviously the work would not be renewed for a long time. The whole mapmaking department closed down; the cartographers were brought in from their missions and dismissed — explorers, too. Though Father retained his position, his entire staff had been cut from under him. John lost his job overnight. Father could not find another place for him, nor could anyone else. We were so sure at first that the panic would be short lived, that other sorts of positions would open up. Time passed. The panic grew worse, not better, as the financial scandals of Grant's administration died down only to give a true measure of the disaster. Longer and longer bread lines formed outside church kitchens. Shabbily elegant men applied for the most menial jobs.

President Hayes, in a series of talks, tried to explain how he had attempted to stabilize the national currency on a "hard metal" basis, which meant very little to those of us who had seen no money at all for a long time. Because John and I had bound ourselves by oath before our marriage that we would never turn to our families for financial help, we were in dire straits. During those years, we never had been able to accumulate enough money with which to purchase our own home. We had to remain at the family board, always welcome there, but it was most humiliating to us. We would have starved otherwise. I discovered that John's thickest surveying boots had holes in the soles — he'd walked so much in search of work. He could find no job at all.

So on a brisk day in February, I took matters into my own hands. I went to see the president.

Mr. Hayes preferred to live in the house at Takoma Park that the Lincolns had called the Summer White House. Therefore I had to go way out to Takoma Park to see him. Without letting John or the family know what I really intended, I borrowed Ben and the buggy ostensibly to put flowers on Grandmother Griffin's grave in Rock Creek Park. (We had a small conservatory on Q Street where I grew flowers in the winter, and I could boast early violets, Grandmother's favorites.) No one could understand why I chose such cold and blustery weather for my errand. Fortunately Grandmother's birthday came that day, and, too, our horse needed some real exercise. My errand had to be that day, for I had been given an appointment I had to keep. Several times on the way, I wanted to call to Ben to turn back. I was frankly frightened, not of Rutherford B. Hayes, Father's old friend, but of what I had undertaken: taking the initiative, something ladies do not do, this time for a man. I prayed I had undertaken something I never would regret.

I remember the president's booming voice as he greeted me when I entered his office. "Come in, come in, my dear," he said as he stood up behind his cluttered desk. "What a handsome young matron you have become."

"Not so handsome and not so young anymore," I sighed. "I am nearly thirty-four."

"Well, well. That's not so aged. But tell me, what brings you way out here on a day like this? Surely not just to pay a visit to an old man?" I held my hands together tightly in my muff to keep them from shaking. How could I tell this friendly, harassed man, the president of the United States, that I indeed had not come on a friendly mission at all, but to ask a favor. But that was exactly what I had to do or fail in my mission — fail John.

"I've come to ask a favor." I could see his eyes narrow, become less friendly. I knew I'd have to resort to a woman's wiles, use every bit of charm I possessed to wheedle some small concession from him, for no doubt everyone who came to him came to ask a favor.

"A favor? If that is possible, Elizabeth. The president isn't God, you know."

"My husband was with the Geodetical Survey Office. You abolished it six months ago. Mr. Beaman has tried to find work, any kind of work. There isn't any work. I know you will be angry with me when I say it is unfair for veterans to have to face this — most unfair that someone wounded at Red River should have to walk the streets looking for even the most menial job, just to keep alive. The men who fought to keep this nation together deserve something better than that."

"You mean to say that one of Burnside's men is in such a plight?" he asked, hitting the desk with his fist. I'd used John's war service, sure that it would strike the right note, for Mr. Hayes *Cottage at* had been a general in the war and something of a war historian *Soldiers Home* ever since. "Your husband is an engineer, is he not?"

ON THE PACIFIC

Rutherford B. Hayes

"Yes, a trained civil engineer, especially trained in cartography," I answered, seeing a ray of hope.

"You're right, Elizabeth. We did have to abolish several whole departments. The country is going to have to wait until times are better to go ahead with many of its ambitious programs. Official boundaries, national parks, rights-of-way — those are things that will have to wait until starving people are fed and housed. I'm sorry this had to happen to your husband. But we had to do it. We're in the midst of a terrible financial panic. I am being blamed on all sides for it. I tried to win the South's goodwill by recalling all troops, and immediately the North raised a howl for dumping thousands of men on an already serious unemployment market."

"I know. Father says it's the worst period he ever has experienced. Certainly it is mine."

"And I don't seem to be helping you, do I?"

"John's unemployment wouldn't mean so much if we were younger, if I hadn't waited so long to marry him and against my family's wishes. You see, he just had to make good to win their respect. Now that respect is all but shattered again."

"But that's not his fault!"

"It's no good trying to tell them so."

I could see that a sudden idea had struck him, and I took heart again. He began riffling through a stack of papers on his desk. "The Treasury Department has been importuning me to appoint a new assistant special agent to one of our newest outpost responsibilities. Your husband has been surveying all over the country. That means he must be accustomed to rough living and all kinds of weather conditions, doesn't it?"

"Oh, yes!" I said almost too eagerly. He looked at me quizzically from under his brows.

"Do you think he would be interested in going to the Aleutian Islands?"

"The Aleutians!" I shivered, remembering where I had drawn

ON THE PACIFIC

that island chain on the map of the Alaskan Purchase Territory. For a moment the room reeled. That was too far away to send my John.

"Actually, it's still farther north than the Aleutians," he continued. "The Seal Islands are in the Bering Sea. We need another agent up there to supervise the taking of the seal pelts, which means a considerable income to our government. That is about all I can think of that might help you out at the moment. The pay is good and there is absolutely no expense involved, so the entire salary could be saved. There is a senior special agent there already. I could appoint your husband to be his assistant. It is a two-year contract. Do you think you could part with your husband for two years?"

Part with him? Wait two years! That did it!

"If he accepts, I will go with him." How bold I must have sounded!

"You apparently do not know where these islands are. I should have explained that I was not speaking of Nantucket or Long Island."

"Oh, I know where they are. St Paul and St George are about 57 degrees north and 170 degrees west, almost within the Arctic Circle."

Mr. Hayes looked at me keenly then, not believing that this delicately reared hothouse orchid of Washington could dream of being transplanted to the frigid zone. He probably thought me incapable of undergoing the same hardships that the pioneer women had been undergoing for more than two generations of trekking across our country. "You know where they are, and you still wish to go with him?" He paused, and he may have been weighing whether or not to forbid me. But he did not forbid me. Instead he said, "Be awfully sure, Elizabeth."

"I am awfully sure, Mr. Hayes," I said, seeing that I had to terminate the interview before he changed his mind. Had I not sworn long before that I never would wait at home alone for John again? I could not bear it if the president forbade me to go. I smiled a grateful smile to Mr. Hayes, as though he had conferred a cabinet post on John, held out my hand to him, and bid him good-bye.

"I wish you luck, my dear," he said as he took my hand firmly in his. "But I certainly would be the first to understand if you backed down on this."

"Never!" I said and I meant it.

To this day, John never has suspected that I had anything to do with his official appointment, the notice of which arrived by courier a few days after my trip to Takoma Park. We had long and earnest debates over the advisability of accepting. He was sure that the position was one for which he was ill suited by temperament and training. I argued that, after all, it was for only two years, during which time he would be able to save the better part of his salary.

"But two years, Libby!" he exclaimed. "To be away from you two whole years! You've sworn you'd never let me go away again, and now you are urging me to go from you to the ends of the earth! I don't understand. I expected tears — remonstrances — anything but this!"

"This time I am going with you."

I can remember that I said it quietly but firmly, and because there was no change of expression on his face, I thought he had not heard. So I repeated, "I am going with you."

"I heard you the first time," he said, and that was all he said for a long time. He paced the floor. I know now that he was trying to find words with which to discourage me, make me change my mind, without ordering me to stay at home. He never had ordered me before, though that was not an uncommon practice in the households of all my young married friends. We never had quarreled. And suddenly I knew we were about to argue, yet both of us wished to avoid any bitterness that we would someday regret. In a flood of words more eloquent than his usual succinct way of expressing himself, he told me all the reasons why I, a woman, could not go. The reasons were consideration for my health and well being, my happiness, and my safety. He hinted explicitly at the provocation my presence would cause men who were hungrily denied their own wives for the years they had to spend in such places.

I would listen to none of his arguments because my mind had been made up and nothing would change it. Always I came back to the prospect of our long separation if I did not go.

"Two years, John! Do you really know what it is like to always have to wait for you?"

"I think I do, Libby. After all, I always have to wait for you, too."

"I'd never have argued you into accepting the position if I had not planned, from the very moment of hearing about it, that I would be going, too. Don't you want me to be with you?"

"God knows how much I do, Libby, but . . ." There was always a "but" and a return to the old arguments about weather, living conditions, the absurdity of an American woman living — or trying to live — among barbarians at the rim of the Arctic: the absurdity of Libby Beaman of Washington, D.C., living or trying to live under primitive conditions, when in her own home and at her fingertips, she had all the comforts and conveniences of the overpampered and was surrounded with the very cultural, intellectual life she would be denied on the Pribilofs.

"That's just it, John," I argued. "We've been surrounded and overwhelmed by my family. We have to start sometime to make our own lives, out from under this roof."

"How well I know we must," John sighed bitterly. He had the look of one trapped by circumstance.

"And too, you know that I have sworn I never would let you go away alone again, no matter where you were sent."

"That, too, I know."

"I hadn't quite counted on the North Pole," I said, trying to bring a little humor, a little lightness, into a difficult, tense moment. "But as you see, I am willing even to go that far to be with you. Good heavens, John, women are crossing this continent every day in nothing more than wagons, on horseback, even on foot. If they can do such things, so can I."

"I like your pluck, my dear, but not your foolhardiness. There are great differences between you and the women who are trekking west. If I thought for one moment that you might come to harm from this proposed mad assignment, I'd turn it down now in spite of its attractive inducements."

"Then you will take me with you." I stated rather than asked.

Together we visited the Treasury Department under secretary in charge of these operations to learn as much about the assignment as possible, also as much as possible about living conditions up there on the Pribilofs. We quite candidly announced that I would be going along, and not once during any of the conversations did anyone put a prohibition upon my going. Meanwhile, of course, there were long and earnest discussions with my family around the dinner table and whenever we were together. Everyone took every possible means and argument to discourage me from going, considering me only slightly less than insane to contemplate such a venture, and hoping, I am sure, right up to the last moment that I would find myself with child and unable to go.

In spite of all my firm resolutions, I cannot even now write of my parting with my family without breaking down.

I realize now that I should have begun this journal the day Charles gave it to me. Writing in retrospect is difficult. Yet I hate to make short, daily entries. I would rather tell a continuous story. So I wait for the leisure moments to write these things that have happened.

We made a harrowing trek across the continent, which I have described in a long letter home. At times we came close to disaster, and I still am amazed that we have no scars from the journey. The engine belched black smoke that covered us so that we looked more like Negroes than like ourselves. The engine also spewed live coals that at one time set the baggage car on fire and, on another occasion, caused two bags of mail to burn. Fortunately none of our possessions were harmed. We never could replace the wonderful gifts of warm things our families and friends gave us. We were showered with lengths of woolens and cashmere, soft warm underclothes, nightclothes of pure wool challis, eiderdowns, wool hose, knee caps, bed socks, nightcaps, and hug-me-tights galore. It is a far more elaborate trousseau than the one with which we began our marriage.

John insists we are taking too many hampers of clothing, that as soon as we arrive on the islands we will sew ourselves into sealskins and never take them off until we leave. He does not look the way he always looks when he jokes. I've had trouble understanding him all the days of this trip. He is gentle and considerate of me but oh, so quiet, preoccupied, and remote — even evasive — not my John. I've asked him what disturbs him.

"The job itself, Libby. I just can't quite see it."

One of the first things the Treasury Department instructed John to do upon arrival in San Francisco was to get in touch with the Senior Agent, who had been home all winter on business and would be going back with us to the Pribilofs. "He can answer your questions better than we can here in Washington," the officer had said. "He's been up there and knows what the arrangements should be." Thinking back now, I realize it was after John's first interview with the SA that he became so silent. When he returned from that interview, John had asked me searching questions about how prepared I would be to face terrific dangers we hadn't thought about.

"How bad really is it up there?" I asked. "Did your superior tell you anything different than the Treasury Department man? There is a house, isn't there?"

"Oh yes, a comfortable little bungalow."

"Well, that's all we need, isn't it? The only thing that could turn me back at this point is for you to tell me directly that I may not go with you."

"And that I never will do, Libby. I'd rather break my contract than go on without you now that we've come this far. That's

ON THE PACIFIC

God's truth. I guess I took the Senior Agent too much by surprise. The Treasury Department had not informed him that you would be going along."

"He didn't say outright that I could not go, did he?" I asked. But what right had he to forbid me? The Treasury Department had not forbidden me, nor had President Hayes. Certainly he had no more authority over our lives than they. But suddenly it was important to me to know just what this man felt about my presence on the islands. "He did not forbid you to bring me, did he, John?"

"No," John said. But it was a long, drawn out, slow no. "He could not have done that. He just cannot believe that a woman is going into that hazardous situation or, for that matter, that *I* would let you."

I remember now how John paced the floor a long time before he spoke again. Then he turned and faced me, rather belligerently for him. "We three are going to have to live together in one small house. Do you realize what that will be like, Libby? Three of us! You and I are not to be alone after all, and this time we will be sharing our lives with a stranger — a man!"

Is this to be my fate forever — never to have my husband to myself?

"But I thought there were plenty of company houses."

"Company houses for company employees, not for us, Libby. As a matter of fact, there are only enough houses for the Aleut families, none left over. We have to live in Government House by agreement with the company. Since talking with the Senior Agent, I've had visions of you cooking and keeping house for another man. I'll not have it. I'll not have it, I say. We should have been forewarned before we got this far."

"But, John, I'm sure we can make some arrangement for our own privacy." I wasn't so sure, but I wanted to sound reassuring. "Let me work something out with the Senior Agent. He may wish his privacy too."

"Not when he sees you, my dear."

"Thank you, Mr. Beaman. It could be that he might find me forbidding. I can be, you know — spinsterish and forbidding. I'll speak with him."

"No matter what arrangements you make, remember I'll not have him sitting at our table with us every meal, day in, day out — or sharing that one living room constantly. I couldn't stand that for two days, let alone two years."

"Is he such a terrible boor?"

"On the contrary, he seems a fine enough gentleman — capable, interesting, and in most ways, far superior to this piddling job we have to do. Yes, I said piddling. I could call it by worse names. He has described it to me. It is beneath our dignity, his and mine."

"No, John, no work is ever beneath a man's dignity if he does it with dignity." But inside I realized this too would be a constant goad, rubbing both men raw — work they did not like, work that might be far beneath their capabilities. "I am surprised at you for saying such a thing."

"It is ugly work and not an engineer's."

"That we knew before leaving Washington. Our job is to make the best of it, the best, too, of what will be a difficult situation."

"You're so accustomed to living with your family, surrounded by loving relatives, that you cannot imagine what it will be like to live in close quarters with a total stranger — a total stranger who is domineering and who is my superior officer."

"We can manage. We can manage. I'll arrange it. When can I meet with him?" I wasn't too sure, but again I wanted to sound reassuring.

"He's gone back to his home downstate until the ship sails. You will not meet him until we are aboard the St Paul."

"Oh," I said, and suddenly I felt very old and very afraid. "All those weeks before we can meet! All those weeks to be harboring ill will and indecision! Oh, John, that isn't like us at all. Let's plan for ourselves. Why, if worse comes to worst, I can cook for us on a little spirit lamp in our own bedroom. You were told that we could get such things up there at the company store — and our food supplies. As for the rest of the house, though it might be nice to stretch out a bit, we really don't need it. We could do without it. I'm not afraid of living in one room for two years."

"You don't know what it means to be cooped up in bad weather in small quarters. It's happened to me often in the field. Men who've been friendly out on the line want to cut each other's throats when thrown together too long in small quarters during bad weather. And weather, Libby, is to be our worst enemy. Three of us, icebound, rockbound, weather-bound! We'll go mad!"

"Then let's not go at all. You could find work here. Perhaps I could, too, until we catch up. We might even settle here. This little place isn't too awful. I don't want you to go on into something you already hate."

"And break a government contract! Why, Libby!"

"You said before that you would."

"But I did not mean it that way. I was quite upset."

"You've been upset ever since your talk with the Senior Agent."

"Facing this uncertain future has upset me. It's all so far out of my line that I cannot understand how I ever let myself in for it."

"We're penniless otherwise. Let's count them as two lost years, then start from there."

"We've lost so many already, dear."

"I know. But things may break for us. Don't let that man bother you. After all, why is he having to do this sort of work unless he, too, is faced with our same problem? Perhaps he will be understanding of that."

"I doubt it," John said, and I could tell from the way he said it that his mind was made up about his superior officer.

May 23, 1879
Onalaska, Aleutian Islands

My Dear Ones,

We are on the steamer St Paul waiting for the unloading of goods which are left here to be distributed to the different stations of the Alaska Commercial Company. We arrived here yesterday afternoon and expect to leave for St Paul Island Sunday morning.

I stood on deck with all the gentlemen when we pulled away from Angel Island. The wind was brisk and the day fair. After we left the harbor called the Golden Gate, we sailed westward for several days, then turned toward the North Star. On Sunday, May 10th, the ship began to go up and down. I laughed and talked and thoroughly enjoyed the new sensation, glad that I had eaten a hearty breakfast to withstand the wind. One by one the young men rapidly disappeared without excusing themselves. From the corner of my eye I watched them dive into their staterooms, unceremoniously holding their hands to their stomachs or to their mouths. I was rejoicing in my own well-being when just as suddenly I too had to follow, much to the amusement of our little company.

On Thursday, a week — to the day — after we had left, my husband reported to me, in my stateroom which I could not leave, that the sea was calmer; in fact, it was so smooth he thought I might try to go out on deck and get some fresh air. Since I was too weak to help myself, he dressed and carried me to my deck chair. Soon I was surrounded by our little company of gentlemen, all expressing pleasure that I was again up and about. They surrounded me with every comfort, but I could endure being up for only a little while before I was overcome with seasickness again. I was obliged to return to my cabin where I remained the rest of the voyage.

The next day began another period of extremely rough weather.

The Senior Agent's stateroom is on the opposite side of the ship. He was first to get seasick. John had stopped in to look after him several times each day. Each time he did, the Senior Agent inquired about me. One day he sent me a note on the back of his personal calling card, which caused my first smile since leaving San Francisco. "Compliments and commiserations of your fellow sufferer, a forlorn and shipwrecked brother who hopes that you will take heart again and fight this battle through with Old Nep. But isn't it enough to disgust an Egyptian mummy? The St Paul goes bravely on, but very slowly, and the haven of rest is still ten

ONALASKA HARBOR

44

days off. Let's get out and walk! Yours Jonahfully, SA." I took heart at this evidence of a human side to my husband's superior.

Sunday night of the second week, a stronger wind came up. The vessel rolled and pitched; the wind got worse on Monday and still worse on Tuesday. There was no rest for our bodies, which were tossed about. For two nights not even the bravest could close his eyes. It was a struggle to stay in one's berth. John lashed me to mine. The sea was fearful to look at, with great waves that broke over the deck, beating against our doors and washing into our cabins. They came with such force that we feared the doors would be battered down and we would all be swept into the sea.

The sailors were on deck, screaming at each other above the noise of the waves, either putting up or taking in the sails. I felt extreme terror for our lives. Yet the captain, the only one to keep his footing, looked in to say that this was one of the easiest voyages he ever had made!

Days later, you can imagine how welcome was the sound of the watch's voice calling down, "Land in sight!" I sprang out of bed, forgetting I had been sick, and looked through the lattice of our door. In the far distance I could see a faint line of something darker than the sky, and I knew it was land.

To my astonishment, as we drew nearer to the mountains I saw that they were covered with snow. I felt better instantly, and as the sea was smoother, I dressed hurriedly and went on deck to watch landfall coming on fast. Great purple peaks arose from the water. Their tops and their gullies were covered with a blanket of purest snow. The biting air coming off the snow was all we could stand. Though the land is desolate and dreary, it seemed beautiful to us. In the afternoon, we sailed through the long Aleutian chain of mountainous islands, which actually are volcanic peaks lifted out of the sea. We sailed into this harbor, and within two hours of suffering all the tortures of the sea, I was walking the streets of this quaint little village nestled among the hills.

This is Onalaska, one of the company's trading posts. There are about fifty to a hundred native families and several American agents, all men. I learned that I am the first American woman ever to touch upon these islands. The knowledge gives me a strange sense of pride and a new strength, in spite of my weakened state. Everyone looks at me with a little awe and a great deal of curiosity.

We are blessed with pleasant weather, so that we can roam about the hills and through the village, which is surrounded on all sides by high, snowcapped mountains. In the distant northwest is a volcano which is usually invisible because of the mists enveloping its summit, but now it is sending forth great columns of smoke which, I am told, it does from time to time.

We took a sail across the bay and climbed the hills. After tramping about a mile, we came to a grove of small evergreens called "Sitka spruce." There were about a dozen stunted trees, the tallest fifteen feet. They resembled the Norway spruce, which I think they are. They were brought from the island of Kodiak, several hundred miles to the east of

ONALASKA HARBOR

45

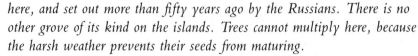

here, and set out more than fifty years ago by the Russians. There is no other grove of its kind on the islands. Trees cannot multiply here, because the harsh weather prevents their seeds from maturing.

On our way back, we picked a large bouquet of ranunculus. The strawberry-shaped flowers came in vivid colors, startling against the snow, and they were sweet scented. We found other flowers in warmer, sheltered crevices where the snow, which fell heavily last night, had not reached. I counted nine varieties in all.

This afternoon we walked along the seashore and were charmed with the abundant sea life: jellyfishes — some purple, some rose, and some white — fish, and sea plants. When we returned to the village, we visited the Russian church, which is very beautiful and was being made ready to celebrate Ascension Day. Its exterior is in striking contrast to the white frame houses and the sod houses of the natives. It has a bright blue, onion-shaped dome that rests on a bright green tower. The frame structure of the church is a vivid yellow.

There are no seals in these waters. The natives hunt the sea otter and fox, whose pelts they sell to the company. The company has a warehouse filled with all kinds of skins found in these parts. The principal catch is the sea otter, whose pelt is extremely valuable. It is a rich and beautiful fur which needs little processing and no dyeing and can be used in its natural state. One pelt, back in the States, can be sold for $100 to $600! The black fox fur is the most expensive. In all, there is about $100,000 worth of fur to be taken to the States for the market.

The Aleuts resemble Orientals more than they do the Esquimeaux of Alaska (there are a few here). They live mostly on fish which they catch in the bay. Cod is the staple. Salmon and salmon trout come in at certain seasons. The latter is delicate eating; we have discovered we cannot get enough of it. Mussels abound on the shores just above low tide. Birds are numerous and delicious. Seal meat, a delicacy, is imported from the Seal Islands.

When I left Washington, I had many misgivings about what was in store for me. But now, after seeing this little village, I am reassured. Even in these few days at anchor, the memory of the horrible voyage is fading. After all, we did live through it. I have, however, begun to question whether those who have written so beautifully of the sea were ever on it.

My next letter will be from St Paul Island, from Government House.

As always, your loving
Lib.

Onalaska. Aleutian Island. harbor.
May 23d 1879.

My dear ones. We are on the Steamer "St Paul"
waiting for the unloading of goods which are
left there to be distributed around at the
different stations belonging to the Alaska
Commercial Company. We arrived here
Wednesday afternoon and expect to start for
St Pauls Island Sunday morning. I mailed a
letter to you while on board the ship and
first starting from "Sancilito" (an island in
San Francisco Bay) where we had anchored for
the night in order to fast all the goods to the
ship to keep them from rolling about.
Sailors are very superstitious and dont like to
start on Friday so I think that was their reason
for starting Thursday before time in readiness
& they had to anchor and finish. The next
morning after partaking a hearty breakfast want
out on deck with the gentlemen & at eight we
am. We started. We sailed along towards the
far where we leave the harbor—called the
"Golden Gate) and entered the ocean. The
great ship began to go up & down. I
laughed & I talked and tried to appear
unconcerned. One of the young men began
to rapidly from the deck struggling with
his stomach. I laughed at him and
turning to one of the men said "I hope
I wont be the first to give up" & I rejoiced
to see the young man dive for dear life
into his cabin. I was the next to follow
amidst the laughter of the more intimate

On thursday & week from the day
he started my husband reported the
Sea so smooth & night it able to
go on deck, being so weak to help
myself he dressed me and carried me
on ... and was summoned
on ... company of gentlemen—
... pleasure to see me out on
they surrounded me with every care, a
but I could not endure it for me a
little while when I was again attacked
with sea sickness and obliged to turn
in again, there I remained for the rest of
the voyage. The next ... whole time
was as sick as ever C. ... my ... so sick,
was on the opposite side of mine ... &
daily enquired after my health, he
one day he sent me this card
which caused the first ... since
... compliment and communication ...
fellow sufferer, H.G.O. A ... and
wicked brother who hopes he will
will take heart again and fight this
with Old Neptune's things but its energy
disquiet—an Egyptian mummy isn't it? the
St Paul goes bravely on slept awfully slow
and the horn of rest is ten days off, ...
Lets get off and walk. Yours Jonah fully
H.G.O.
Sunday night of the second week a
strong wind came up the vessel pitched
& rolled and all day monday & tuesday
night was the same motion & no rest
the body, two nights we could not shut
our eyes as ...

48

great waves dashed on the deck & eating
dashing against our doors with such force
in fact it would wash us off. The
sailors were all on deck - screaming at
each other while pulling up or lowering
down the sails. I never ___ in such ___
in my life and yet the Captain
said it was one of the best voyages
they had made. For two twelve days ___
___ of sight of land. Here exceedingly
___ were the words "land in sight". I
___ out of bed to see if I had
___ right — ___ in the far distance
a faint line of something dark
___ it was really land. The sight ___
___ new life in me — I felt better
___ the sea was smoother. I went
___ again to feast my eyes on
___ ___ coming into sight. To my
___ ___ the ___ drew ___ to the
___ ___ they were white with —
___ arose before us all
___ ___ of pure white snow
___ ___ from there, was almost
___ ___ though the land
___ ___ it was beautiful
___ ___ we sailed the
the ___
___ ___ ___ islands
We sailed into ___ ___ volcanic mountain
little village nestled ___ among the hills
& this was "Analaska" ___ ___ ___
trading posts. There are ___ of ___ ___
notives & several agents. ___ ___ ___
here but the notives ___ the ___ ___
& call it the company. ___ ___

a ware house filled with all kinds of
skins found in that part of the country. The
principal catch is the sea otter - the skin of
which is very rich and beautiful as it can
be used for the natural state they are
worth from $100. dollars up to $600 they
breed a fine stock fox which is the most
expensive. In all they have about a thousand
thousand dollars worth of furs stored up in
this ware house ready for the market.

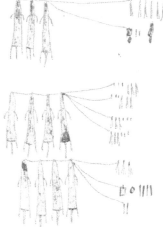

The he ship is our hotel. Aside from the dormitory for the
men of the Alaskan Commercial Company, the army
garrison, the navy garrison, and the natives' homes and
warehouses, there is nowhere that a white woman can stay. The
company only recently has built the frame houses for the Aleuts,
one for each family who would consent to move in. There has
been some trouble about convincing the natives that the new
homes are preferable to their sod *barrabkie* built half underground.
But they have begun to take to civilization rapidly now and will
feel quite at home soon. Their cousins, exported to the Seal
Islands one hundred years ago by the Russians, have been living in
modern frame houses for more than three years, which has put the
Aleutian Aleuts to shame. Their cousins in the Seal Islands earn
more than they do and now can buy luxuries. They refer to their
Pribilof cousins as those "bogatskie Aloutov," those "rich Aleuts"
that I am going to live among.

I could make no entries in this diary during all the wild days of
the voyage after the first storm broke. Had the trip been a smooth
one, I do not know what our days would have been like, aside
from promenading and writing and a few attempts at
conversation. Days are endless; the sea, monotonous; and the
passengers one does not know, boring. The men are nice enough.
They would prefer to tell rough, wild tales of war experiences, of
prospecting for gold, or other adventures. But when I am around

MAY 23rd

ONALASKA HARBOR

51

they speak only of their families, which they have had to leave for six months, a year, or two years at a time, according to their contracts with the company.

The Senior Agent seldom has been a party to any of this. He has kept to himself most of the time. The men do not consider this rude or snobbish, and they respect his desire for privacy. He says he is busy writing. I was, of course, pleased to get his little message in midvoyage. It was such a human gesture and helped so much when I was sickest. I felt as though our common misery and fellow suffering had wiped out his displeasure with me. John's ministrations to him must have won a measure of gratitude that would make our relationship more congenial during the rest of the trip. Instead, John has been annoyed by the note and feels as though I have counted too much on its momentary friendliness.

He may be right. Since we have been lying-to in port, the Senior Agent has been gruff again and unapproachable, as though he never had written the little note or is ashamed that he weakened enough to do so. He goes about his own affairs, seeing men in the village, or remains secluded in his stateroom.

The company men are busiest. But some of them have been kind guides and escorts, taking us all over this area and explaining as much as they can about the activities of the company and their arrangement with our government.

I've written several letters home from here because there is the possibility that they may get there faster than if they go back on this ship. Though the Senior Agent was right about letters not reaching home until August if they go back on the St Paul, he failed to mention that occasionally a few of the Coast Guard cutters that patrol these waters put in at towns along the coast where overland stages now connect with cross-country mail stages or with the Union Pacific Railroad. Most of the men here risk their letters this way and often find that they beat the letters delivered from the St Paul by many weeks. I, too, am risking a batch of letters. "It's chancy no matter what way you send them, Mrs. Beaman," one kind guide said.

The air is biting cold aboard ship. It sweeps down off the mountains and across the bay. Yet in the sun of midday, I feel a hint of warmth. The islanders say they seldom have seen this much sun, though it does get warm in spite of the mists in July. My clothes so far are adequate. Whenever I get too cold, I add another layer. I look with longing at the warehouses filled with luxurious furs, which we could purchase here for only a fraction of what they would cost back home. I could have them heaped upon me like the wealthiest ambassador's wife in Washington. I could, that is, if I cared to have every dog in town follow me. All the furs up here are uncured, untreated, and laid away only in salt until they are shipped to New York and London to be properly processed. The stench around the warehouses is only slightly worse than that around some of the natives' homes.

The natives, until warmer weather arrives, are still in their winter clothes of native-cured sheared furs, worn with the fur side toward their skin. They do not seem to mind the odor at all. I shall continue to live in woolens until some distant day when we may have enough money to purchase a fur coat in the States! Strange, isn't it, with all this wealth of fur around us?

I cannot write long because my fingers are cramped and **MAY 24th**
tired and cold from writing letters to all our friends and relatives while we wait for the *St Paul* to continue on its way. The last of the supplies for Onalaska were unloaded yesterday. Then the ship began to take on the huge cargo of pelts and whale oil. This is because it will not be stopping here on its way back to the States. This is Sunday and all the warehouses are closed. No one is working except our crew in preparation for casting off. I should have liked to stay and see how the natives celebrate their Ascension Day. I know little about the Greek Orthodox Church, which seems to have taken a firm hold on these people. The church building is an extravagant structure out of all proportion to the simple, humble way of life in this little town.

A final shout brought us all on deck to the landward rail. The entire village was at the wharf to see us off before going on to services at their church. As we sailed away, we could see them forming a procession and going toward the church. Captain Erskine invited John and me to the wheelhouse to watch him maneuver the *St Paul* out of the sheltered harbor and into the treacherous waters ahead. John argued with him that using the engine would save him a lot of trouble, that it would make the ship cut the waters instead of riding the waves, especially in the storm, especially if all sails were down. I could tell by our captain's expression that John was speaking heresy. Captain Erskine argued back. John said he studied such things at Rensselaer. The captain said he'd sailed the seven seas and ought to know what's best. John said that someday there will be engines powerful enough to drive big ships faster than sails can. In fact, sails won't be needed at all. Captain Erskine said that he hopes he never lives to see that day . . . that John is engaging in silly speculation . . . that there always have been sails and there always will be sails — the most beautiful and dramatic sight in all the world!

We could see that the captain had to begin to concentrate on getting us through tricky waters, so we left him to his wheel and his sails. Not once has he resorted to the auxiliary engine. We will put in at sheltered coves each sundown, for we are among submerged mountain peaks, reefs, and strange currents. These currents change from year to year, which is why we must sail so far to the west. We cannot navigate the currents in the dark until they are charted for this coming summer. No longer are we in the open Pacific with a clean, broad path to the North Star. After we have gone through the strait between Kamchatka and Attu, which is also a vicious channel but the least treacherous, we will again have open waters until we near the Pribilofs. The waters of the Bering Sea may be open, but they will present the wildest Arctic storms for three days, if we are lucky, and for many more if we are unlucky. There will be icebergs in that open sea, and fogs and pirates, too.

When we left the wheelhouse, I found the Senior Agent sitting in the deck chair next to mine.

Bidarrah and Natives, St Paul Island, a watercolor by Henry Wood Elliott

Onalaska Harbor — where great purple peaks rise out of the water.

I should have written down our conversation as soon as it was over. But when I came in to do so, I heard shouting and much running about on deck. John came to the door to announce that we had come into the wake of a company whaler which either had sighted or already had harpooned a huge Orca gladiator, one of the largest of all whales and known as the "killer whale." I hastened on deck to watch the excitement.

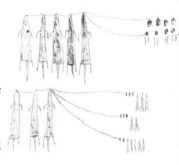

The monstrous mammal, with its giant dorsal fin just above the surface of the water, seemed as big as the sturdy little ship which was either chasing it or being towed by it. We were not yet close enough to see. The whaler was going at a tremendous clip toward a black, perpendicular cliff with only a narrow shelf of beach under it. We could see her sailors frantically tacking and taking in sail to slow the vessel's headlong plunge toward disaster.

"That whale is almost as big as the ship," I exclaimed.

"That's why they have to run it aground," Captain Erskine said. He had joined us on the foredeck to watch. "They can't take it aboard or even drag it alongside as they do sometimes. There are probably natives on this island who can help with the killing and the flensing. We'll stand by for a while to make sure our friends don't get into trouble."

We could hear shouting from the cliffs and could see natives waving to the men on the ship. Two *bidarrahs* (large skin boats) carrying six men each came from around the cliff; our captain explained that there was probably a village and low landing on the other side of the island. The whale, which had been harpooned, was thrashing about furiously in the shallower water, fighting the cornering maneuver of all three boats.

"It's big enough to capsize them," I said.

"And so it could," one of the men explained. "But whalers know their business and won't let that happen. Even if it doesn't yield as much oil as its next largest cousin, an Orca is a prize — especially for the natives — because of its great supply of meat. Helping to corner it is sport for them, and they know the company will pay them for their labor."

"A pleasant arrangement all the way around."

"The company always has maintained a fair way of dealing with the Aleuts. Freebooters of other nations have not always dealt as fairly, and the Aleuts recognize this. That's why they've come out so readily to help." And help they did, in their light, easily maneuvered skin boats. If Orca lashed out in one direction, a bidarrah, with full sail and each man paddling like mad, dashed directly at him. He would veer and thrash in another direction, only to be confronted by the other little boat or by the whaler.

"If they can get him nearer shore or wedged into that cove," our captain said, "they can shoot him in the eye and finish him off. The greatest problem is the reefs. Believe me, there's no time to study charts. Last year's could be different anyway, and there's still a lot of ice. The mate's one busy man taking soundings." We could see the mate taking soundings and could hear him shout, though we could not hear what he said. Captain Erskine continued, "When I was a youngster, I wanted to be a whaler. Some of the lads I grew up with tried to get me to join them on freebooter crews. Their tales of excitement were enough to turn anyone's head. But my father was an officer in the U.S. Navy and insisted I take the gentleman's way to sea."

"Such trips as these, I should think, are excitement enough," I said. "I warrant you're glad now you didn't take to whaling."

"Oh, yes," he sighed, and in that sigh I recognized all his life's longings and his regret that he had chosen the gentleman's career. It explained also why we had lingered so long to watch the action.

The whale, exhausted from loss of blood and energy, was giving less fight. We watched the men throw the harpoon lines to the Aleuts, who could run them ashore in their light boats. They were not strong enough or numerous enough to haul the monster onto the narrow ledge of shore. But they could secure the lines around great boulders to hold Orca as close as possible until the ebbing tide ran out from under him and left him high and dry. Then they'd have to work fast, before a rising tide, to get him flayed and sectioned in small enough portions to remove for further processing. They had a whole night's work ahead of them in the light of whale-oil flares.

"More work than some of them do in a whole year, I'll warrant," one man said. "Aleuts never expend much energy if they can help it." We sailed away from the scene after a final exchange of shouts and after the whalers ran up signals to reassure us that they were in no danger. The air was luminous as the sun, setting behind orange mists, cast a golden glow upon the sleek mountain of Orca's heaving flesh. The Aleuts and the whalers, who had gone in to land in a lighter (a barge-like boat used in loading or unloading boats like ours), looked like so many pygmies dancing around their monstrous catch, seeking the most vulnerable spot for finishing him off. Our last view of him was of his great yellow gill rakers turned toward us in a nightmarish grin I shall not soon forget.

"Last summer, one Orca's stomach yielded fourteen fur seals, one walrus cow, twelve porpoises, and a load of smaller fish, all larger than a man and undigested," one of the men said. "And that's not the greatest yield we've had on the island. But so far, no one has found a human inside."

"Except in the Bible." And the old argument began about whether the story of Jonah could be true or not. Those whalers who have had experience with Orca thought it could be true. Orca regurgitates the fur pelts of huge seals almost intact because he cannot digest them.

"Perhaps Orca found Jonah too tough to digest," said Captain Erskine.

I was about to record my conversation with the Senior   MAY 26th
Agent when the whale episode took place, and I recorded that first. I find I often set down the more trivial first, hating to approach the more difficult and disturbing experiences until I absolutely have to. I had the conversation alone, for John, having seen the Senior Agent before I did, excused himself and dove amidship on some slight pretext.

The Senior Agent rose as I approached him.

"Unusually calm weather for these parts," he said pleasantly enough. "For which I am grateful. I was never good as a sailor."

"And I, who've never sailed before, discovered I'm not a good one either," I said, hoping this shared truth might make matters simpler between us. "You're right about this pleasant day, a relief after all we've been through. It also seems much warmer."

"The Japan Current," he said, seeming to enjoy instructing me. "It sweeps in under this chain of islands. But the warmth won't last once we've reached the straits. That's why I am taking advantage of the sun. We will have so little where we are going. I wanted also to have a little talk with you, Mrs. Beaman," he said more formally, and I thought the chill already had set in.

"I've also wanted to talk with you, sir. A woman is naturally curious about her future home and housekeeping."

"There will be no housekeeping details. Mrs. Mandrigan, one of the more intelligent Aleuts, does all the housework, even carries in the water."

"That's not what I meant," I said, "though I do expect to do my share of work. I meant our actual living arrangements. Mr. Beaman tells me Government House is rather small for three to share."

"Quarters are small and built for only two male agents to occupy. We will have to arrange something to our mutual convenience. Fortunately there are two bedrooms, so we'll not have to convert the living room into one. We need it for an office." Then he turned to me and asked abruptly, "Mrs. Beaman, why have you insisted on coming up here in spite of every warning?"

I looked at him aghast for a long moment. I could not remember any warnings or prohibitions. But couldn't he see why?

"I wanted to be with my husband," I answered quite simply. What use to explain the long years of separation?

"Didn't your husband insist that you stay at home after my first conversations with him in San Francisco?"

"He did not insist."

"And, of course, he couldn't order you to stay at home," he said with a sneer in his voice as well as on his lips, contempt for a weakling too plainly written in his eyes, contempt for me, perhaps, for being the domineering woman intent on getting her own way. What could a man like this know of lonely longing for a loved one? "Why, Mrs. Beaman, I would no more think of bringing my wife into this life than I would of taking her to the moon or of subjecting her — or anyone I love — to such a hazardous adventure on a treacherous sea, to the Arctic climate, and to such primitive living conditions. Living on the Pribilofs, Mrs. Beaman, means an attempt to survive against the worst possible conditions any of us Americans have yet had to face. Many of the hardiest men have not survived. I explained all this to your husband in no uncertain terms. I described what was in store for him — the weather, our living arrangements with the company, the bestial nature of the work we have to supervise, work that makes beasts of the men who do it. No lone white woman should ever be permitted on the islands. Your husband knew all this in good time to send you back to Washington."

And that, of course, my husband never would have done. I was angry as well as embarrassed by his bluntness, for never in all my nursing days and in my work among men had I been spoken to so bluntly. And, too, I wanted to rise to John's defense. He blamed John — not me — for my being here. A flood of invectives rose to my lips. I was ready to charge him with rudeness and unfriendly treatment of two people before giving them a chance to show their own goodwill. But some few words he had said struck home with an awful force. So I did not let loose the flood of hurt pride and accusations, which would only have lowered his respect for me still more and would have gained us nothing more than additional ill will.

Suddenly, it seemed so clear to me just why he had acted as he had. I could be wrong. Let me say I want to believe I am right. My knowledge will alter nothing, make matters no easier. But in my mind and heart, I will feel easier because I think I understand. He has to act this way consistently — he will never be anything but rude and gruff and unfriendly. That is his self-defense against me, not as Elizabeth Beaman, but against me as a woman coming into his exclusively male world. He must have had some hard times over this fact. He must have weighed the situation carefully and then chosen exactly how to play his part, not only for his own security but for all of ours. Thank goodness I did not speak up in anger unwisely.

I had to admire him while I hated him.

"No matter what you may think of Mr. Beaman, the fault is mine, not his, that I am here," I said coldly. "I did not beg or cry until he gave in and let me come along. You would not understand why I have said firmly from the beginning that I would go, no matter how black a picture you or he or anyone else painted. So no matter what happens during these next two years, the fault will be entirely mine. If I've been too headstrong in this, then I will have to take the consequences. I am prepared for that."

I watched the steel bars in back of his eyes drop a little — not all the way and not for long.

"The consequences! You are too gently bred to know what you are saying, and you are too gently bred for life up here."

I smiled a wry smile at that but felt a warm glow of gratitude that he should recognize the fact. "But physically hardy withal," I said. "I nursed at Hallowell all during the war; that was a grim and hazardous experience, and I survived. I've never been sick a day in my life until this seasickness struck."

"Seasickness is another kind of sickness entirely," he said hastily in his own defense. "No doubt you are a hardy woman. But it isn't physical hardihood alone we have to have up here. Life on the islands requires strengths we haven't got."

"I thank you for your frankness, sir, and your warnings. I think I understand. I know you will want me to go back on the St Paul.

But nothing you have said will make me turn back now. Nothing frightens me or makes me wish I had changed my mind before we left Washington. We've come this far. I mean to go through with it." I wanted to add: *Therefore I wish we could be friends. The two years would be pleasanter.* I did not, because I realized that friendship, or even a friendlier attitude, was a prize to be earned. He sighed. I could tell that he finally had given up hope of turning me back. Instead I said, "Now we can get down to planning how we are to manage living under one roof so that we will be the least bother to you."

"Oh, we'll manage to get the house patched up to suit Mr. Beaman. He seems to think he is going to have to share you with me," he said in a coldly dispassionate way but in a tone that implied (I am sure it implied) share me in everything! I blushed. I could not hide the blush or my confusion.

"Oh, no!" I said without stopping to think before speaking out. "He's only afraid I'll have to cook and keep house for the two of you. That, he would never permit." I felt the spread of my blush down to my toes, and I could see that he was amused at my confusion even though he remained cold and smugly superior.

"As I have said before, there's no housekeeping to do. The widow Mandrigan will look after everything for all of us, as she has been doing for the agents these past several years. We will have to divide the house into two separate suites. There aren't many men up there good at carpentry, and unfortunately, there's not an extra stick of lumber. As you know, every inch of wood has to be shipped from the States or Alaska. I should have seen to the loading of some lumber at San Francisco. But frankly, Mrs. Beaman, I never dreamed for one minute that you actually would come along." He then proceeded to draw a rough sketch of the floor plan for me, explaining what he thought might work out to give us each as much privacy as possible.

His drawing of the house showed a tiny box, all on one floor, with a small, central, square hall; two bedrooms; a living room, which serves as an office as well; a dining room that opens into the living room with a wide archway and no door; and a small, dark, poorly equipped kitchen. The SA proposed cutting the dining room off from the living room with a wall, since it has a doorway to the narrow hall that runs from the front hall to the kitchen and is opposite the bedroom he will let us have. This would give us a private sitting room.

"But that would give you no place to eat," I protested. "Mr. Beaman and I could manage with the bedroom alone. We don't need anything else but the use of the kitchen when you do not need it." I was bound to insist that there would be no joint dining. "Does Mrs. Mandrigan also do your cooking for you or have you been doing it yourself?"

"We wouldn't think of letting Mrs. Mandrigan touch our food!" he said, but he said no more. I assumed that he and the assistant agent had been trying to cook for themselves. John could be right about thinking that the SA would want to join us at table. Men hate to do their own cooking. Perhaps a short time after we arrive there, he'll make some sort of bargain about the joint use of the dining room in exchange for sharing meals with us. However, he does not look like the bargaining sort. My problem will be the cooking in any case — I'm not a very good cook.

"Mr. Beaman did understand you to say that we would not have to take food supplies with us, that we can purchase whatever we need at the company store?"

"That is correct. The store is usually well stocked with staples, nothing fancy. We depend on the wildlife right there for the rest of our diet."

"Then in that case," I said in a tone that must have seemed like wishing to terminate our conversation, "I shall try not to upset the islands too much by my presence. I have been made aware of some of the problems. I shall keep to myself. Our quarters, I am sure, will be worked out to everyone's satisfaction so that I will not be in your way. I assure you that I have come up here for no other reason than to be with my husband and to look after his comfort alone."

"That's what you may think," he said, rising and seeming to tower over me. "Remember that I am the senior agent, in all ways responsible for whatever happens on the Pribilofs. I cannot always be at your side to protect you when your husband has to be away from you. It won't always be a matter of your looking after your husband, but of his looking after you. There is work that takes us far afield for days at a time. I do hope everything will work out as you so optimistically think it will. Believe me, Mrs. Beaman, I have no other motive for frowning on this adventure of yours than a concern for your own well-being and the good name of our government services in the Pribilofs!"

He stalked off to his stateroom. I have said nothing of this part of our conversation to John. Dear knight in shining armor! He'd go right over and fight his superior officer. Indeed, I'd be starting all the troubles that he has foreseen and has been franker about than any other man who has spoken to a lady.

The Senior Agent still thinks he can make me return to the States with this ship when it goes back.

I will not return.

Sea Moss

We've had a rough and turbulent three days, all of us seasick and frightened. At first there were the terrifying mountain islands to sail between, with their jagged, black precipices coming down into the waters and their glaciers breaking away and falling into the sea in great roaring avalanches of rock and ice, so near at times as to rock the ship. We were like a bit of chaff in a whirlpool. There were sudden storms, tidal swells that all but dashed us against those perpendicular cliffs, and shallows where least expected; most treacherous of all were the currents and countercurrents forced between the close islands, apparently of warm and cold origin, for the fogs they formed have been the most hazardous.

The greatest warm current, the Japan Stream, squeezed itself between Attu and Kamchatka after having swerved in under Alaska and back westward under the Aleutian Chain. Where it hit the bitterly cold waters of the Bering Sea, dense fogs and turbulent storms formed, making this the most dangerous stretch of all the trip to navigate. We were sailing through banks of fog that opened and closed, and though we'd begun to get a faint odor of land, no land was yet in sight. Birds, too, came out to greet us. They wheeled about our mainmast by the thousands — all kinds: terns and auklets, gannets and gulls, and many others I did not recognize. They were noisy greeters, at times deafening. We could not hear each other speak. We did not speak. We were too full to speak. Our destination was so near.

"Land ho!" the watch called down. "Land ho!"

So near, dear Lord, so near, and yet we are not there, not really there until our feet are on the land. We ride at anchor, straining at the anchor buoy about a mile from the village of St Paul. A dense fog lies over us, lies over the Bering Sea.

The captain said that it is sometimes days (once two weeks) before he can land. "Not this time, fortunately. The sea is calming," he said when he saw how disappointed I was that we could not go in immediately. "We did at least find the anchorage, and that is something. I've also spent days hunting for it. By tomorrow the sea will be calm enough, I think, to send in the lighter, the first time with only crew aboard because there's still so much loose ice in the harbor. They'll have to chart a course and tell us whether it's safe enough for passengers to follow."

"You mean the ship doesn't go in to the wharf?" I asked, aghast at the thought of having to climb down the side of this heaving vessel into a tiny boat bobbing at its side.

"She can't. Water's too shallow. This is the shallowest water I dare draw, and it's the only safe anchorage for the island. Unfortunately there are no sheltered bays up here. We always take our chances with fog, storms, and changes — volcanic changes, that is — in the shallows. I hope for your sake, Mrs. Beaman, that the day will be calm and clear tomorrow."

I do too. The hours of waiting are longer than any I've had to wait before. The sea is still too rough for me to write legibly. But let me try. We've little else to do during these disappointing hours. We did catch a glimpse of our future home before the fog blanket descended. It was in those same few clear minutes that Captain Erskine performed the miracle of finding and anchoring us at the buoy. Miracle it is, indeed, when one thinks of how he manages to find these tiny pin dots on that map I once traced of the Alaskan Purchase. Navigation is still an incomprehensible science to me. For one thing, neither Captain Erskine nor the ship's mate has once been able to take an astral fix because of cloudy skies at night; not even a solar fix has been taken since we saw the Orca. They've navigated entirely on calculations, the careful computations on their charts, accurate timing, compass readings (which because of the closeness to the North Pole are erratic), and by recording every degree of every single turn of the wheel, as well as sounding constantly with the lead line and straining their ears for the sounds of seals and breaking surf.

"When I smell seals," our captain jokes "I know I've come in too far. I arrive by smell."

We know otherwise. We say a private prayer.

Speaking of smells, the cold winds from land come toward us

Three Alaska Commercial Company cutters off Novastoshnah, St Paul Island.

OFFSHORE, St PAUL ISLAND

laden with earth odors, seaweed rotting, animal debris, fish and rotting fish, and, above all, seals. *Pahknoot,* the Aleuts call odors. "You are getting the pahknoot of the Pribilofs," one gentleman informed me. "Something you will have to live with. It never goes away."

"How horrible," I said.

"Lady, you haven't smelled anything yet. Wait 'til you're right in it."

A few days ago, when we came through the straits, we were all asked to look out for pirate ships. They linger about the narrows where the great herds of migrating seals have to squeeze through from the Pacific into the Bering. There pirates can do their pelagic killing with the greatest of ease. Our government has been trying to stop this illicit trade that has decimated the seal herds considerably through the years. But this time we saw no pirates. In fact, the straits were so violently rough, I thought we'd never see another day.

"There's always plenty of excitement if we catch any pirates at it. We're permitted to use guns and we have, often," Captain Erskine said.

"The storm is enough excitement for me," I admitted. I was thankful that we didn't have to go to war with anyone over the seals, though I could see that the men were itching for a good fight. There were other excitements they watched for — treacherous icebergs, and we saw many — but no polar bears,

Village of Sᵗ Paul, a watercolor by Henry Wood Elliott

AK. ARTS AND ILLUS. COLL. ALASKA STATE LIBRARY

OFFSHORE, Sᵗ PAUL ISLAND

which would have interested me more. We did see whales —
which also linger at the narrows because seal meat is a favorite
meat — and sharks, as well as other ships. In all this great waste
of frigid waters, anything makes one feel less small, less lost.

I wanted to know if it was my imagination or if the water of
the Bering was greener than that of the Pacific. And if it was
greener, was that because it was shallower or colder or what? To
me, it appeared to be a brilliant green.

"It's sweeter," a fellow passenger answered. And in response to
my raised eyebrows, he explained, "Seawater is always less salty,
so it refracts light differently. That is why seawater is greener than
ocean water."

I suspect the main reason we all stayed on deck today, in spite of
the chill and the stormy sea, is because we wanted to watch
landfall, and fortunately, we had our brief glimpse of it — a bleak,
cold, inhospitable-looking mass of rock, here at the other end of
the earth.

We came in from the south, ignoring St George, which would
have been the nearer island but is too stormy to approach at this
time of year. The *St Paul* visits it only twice a year and then
merely to load pelts, of which none is ready now anyway. S^t
George lies about thirty miles southeast but seldom can be seen. It
appears, I am told, still more formidable and inhospitable upon
approach. St Paul has bleak, sharp contours relieved by soft,
rounded, worn down hills. Inland there are snowcapped peaks and

*Village of St Paul and
Lagoon, a watercolor
by Henry Wood Elliott*

OFFSHORE, St PAUL ISLAND

deep violet shadows ending sharply in pinkish sand dunes, vast, vivid patches of grass, and rocky shores where great chunks of greenish ice are piled in mountainous heaps. Low beaches sweep inland to high bluffs of perpendicular rocks with flat plateaux on top. Some cliffs drop directly into the sea with shelves of rock at their bases, undercut by waves and tides. On these and on the beaches are thousands and thousands and thousands of male seals. From the ship, they appear to be black blobs restlessly swaying or moving back and forth between the water and the land. The sight is incredible. I had heard descriptions, but my wildest imaginings had not prepared me for such a sight.

These teeming, restless, barking, roaring hordes, then, are to dominate our lives.

"The groupings are called 'rookeries,'" John said, reiterating some of the lore he had gathered on the way up. "Don't ask me why, unless from a distance they resemble the hordes of noisy rooks we have at home." In that brief moment of seeing them, they presented a dramatic, fascinating sight.

Our approach, even from a mile away, had stirred up another overwhelming sight. Millions of seabirds wheeled into the sky from every nook and cranny of the cliffs. We could hear, and still do hear, their screams and squawkings above the surf pounding over the ice and against the rocks. The birds drown out the barking of the seals.

The village of St Paul, visible for only a few minutes before the fog closed in, presented a pretty picture. It is built up a steep slope away from the harbor, where the small boats of skin called *bidarkahs* and the bidarrahs are pulled up on the little wharf. Low hills surround the village, and one hill drops in a sheer cliff just to the south of the buildings. It drops 300 feet straight down to a narrow shelf where there are seals, the smallest rookery on the island, I am told, Nah Speel. Government House, our home-to-be, sits high on the central slope overlooking the roofs of the other houses. But it is not Government House that dominates the scene. The vivid blue onion dome of the Orthodox church gives cohesion and charm to the scene and gathers unto itself the neat white frame buildings of the Alaska Commercial Company and

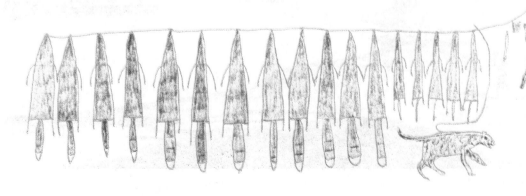

GOVERNMENT HOUSE, St PAUL ISLAND

66

the eighty white frame houses of the eighty Aleut families it serves.

To the left of the village, I could make out a long spit of sand, seal inhabited and parallel to the shore, enclosing a narrow lagoon which extended inland and seemed to broaden out beyond my vision. "That's Lagoon Rookery and its lagoon," one man said. "It does broaden out into a saltwater lake inland. That vast stretch of green grass between it and the first houses is the killing ground. That is where we drive the seals to be killed."

"How awful!" I said. "Right under the villagers' eyes!"

"Right under their noses would be more correct," he countered. "You at Government House will be spared the sight of the killing because of a fortunate rise in the land. But you'll not be spared the smell. St Paul is a smelly place in which to have to live."

"So I've already discovered," I said. "Even out here, the pahknoot of the island is strong."

Vicele Mandrigan

W hat a long day this has been! But here we are, at last, in our own room in our own home on land — not dry land, but land again.

MAY 28th

I was touched by the reception we received at the wharf this afternoon. We've been touched by all the little courtesies since.

About midmorning the mists cleared, and the waters calmed enough to send the lighter in with a complement of ship's crew and two company men who volunteered to brave the rough waters. Captain Erskine informed us that they would signal whether the waters were too rough for passengers. "Women and children first," he smiled, and from that I gathered that I would be in the first boat load to go ashore. We watched the lighter go into the mists that moved across the landscape. We watched it land and saw a crowd spring up around it. We watched the exchange of words with people on shore, and though we could not hear them above the roar of the surf, we knew that everyone was waving out to us and shouting. Signals were run up on the mast of company headquarters — favorable, I assumed, because Captain Erskine came to us first and said that we should stand by for the lighter's return. Our baggage would go in on a later load.

Almost as soon as the ship's crew landed, many Aleut men and boys leaped into their skin boats, hoisted sail, and came hurrying out to surround the ship. These native boatmen seemed not to mind the rough waters at all. They surrounded the ship, waving and shouting and singing in a gay and gala way.

"The welcome is for you, Mrs. Beaman," Captain Erskine said. "The natives do not usually come out to demonstrate like this." I took out my handkerchief and waved it to the men in their little boats. Immediately there was a roar, and they all broke in Russian song which one of the men at my side translated for me; it was a song of welcome to a brave soldier who had just returned from the war. How appropriate! I looked to John with tears in my eyes. His face was grim and set. I looked to the Senior Agent as soon as I was sure the tears had cleared from my eyes. His face was impassive. But he nodded to me in such a way as to indicate that the welcome was for me. The bidarrahs and the little bidarkas bobbled about on the huge waves for nearly two hours while we rode at anchor awaiting the lighter's return from shore. (An adverse wind was delaying it.) I said that I could not see how those flimsy little boats could stay afloat in such rough waters.

"Oh, their boats seldom capsize," Captain Erskine pointed out. "They're made of skin stretched over a walrus-bone frame, curved inward enough so they can heel over at a goodly angle before they ship any water. The boys, however, really are showing off for you today. Ordinarily they're too lazy to fight the sea. They fish only in calmer weather." These same lazy boys moved in close and staunchly held the lighter steady for me to climb in — no easy task for them or for me. In fact, I was terrified. There are some events for which a woman is not properly clothed, and this was one of them. My skirts blew out from me like a parasol and threatened to be torn from my waist.

The wind whipped the little sailboat like a bit of chaff on the surf and threatened to dash us against the great blocks of ice floating loose in the waves and through which we were trying to pick a channel to shore. I was relieved when we bumped the wooden wharf and threw a towline to many waiting hands. Terra firma at last! S' Paul — our Arctic home.

Mr. Morgan, the company director, stood on the wharf and handed me out of the lighter and onto the dock with all the grace and concern of a well-trained courtier. He introduced John and me to several of the people standing about trying not to seem too curious at the appearance of an American woman on the boat. I was introduced, amongst much confusion, to Mr. Redpath, Dr. Kelly, Mr. Moulton (whom John is to replace), and bearded Father Paul Shishenekoff in his black cassock and tall, black priest's hat. "Father Paul," as he is known to the island, wore a beautiful large pectoral cross on his ample bosom and leaned on a shepherd's crook as though he were an icon right out of the Old World. We also met Phillip Volkov, the chief or *tyone,* his wife, and Mrs. Mandrigan. I can't remember all the others. A well-dressed little boy stepped out of the crowd and timidly handed me a bouquet of flowers, while other children peeked from behind their mothers' colorful calico dresses. Everyone was agog at this strange new creature who was white like the company men but wore skirts like a woman. The air was warm in the hazy midafternoon sun, and our reception was full of a warmth I had not expected. I had anticipated the unfriendly stares of men who would be resenting my invasion of their privacy; I had been anticipating the same sort of welcome I had had aboard the *S.t Paul*. Instead everyone was dressed in Sunday best to make me feel at home.

The bidarrahs had helped bring in more of the passengers and our luggage. Mr. Redpath, assistant to Mr. Morgan, began to busy himself with our possessions, enlisting several young Aleuts to carry them up the hill to Government House. At this point, the Senior Agent, who had leaped ashore from one of the native boats, joined us and also was given a cordial welcome by the tyone and others. When he saw that Mr. Redpath was about to escort us up the hill, he said, "Charles, please allow me to do the honors. I should like to be the first person to welcome the Beamans to Government House." He then stepped ahead of us, and we followed him up a jagged but well-worn path to our new home. The entire village fell in behind us like some ancient religious procession winding its way up a hill to a shrine. The Senior Agent's gesture was the first, I am sure, of many to come that must be made for appearance's sake.

He had hurried ahead of us up the hill so he could arrive first at Government House. There he turned at the doorway and swiftly removed his hat and topcoat, tossing them aside so that he appeared to be the master of the house welcoming newly arrived guests. He greeted us most cordially and invited us into the living room where an oil-burning Franklin stove gave forth warmth and hospitality. I cannot believe there is this much comfort so far north, so far from civilization.

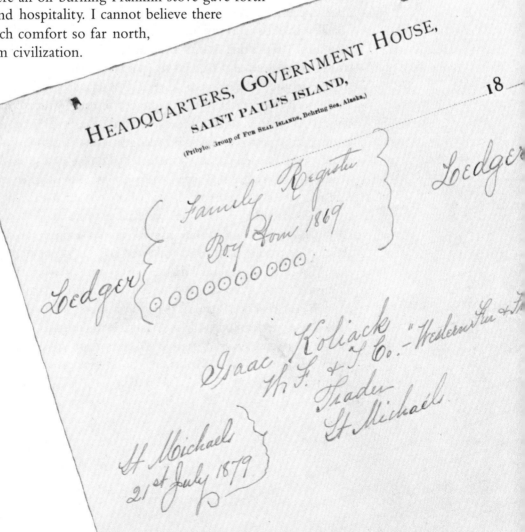

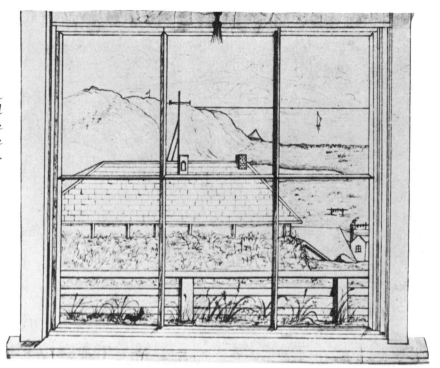

From our sitting room window, we are spared the sights of the killing ground by the hill.

"This is to be your home, you know, for the next two years. I hope you will be happy here," he said and smiled broadly, a beautiful bit of acting for all those who stood close by.

"Yes," I said, and that was all I could say for a long, long time. I was too full for words. I went to the window and looked out upon the bleak rocks and at the ship riding at anchor in the bay. For all his outward cordiality, I knew he wanted me to go back on that ship. I remained a long time at the window until the misty landscape cleared and I dared to face him again.

The babble of many people speaking in a strange tongue announced the arrival of our baggage, borne on the shoulders of several Aleut men. Each was eager to be the first to present his burden to us and thereby gain recognition; since men up here never carry burdens, each wanted us to know he'd done a noble deed just for us. John wanted to tip them, but each, in turn, refused with a shake of the head. I noticed our host's slight, wry smile. There will be so much we'll have to learn.

"This room is exactly like mine," our host pointed out as he showed us to our bedroom, followed by our Aleut helpers. "I see that Moulton, the agent who stayed up here all winter, has had it all cleaned up for you. Men don't live as neatly as they should, Mrs. Beaman. I was afraid we'd find a mess. The Aleuts have little sense of cleanliness. Mrs. Mandrigan, though awfully slow, is in that respect a superior native. Moulton must have made her hurry. That was Mrs. Mandrigan's son, Vicele, who presented you with the flowers."

GOVERNMENT HOUSE, S*ᵗ* PAUL ISLAND

70

I looked down to discover I was still holding them, though much too tightly. I had crushed their fragile stems.

"You will want a little time in which to get settled here," he continued in the same dispassionate voice but certainly with considerable thoughtfulness behind what he said. He left us standing in the middle of our bedroom. "I will show you the rest of the house later, whenever you are ready," he cast back over his shoulder.

John took me in his arms wordlessly. We clung to each other, too full for tears. "I'm sorry I got you into this, Libby. You'll never know how sorry."

I wanted to cry out that it was I who had gotten him into this, not the other way around. But suddenly I realized that tears and a sad face would get us nowhere, would make matters worse. *It is up to me to make the best of everything and to do so with good grace. We will never survive the two years and keep our sanity unless I do.* I broke from John's embrace and looked around our room.

"But, John, this is a lovely room. We should be quite comfortable and happy here." John, expecting tears, looked at me in surprise. We began to unpack and try to settle in.

This room is not exactly what one would call lovely. It is terribly plain. But it has possibilities for improvement. It needs, most of all, a feminine touch. While I can't hurry right down to F Street to get drapery and other yardage to brighten and soften its austerity, I can send back to San Francisco for what I need, and the *St Paul* will bring it back in mid-July on its next trip. The room is not large — but large enough for the two of us — square, with two windows that look out on the rise of earth inland. The woodwork is stained dark, as is the floor. There's a nondescript beige paper on the walls, stained and coming loose above the asbestos shield in back of the iron stove. I think that overheating the stovepipe has been responsible for that. The asbestos should be extended to the ceiling. I'll feel safer if John tends to this. There are two small beds instead of one. One looks newer than the other and probably was hastily brought here from somewhere while we were still riding out the waves offshore. They were neatly made up with clean, unpressed, unbleached muslin sheets, gray army blankets, and pink damask spreads. Wherever the pink spreads have come from, they are the greatest surprise.

The furniture is good, sturdy, mission oak: a chiffonier, no dresser, a huge wardrobe, a small table that we are using for a desk, two straight-backed chairs, a washstand with huge china basin and pitcher for hot water, and on the floor, a good rug of a rather nondescript conventional flower pattern. Men chose all this, it is obvious, and none ever expected a woman to be living here. Yet I'm sure that I can live here.

I am happy, now, that I did bring all those hampers John wanted me to leave at home. In some are linen sheets and soft wool blankets, full size though, so I hope we can find or build a double bed. I brought our soft bolster, slips for it, the large eiderdown that I quilted for my hope chest, and the silk crazy quilt which Sister Carrie and I made during that last carefree summer vacation of hers, before she went back to Vassar and the diphtheria epidemic that took her away from us. I thought again poignantly of Carrie as I unpacked the vivid quilt. Should she have gotten married in her freshman year as she wanted to do? And if she had, what would her life have been like by now? Each brilliant scrap of silk — they are intricately featherstitched together, some embroidered or painted as we fancied — is a memory of a ball or a party or a gala affair we attended, for the scraps are from our gowns and dresses. These are the gay, lovely memories I shall have to live on in this gloomy land of dirty skin coats and shapeless Mother Hubbards. Thank goodness, too, I brought two irons!

The windows are my greatest problem and will continue to be until I can do something about them. At the moment, they have two of my sheets tacked over them. There are no curtains or shades at all. That's first on my list. Though Government House stands on the hill, away from the village with no road past it, we simply will have to have shades and curtains for privacy. I realized that just after we began unpacking yesterday. I heard a slight noise outside our windows and looked up to see half the village with their noses flattened against the panes! Everyone was fighting for a place to watch what we were doing. I was aghast when I discovered that we could not pull a shade or close ourselves away. I went to the window and made a shooing gesture. They all fell back a ways — men, women, and children. Then they moved back to their places by the windows as soon as I returned to the task of unpacking and storing our things in the wardrobe. I shooed again. I wanted John to hang up sheets immediately, but we could find no hooks or rods or anything to hang them over.

"I'll go find a hammer and some tacks," John said and opened the door to the hall. Vicele fell into the room on his face. He had been peeking at the keyhole in which there was no key! Right behind him was his mother, and behind her were the Aleuts who had brought up our baggage. Vicele probably had been relaying information to them about what he saw, or he had been changing places with them. The Senior Agent came out of his room at this moment and issued a peremptory command in a strange tongue. Everyone instantly retreated to the living room. They stood about awkwardly as though they did not know what to do next.

"There is a native reception committee waiting to meet and greet you officially, you and Mrs. Beaman," I heard the SA tell John. "I've told them that they would have to wait until you were rested and until you were pleased to come out, which might be a long while. The Aleuts are a patient people. They'll wait forever. I will admit they've waited more quietly than usual. Remember, some do understand English and what I am saying, though most will tell you they speak only Russian. I think they know more English than they let on. When should I tell them to come back?"

I came to the door and said we were ready to meet them anytime.

Tyone Phillip Volkov and his little wife, Maria, were standing near the door to the living room in the front hallway. He is the tallest and oldest Aleut on the island. The Aleuts have a well-ordered system of government under chiefs of their own choosing. The chiefs are subject to removal by the will of the people whenever they choose. There are even subtyones who act as foremen when the killing season begins. Tyone Volkov, however, is the spokesman for the Sr Paul Aleuts. He exercises a kind of patriarchal supervision over the affairs of his people but has no power to enforce his authority beyond the expression of his will.

Most Aleuts are stocky and below medium height, with coarse black hair which grows long and lank down to their shoulders. The tyone, like all the others, is copper colored and has only a hint of chin whiskers, which he never has to shave.

Tyone Volkov was wearing a well-tailored black broadcloth suit in the best fashion. His wife — extremely short with bright, beady eyes — had made an attempt at a neat chignon with her scraggly locks. She was dressed in a housedress of bright printed cotton, a fashion most of the women have adopted in preference to the shaved sealskins they used to wear beginning at this time of the year. It is chilly, so they wear skin coats over their dresses; they can take the coats off indoors where it is too warm. In winter all natives wear heavy sealskin clothes with the fur turned toward their skin. We may have to, also.

Both the tyone and his wife speak a little English. But for fear of not being understood, they had George Butrin translate for them. Mr. Butrin is a native Aleut who was educated in Vermont and who now teaches in the school. He translated swiftly for the tyone while the tyone's wife stood shyly by, not saying a single word but beaming because she was in the center of the formalities. Women are held in very little regard here, and if I had not been present, there would have been no native women present.

"Our people," said the chief, "are very happy to have an American lady come to live with us." The reception seemed to be for me, because most of the conversation was directed to me. I was not so sure about how happy the people were, but I was sure I would be providing considerable diversion for a long time. Like children, all of them were curious about me and would no doubt follow me about, as the natives had at Onalaska, for some time to come.

GOVERNMENT HOUSE, Sr PAUL ISLAND

"I am happy to be here," I replied with warmth for their friendly gesture.

"We are, as you can see, very Russian. That is because the Russians were in these islands a long time. We do want to know more about America. It is very new, yes? Russia is very old and very civilized. We try hard to be civilized like Russians."

"We think we are very civilized, too," I said, having difficulty hiding a wry smile at the remembrance of some of the men's descriptions of how the company found the natives living when first they came up here. "Perhaps there are many ways of ours that you would like to learn, now that you are Americans." I doubt anyone has pointed out to them that they *are* Americans. Possibly they are a link between the American Indian and the Asiatic, but certainly they are indigenous Americans from long before our ancestors came from Europe.

"I should like that for my people very much, Mrs. Beaman. But they do not want it for themselves. They were happy when the Russians were here. Even Mr. Butrin here, who has been to your country, did not always like your ways; he prefers to teach in the Russian language." Butrin smiled a sheepish smile as he had to translate this. But I thought of what a frightening place the States must have seemed to this simple Aleut, and I could forgive him for not liking our ways. He had been introduced to an overdose of civilization too quickly. The rather sullen expression on these people's faces may be natural, but it also could be from too much forced civilizing. I have no missionary zeal in this respect.

"Are not the people happier now that they have these nice new houses that were built for them last year? The houses are so much nicer than the earthen dugouts I saw in Onalaska. And don't your people make more money now that the Americans are here than they did when the Russians were here?" John asked. He had been bristling with indignation at the implied criticism of the country from which he came. I saw a warning flash in Butrin's eyes, and he explained something to the tyone. They must not criticize America, I think he warned.

"That may be true," said the tyone. "But my people never have wanted more money. They cannot spend all they make. If one gets more of anything than another, he shares. It always has been so with our people long before the Russians came. They never want what others have. They never will learn the value of the things you possess." He paused. I realized for the first time that these people must have their own traditions and legends, a whole folklore perhaps, now buried or completely intermingled, as is their language, with the Russian. He continued. "My people do not want to learn English. I am sure the company men will ask you to teach English. They asked every agent, both the *precashchik* [senior agent] and the *predovchik* [junior agent], to try to teach

English at the school. The language is too difficult. It confuses. We are a simple people, Mrs. Beaman."

I assured the chief that I had not come to the islands for the purpose of changing their ways. I could see relief written in everyone's eyes. Our conversation became more relaxed, less stiff and formal after that. The old man probably did want new ways taught to his people. But he knew that they had to develop slowly. He felt, because of the ten-year military occupation, that they had been treated like a defeated people. Inherent was some sort of racial pride. They resented the American influence as once, long ago, they must have resented the Russian influence. Who knows? But since the formal call, I have a certain respect for these natives I've come to live among.

The call confirmed what the men on shipboard had told us. Russian Aleuts they are, and Russian they will remain for a long time. Although their chief is amenable to American ways, the real power over their lives and thinking is their church, which has gained a tremendous hold over them. More especially, their priest, Father Shishenekoff, has gained an unshakable allegiance from them. It is he who has tried to undo all the good the company has done for the natives. He does not want the children to learn English for fear they will forget the Russian liturgy, which is far more important to him than their physical well-being is. Actually, he does not want them to learn English for fear that it will open to them the gates of progress and change which would lessen his hold over them. He seems to take his orders not from God but from some archiepiscopate in Russia.

I do not wish to belittle the church. Its simple faith seems to have had a good influence on the natives. I could see that at Onalaska and even more so here. The Aleuts are extremely devout, not only by outward gestures but within themselves, like the humble Russian peasants. Their devotion to God should be encouraged. It is just that their priest is such an unfortunate example. We were warned, however, that little could be done about Father Shishenekoff, for he is the brother of Father Innocent Shishenekoff, archpriest for all the Aleutian Islands. Both are the first native Aleuts to have been ordained as priests, having studied at the Russian seminary in California.

I am surprised that these two men were not converted to American ways while in our country. However, they may have been kept completely isolated from the world in their monastery, located at a Russian settlement near San Francisco. Mr. Morgan told me in confidence that Father Paul is not known to smile except when he has a bottle of whiskey before him. Then a sickly halo seems to surround his head, as on an old Greek icon. The fountains of his soul seem to be stirred to their deepest depths — not the holiest depths, but the most evil. He is also known to be

GOVERNMENT HOUSE, St PAUL ISLAND

an inveterate gambler. His bank account with the company bears witness to this. He is the wealthiest individual on the island.

Before Father Paul came to Sr Paul, a visiting priest would come by boat once a year to solemnize all the weddings, christenings, and burials that had occurred during the year. Sometimes if the weather proved bad or the landings impossible, he did not get around for more than two or three years. That never deterred life from taking its natural course. The natives, however, felt better if their marriages were officially sanctioned by the church. Often they had to bring their suckling babes to their own weddings.

When the tyone welcomed us, he did not mention Father Paul or their differences of opinion. He is a faithful member of the church, but he knows that even the priest, like everyone else, is subject to the laws of the United States and the local regulations of the U.S. Treasury Department. What he does not realize, in his simplicity, is the subtle means used by the church to retain allegiance to Holy Mother Russia.

When the formal reception drew near its end, all the natives who had crowded into the little house filed out, allowing those who had stood about outside to file in and shake our hands. Finally, there had been some form of contact with every individual on the island, and the tyone, well pleased, decided to take his leave.

The tyone's little wife, who had said not a word all this time, came up to me and, with a feminine curiosity that must be universal, fingered the cashmere of my green dress appreciatively. A smile spread across her placid face. Then she felt down over my waist.

"No babies?" she asked in English. I went red with embarrassment to be asked such a question in front of all the company men and our host. But she seemed not the least bit embarrassed. I shook my head sadly. She shook her head in sympathy. Then the two, with great formality, took their leave.

I am quite sure that my new friend was trying to find out what keeps me slim where she is biggest. These women know nothing of stays and shams, which add a gentler grace to the female figure.

The entire population followed the tyone and his wife down the hill. Even Mrs. Mandrigan and Vicele went with them. Mr. Redpath, who stayed behind, laughed as he watched them.

"No doubt some sort of celebration has been brewing. The first arrival of the ship with fresh food is always excuse enough. But a white woman's arrival on the island is a tremendous event they'll not get over for a long time."

"They haven't been making *kvas* [an alcoholic beverage] while I was away?" the Senior Agent asked. "There won't be trouble tonight?"

"You know there's always some kvas cached away, no matter

how vigilant we are, SA," he answered. It was the first time I'd ever heard the Senior Agent referred to familiarly. "I don't think there'll be trouble. They couldn't have made much of the stuff because we ran out of sugar and flour early. I've been waiting to tell you how desperate the food situation has been, but that will keep. Believe me, the *St Paul's* early arrival seems like a miracle." He turned to me. "You've brought the islands good luck, Mrs. Beaman." I smiled unbelievingly. To whom or what had I brought luck ever since that mad trip to Takoma Park? "You brought the ship here with fresh supplies of food. We haven't had anything fresh until the seals hauled up last week and the birds arrived. There's been nothing else — not even staples. Now we can have a feast to which you all are invited." He must have noticed my slight hesitancy. "Oh, I assure you we'll not have seal meat tonight. We'll introduce you to that another time."

Ever since Washington, I had been steeling myself against a first taste of seal meat. We had been told that it would be our staple diet while here and that, unless one ate it, there would be little else but birds for red-blood meat. I guess I kept thinking we could avoid having to eat it. I showed my relief. I was really more relieved that I would not have to cook a meal our first night on St Paul's Island.

"How kind of you," I said.

"Thank you for your cordial invitation," John said, and the SA said, "Thank you, Charles. We will be down on time." The SA had included us quite naturally. For appearance's sake? I liked the inclusion just the same. It made us both feel as though we belonged.

After Mr. Redpath left, our host showed us the rest of Government House; there was not much to see. Just as he had described it to me, the living room opened with a wide, arched doorway into a dining room which had a door opposite going into the kitchen. The SA only pointed to the kitchen, making no attempt to light the whale-oil lamp to show me that room. I decided to explore it in the morning. What little I glimpsed of it did not look promising, but I saw a door into the hallway, so we can get to it from our room whenever the SA isn't using it. I think a spirit lamp in our room would be handier. The dining room, if closed off, could be made into a sitting room for us, and we could put the spirit lamp there. John insists he could never survive two years of cooking on a single burner. Anyway, we cannot have the sitting room until wood comes from Alaska on the *St Paul's* next trip in July.

Fortunately, the season is going into summer, so we can spend some time outdoors at midday and not feel the confinement of a single room too much. The picture is not altogether dismal, though John continues to look at it gloomily. He plans to suggest in his first report that separate quarters be built for future assistant agents. He is a firm believer in privacy, because we've had none during our married life.

He also knows me well enough to know that I couldn't prepare meals for just the two of us and not invite the SA to share at least some of them with us. We will have to share the living room or remain in our bedroom more than we'd like.

The SA is knocking now. We are going down to the company lodge together for our first dinner.

MAY 29th

Dinner was at eight o'clock Pacific time, which we observe here, though I am sure we are west of another time meridian. The sun hung on the rim of the Bering Sea like a pale, silvery moon behind the thick folds of mist as we walked down to the company buildings. Soon the sun will be with us all night, and there will be no actual darkness until the Arctic winter sets in. Then we will have no light at all until spring. I hate to think of this. In fact, I've refused to think of it until we arrived here. We find that the winter's dark and cold are the facts that dominate all life up here. Winter is the event for which everyone spends all the other days of the year in preparation.

The Alaska Commercial Company has a group of buildings near the wharf, some no doubt taken over from the army garrison the United States had here for ten years after the purchase. The Lodge, as the men call their living quarters, is a large, two-story frame building much like an army post barracks. It is well built, neatly painted white on the outside, and provides comfort and recreation on the inside. The whole upstairs, I am told, is for sleeping quarters, dormitory-style, and private rooms. The whole downstairs, except for the kitchen across one end, is a single large room with two long tables that can seat as many as ten each. The rest of the room is a comfortable lounge. There are potbellied stoves in each corner and a long buffet near the dining tables. The tables last night had white linen sheets on them for tablecloths, about which there was much laughter and comment. Thus I know the tablecloths are not usual and were brought out just for me. It seems that one of the rookie sealers, who came up last year on a two-year contract with the company, found them at the bottom of his trunk when he arrived and had hidden them from the eyes of the other sealers, who would have teased him unmercifully about them. His wife had lovingly included them without his knowledge. But since he had proved himself an able sealer during the past year, he felt safe enough in producing them for the occasion. "They are the only carefully pressed linens on the whole island," Mr. Morgan commented. "We haven't bothered much about pressing anything up here. But I think all that will be changed by your presence, Mrs. Beaman."

What amazed me most, and encouraged me most, about our stay here was the sight of books. The walls of the Lodge are lined from floor to ceiling with books, more than 1,100 of them, which Mr. Morgan cordially put at our disposal. The greater miracle is that they are such good books, all the classics, contemporary commentaries on the War Between the States, sea stories, many books in Russian (which a few of the company men can read), a Russian dictionary and several Russian grammars, some light fiction, and some scientific works but no geological or botanical guides for this part of the world. Perhaps there are none. I will send to San Francisco for whatever might be helpful in understanding and describing these islands.

The men tried to outdo themselves at being courteous to me. Their table manners are excellent, not boorish at all considering the rough lives they lead here. With the arrival of the St Paul, the full complement of sealers is now here for the season, fourteen in all tonight. Four of them will go to St George in a day or two in a company cutter. With Captain Erskine and the three of us, the two tables were nearly filled for dinner; eighteen Americans, thousands of miles from Washington on a volcanic rock in the middle of the Bering Sea, less than a thousand miles from the North Pole and not many miles from the Arctic Rim whose weather we enjoy. Something to make each of us pause and think!

John was asked to say the blessing. The food tasted wonderful. It was the first meal (except for one we had on land in Onalaska) at which the table had not moved away from me or skidded toward me while I was trying to eat. Meals aboard the St Paul were nightmares and only helped to prolong the seasickness. I think I would have gotten used to the rough seas otherwise. The SA commented that he never could get used to them. He also enjoyed his first stable meal and seemed to be in a more genial mood than we had seen him before. He was back among the many friends he had made last year.

After dinner, Mr. Morgan joined John and me as we looked over the books. I already had selected several to take with us, including a Russian grammar. "You don't have to carry so many at one time," he said to me, "because I am going to suggest that you and Mr. Beaman take all your meals with us down here. That will save you from having to cook under difficulties up there. I know how inadequate the facilities are. You also would have to purchase all your supplies from our store, which would be an embarrassment to us. The company does not want the government agents to have to purchase necessities to live here."

Government House, St Paul Island

"But I'd be breaking in upon your privacy as gentlemen," I said. "Your men will resent my presence, I am sure."

"Libby," John broke in, "Mr. Morgan's offer is the kindest one I've ever heard of and a solution to all our problems. We will indeed be most happy to accept your gracious offer, Mr. Morgan, and are grateful for the invitation."

"Indeed we are grateful, Mr. Morgan," I hastened to say. "I was only thinking of the awkwardness my presence will create."

"I am quite sure it will have a salutary effect on the men. You can see how they behaved like gentlemen tonight. I have a feeling that your presence on the island is going to have a good effect on everyone. We've needed someone like you up here. I am only too happy to extend the hospitality of my company's mess and library to you both."

We thanked him again and made sure of the exact times for the meals so we would always be on time. We neither wanted to keep them waiting nor did we want to hang about their lounge by arriving too early.

I still feel that I shall be intruding on their privacy. But I already have had breakfast and the noon meal there today, and they all have seemed as cordial as they were last night.

A few years ago, our Treasury Department leased the seal, seal-oil, and fishing rights of these two islands to the Alaska Commercial Company, an American concern that had been spreading its fur and fishing trade and whaling operations all along the Pacific coast out of San Francisco. As part of the lease agreement, our government imposed a bounty on every fur-seal pelt taken. For that reason, the Treasury Department has sent special agents up here to count the pelts taken by the company and, in the name of the United States, to administer the islands and inspect foreign ships that come, or are driven by storms, into these waters from the open seas.

There always has been a great deal of pelagic pirating of fur seals, especially when the seals migrate in the spring and fall. Almost all nationalities are guilty, especially the Japanese, the Dutch, and the Portuguese. These pirates are intrepid sailors who would risk anything for the valuable booty of the seal and whale oil, rare sea-otter pelts, and fur-seal pelts. Pirates are not selective about which seals they kill. In fact, they prefer the pelts of young females, therefore becoming the greatest threat to the herds which our government spent ten years to reestablish after the Russian depradation.

The Alaska Commercial Company has tried to keep the waters clear of marauders but, finding the task too difficult, has given up. Finally, the company has asked the government to send Coast Guard vessels to patrol the waters. This is, however, a vast sea, and the United States has so few patrol ships that pirates often get away with tremendous hauls. While our Coast Guard has the right to challenge and even board vessels caught killing the seals in the water, it usually only warns them, then lets them go. We take severe action only when a ship is within our territorial waters.

The men of the Alaska Commercial Company seem to be an unusual lot. The temptation to personal gain must be great. There is a wealth of white and blue fox, occasional bear, and the precious sea otter — all of which can be trapped and sold privately. But none of the men seem interested. At least in this short time of observation, I've seen no evidence of any private business deals. The men leave the trapping to the natives for their private gain. Aboard the ship, I had heard hints of illegal operations which so far are completely unfounded. The treasury agents are extremely vigilant. It would be difficult to get away with anything if anyone wanted to. I like to believe the company would rather be entirely aboveboard in order to retain its lease along with its good name. I could be wrong.

The company has the islanders' welfare at heart. It has done a tremendous amount of good in its short time here. Its relationship to the government agents also is unusual. I should have thought the men would resent what amounts to spying on their operation. Instead, they're cordial and cooperative. Mr. Morgan says they realize that the agents have to be in this grim place because of them. John and I are particularly grateful for the eating arrangements. Now I won't have to cook.

I've spent the few warm midday hours walking about with John, getting a firsthand impression of the village and its immediate environs. One can't go far beyond the village limits without running into some natural barrier. We must stay fairly close. I plan to write descriptions in greater detail during the winter months when I shall have little else to do. Our walks give me the only opportunity to be alone with John. Somehow I feel as if the walls of Government House have ears, so we avoid the intimate in our conversations. Strangely though — on our walks we seldom talk at all.

I thought it strange at first that the SA had not mentioned the dining arrangements when we were aboard the St Paul, but today he told me that he had not been sure whether Mr. Morgan would renew his invitation of last year, and if he did, whether it would include my husband and myself.

"It's the only way we can feel safe about what we eat," he said. "Mrs. Mandrigan may be clean about herself, but I wouldn't

Primrose

vouch for her food handling. The rest of the natives are worse. You'll see."

"But I had thought I'd have to take care of our own meals."

"Why bother when you'd have to get the food from the company store? They'd be embarrassed making you pay for it."

"I'm grateful," I smiled ruefully. "I'm not a very good cook."

Mother had Tissie take me in hand before my wedding to teach me at least the fundamentals. Though I never had been interested in cooking, I made an attempt to learn something in case I went with John. Instead, I stayed under the family roof after our marriage, and Tissie continued to provide beautifully for our wants, so I forgot what she had taught me. Mr. Morgan's comment about having to purchase provisions at the company store gave me my first jolt. I wouldn't know how to begin to provide. How inadequate I would be trying to market for the two of us! I made all this a humorous confession to John as we walked. He didn't smile. But he did say, "I suspected as much."

We've since arranged, however, to have a small continental breakfast in our room, preferring that to the huge breakfast at eight o'clock at the Lodge. Actually, breakfast is a sort of midmorning meal for the men who rise early and prepare their own tea or coffee before going into the field on their various labors. It is much too big for me, and, as John prefers a lighter meal, he has agreed to breakfast at Government House. Therefore I am fixing up the kitchen and have purchased some few supplies at the company store: tea, tinned milk, and sugar. Our oven is impossible, even if I knew how to bake, so after supper at the Lodge, Cook gives me a little bread or rolls he has baked each day to bring up to Government House. Cook is the cook who was here with the occupation troops. He married an Aleut woman and settled here. Naturally the company was only too glad to get him for their Lodge, and he is a good cook by every standard. John will take the noon meal with the men. I have seldom eaten anything but tea and a bisquit for lunch, so I plan to stay here and nibble, unless there is a special occasion down there or unless I get particularly hungry. In this way, I shall be in the men's sanctum only once a day and at a time when they can get cleaned up from their bloody labors.

I have seen to an ample supply of tea things for afternoon *chia* (Russian for *tea*), which is taken more seriously here, I do believe, than in England. It is as much a social occasion as it is a fourth meal, taken before the late dinner. John insists that we will not take tea at the Lodge, but will always provide it for anyone who wishes to drop in at Government House. Since I always have loved the custom of afternoon tea, I've been happy about being able to serve it myself. I am happy, too, that I did not bring my silver service and Sèvres teacups as I had wanted to, feeling I might be lost without my intimate possessions around me. Here, chia is served from a steaming samovar and in tall glasses, of all things! Had I instituted a silver service and delicate cups, I surely would have been accused of putting on airs.

There are any number of samovars used as decoration around the Lodge on top of the bookshelves. Mr. Morgan says the Russians left them, and the army didn't want them, so they collected them and gave one to each family that did not have one. The rest they've put around the Lodge, and each new bride, when she sets up housekeeping on her own, may choose one for a wedding gift. I've been given my choice also, a lovely, shining brass affair with many medals stamped on it for all the awards it has won.

I intend to encourage the village women, not the men, to drop in for chia. Because women are held in such low esteem, I plan to make friends with them and encourage them to let their men do more of the physical labor for them. I've been watching them lug the great buckets of water from the only source of drinking water, more than a mile away, while the men sit idly by whittling fishhooks and walrus spears. I shall start with the tyone's wife. But first I shall have to spend some time with that Russian grammar and dictionary. What a complicated language it is, with its Cyrillic alphabet that looks like Greek and isn't. I remember what a hard time Charles had learning the German alphabet before he went to the Hanseatic League as an attaché at our legation there. Well, Russian is still more barbaric, and I never was good at languages.

I've been on St Paul long enough to have explored every inch of it, for it is not very big — only twelve miles long and scarcely six miles wide. Yet I've seen precious little of it. Walking over it is nearly impossible, though I see in the log that Mr. Elliott did manage to explore almost every inch of it in three successive summers. The best way to see any of it is to go by native boat or company cutter to a likely beach (and every likely beach is a rookery), disembark, and explore inland as far as one can go. The inland terrain is so rough — full of ravines and sudden chasms, craggy upjuttings and slippery, lichen-covered rocks and boggy areas around little lakes — that walking is treacherous. So far I've cajoled natives only a few times into taking me in their boats on the calmest days, so I have seen a few of the more famous rookeries.

JUNE 10th

Sea Life

Sorbus Sambucifolia,
a pencil drawing by
Frederick A. Walpole

The dunes and the high plateaux are my favorite places to wander. They have a certain strange beauty about them that John cannot perceive, but seeing that beauty keeps me from being lost here. Sand seems to play an important part in the formation of St Paul, according to Mr. Elliott's notes in the log. There is no sand at all on St George, so the two islands are entirely different in aspect. I love to watch the changing colors of the dunes. The sands, when rainwashed, are pink until the mists clear and a weak sun comes out to tint them other hues — lavenders and beiges, with black basalt outcroppings and reddish tufa. When winds momentarily scurry across the dunes and dry them enough to eddy the sand, it becomes almost white and glistening, then pinkish again. On the seals' parade grounds, the sand has become hard like cement and is almost the same color, but it is polished by the constant passing of thousands of bachelor seals. The sands at the water's edge are steely black and blue, drying out to purple and browns, grays sometimes, and even reddish tints where the volcanic tufa is newest. The wide avenues the bachelors make to their parade grounds on the plateaux are more easily drained and therefore almost always a pink-beige with, here and there, a startling outjutting of some dark basaltic rock to break the expanse of pastel color. At this time of year, most of the dune tracts have patches of the most vividly green grass I've ever seen. The mists and the rains are responsible, and because there is so little sun, these grasses — the wheat-like Elymus especially — never scorch or turn brown until the first frost strikes and withers all the island.

In among the tussocks of green are patches of the most vivid flowers imaginable — poppies of all kinds, muscari and musci, ranunculas, wild mustard, chickweed, lupine, painted daisies, violas and violets, anemones, and many, many others among tall ferns, which are almost tropical in appearance.

According to Mr. Elliott's map on the living room wall, there are innumerable little freshwater lakes but no streams. I located some of these lakes on my walks. They are indeed beautiful, clear to their very bottoms, with pure water that anyone can drink. They have no reptiles in or around them, thank goodness! On clear days, they reflect the vast heavens above them and the cones of Boga Slov or Kamminista and the other high peaks of the interior. Each lake contains little varicolored fish that are beautiful. Clouds of pale blue butterflies float over the waters, and at the edges of the lakes are pond lilies and water hyacinths and other flowering water plants I do not know. One can scarcely believe we are so near the North Pole, except for the chilly winds that plague us even at this time of year.

I've not yet seen Great Lake except at a distance. It cuts Novastoshnah Rookery off from the rest of the island, because one cannot get around the lake by foot. Because I've had to explore St Paul by boat rather than on foot, it remains for me a series of rookeries strung along the coast. The interior is still much of a mystery.

If one goes clockwise from the village, by boat, and observes the rookeries from the water, Lagoon would be first, just as we saw it from the St Paul when we arrived. I can look down on Lagoon from the front of Government House. It is not a very big rookery because it is not well drained, and seals must have a well drained area for breeding grounds.

Beyond Lagoon, around a sharply pointed cliff that juts into the sea, is the nearest thing to an actual bay that the island can boast. It is called English Bay and is merely a slight indentation in the contour of the coast, about two miles wide. English Bay has two of the island's largest rookeries, Tolstoi (which means *thick*) and Zapadnie, with almost nothing to indicate where they are divided. Tolstoi is one of the greatest hill-slope breeding grounds in the world, with seals solidly massed inland and upward on a steep grade for more than 500 feet to the parade grounds above. On this hill, and on the cliff that falls at Tolstoi Point, also are massed more white foxes than anywhere else. They live in every cranny and under every overhang that birds do not occupy, and of course, their food is the dead and dying seals. The white, graceful bodies of the foxes moving among the glistening, swaying bodies of the

*Tolstoi Rookery and
English Bay,
watercolors by Henry
Wood Elliott*

seals is a sight one can't soon forget.

Between Tolstoi Rookery and Zapadnie is a wide sweep of sand, moving inland and upward from the water's edge — ideal, one would think, for seals to live on. But this is loose sand, which the vicious winds whip up into the eyes of the seals. They do not like the biting, cutting sand, so they do not live on this smooth area but crowd into two rocky sections of Zapadnie. They divide into the two sections because there is a rocky area in the middle of the beach under Zapadnie's cliffs where a vast herd of hair seals breeds. The two clans of cousins never fight, but they never mix. Zapadnie, the second largest rookery on the island, sweeps up from its coastal shelf onto a plateau above cliffs that fall steeply into the sea beyond. The bachelor seals come and go to this high grassy plateau with its ancient, wind-etched wooden crosses and tattered icons that mark an ancient burial ground from explorer Gerasim Pribilof's time. There was a village here, founded by the men he left while he returned to Russia to report his wealthy find.

In this same grassy area are the only berry bushes that actually bear ripening fruit each year, the *moroshka* and the *sheksah,* both rare delicacies which the Aleuts relish. The entire village camps out here for a few days in August to gather the berries, staying until every last one is picked. For the Aleuts, it is a holiday they already are talking about and planning for. Here also are the great patellas of *Archangelica officinalis,* which looks like a huge rhubarb. It is slightly sweet, and the natives crunch the stems like celery.

The other half of Zapadnie, beyond the hair seals' rocks, rises more steeply to another parade ground above Zapadnie Point. The point is the beginning of a high cliff that has no coastal margin under it and that extends for several miles to Seethah, or Southwest Point, where land is again low enough to support a few seals. There are no seals again for miles because of a sheer escarpment going north-northeast, then suddenly eastward all the way to Novastoshnah — Northeast Point or Northernmost Point — the greatest fur-seal rookery in the world, with a million seals!

Just as Mont-Saint-Michel is separated from France, so Novastoshnah was once an island separated from S[t] Paul by tidal waters. But the narrow neck of sand has lifted enough to remain above the tides. The land mass is now permanently connected to S[t] Paul. It is still accessible only by boat, because Great Lake lies across the neck of land, with only a narrow margin of rock to keep it from becoming part of the sea. Like all the other lakes, it is the crater of an extinct volcano raised above sea level. Over time, because of the incessant rains, it has become entirely sweet. If Novastoshnah Rookery could be viewed from Great Lake, it would be one of the most dramatic sights in all the world.

Nowhere, nowhere else could there possibly be so much teeming life. Every inch of earth is covered with writing, barking, roaring, fighting fur seals, hair seals, sea lions (who are tawny in contrast to the seals), foxes, and thousands of birds. Novastoshnah has its own gentle rise from the sea, a central hill, a small lake, a volcanic peak, and a cross on the hill to mark where a village once stood. The company maintains a barracks here for the men during the killing season. Since the seals cannot possibly be driven back to the village killing grounds, the company men have to stay here until their task is done. There is also a salt house or "kenching house" for storing the pelts until the *St Paul* or company cutters come to collect them.

I must revisit Novastoshnah and try to sketch it in such a way that others can catch its drama. It is a majestic scene. Seals line the shore in an unbroken chain from Novastoshnah down the entire eastern shore to the southernmost tip of the island, with great rookeries at Polavina, at Lukannon, at Ketavie, and at Reef Point, which is just south of the village. I've not seen them all. Each has its special characteristics, each its own fascinations. I'd like to visit them often — and long enough to study them.

It is not only the rough terrain that prevents my explorations but also the weather. The weather is in a continual conspiracy against us. There are only two seasons up here: winter and the rainy season. From May 1 to October 1 is the rainy season. The rest is winter. Thirty-five inches of rain falls during the rainy season. That leaves little time for anything but fog and, on rare occasions, a weak sun. The winds blow constantly, though I am told they are mild now as compared to what they will be in winter. Even now I cannot always stand up against them and find myself often staying indoors to live on tea and bisquits instead of going down to the Lodge for dinner.

In spite of the weather, I have managed to make my way inland a short distance and occasionally to the southern tip, Reef Point, past little lakes and conical peaks and great green grassy stretches where, to my surprise — the first time — I saw cattle grazing just as they do along the Potomac. I had forgotten that we had brought up cattle in the hold of our ship — cattle and sheep and hogs; the latter when seal-fed are, I am told, particularly tasty. None of these animals can weather the winters here, so the company cannot always have fresh meats. The animals will be killed at the time of the first permanent freeze so that the carcasses can be frozen instantly to hold throughout the winter. Some parts, of course, will be smoked or dried to preserve them. This small addition to the menu helps vary it from the eternal processed seal meat and tinned salmon, the standard diet for winter.

In the log, Mr. Elliott proposed importing Siberian reindeer — which could survive the winters here and multiply — so the company and even the islanders would have a better supply of fresh meat. So far, no one seems to have tried experimenting with reindeer, though it sounds like a good idea. When one stops to think that each Aleut alone eats from one-and-a-half to four pounds of seal meat daily the year round, supplying even this small village with enough red-blood meat is quite a problem.

The seals begin to leave the islands in September; the immediate fresh supply of meat leaves with them. Long before the seals go, the natives are given permission to kill a certain number of bachelors and male pups. They dry the meat in a way that preserves it for them, on their walrus-bone drying frames called *laabas*. (I don't like the look of the meat that was left over from last year.)

Seal meat, though tasty, is difficult to prepare, Cook tells me. I am going to watch him prepare some soon.

June 12, 1879
Government House
St Paul Island

Dear Ones,

The weather, always first in conversation (second, the seals), continues mild at midday, with cold, torrential rains or fog most of the rest of the time. There is no sun, though it must be somewhere behind the heavy banks of mist, because we are living in the "land of the midnight sun." I have written you in another letter (and they already have piled up waiting for the St Paul next month) that we arrived too late to witness the most dramatic scene this island has to present, that is, the "hauling up" or the arrival of the male seals, the bulls, known as seacatchie *(singular,* seacatch*) and a few days later, the bachelors, known as* holluschickie *(singular,* holluschak*). They haul up in the tens of thousands early in May.*

I have planned to write all my observations about the seals in a separate book, which I shall call The Seal Book*. I have planned to devote the winter months to this, adding to it next spring when I personally can observe the great hauling up of the males. In the meantime, I find that it is impossible to write you of our lives here without referring to the seals or some phase of their lives which affects ours. So until I can send you a more detailed account, let me explain what little I have learned, as well as our reason for being here.*

There are many kinds of seals in the world — hair seals, harp seals, barking seals, sea lions, sea cows, and walruses — all related. Many can be found in our own coastal waters. But the fur seals belong exclusively (with the exception of a few thousand that go to the Commander Islands, about seven hundred miles southwest of here and still belonging to the

Russians) to the Pribilofs. Our two islands — St Paul and St George —
owing to their isolated position, their moist climate, and the configuration
of their shores, seem to have been particularly designed by the Creator for
the propagation of the fur seal, Calhorinus orsinus. Until a few
hundred years ago, Calhorinus could be found only in the South Polar
regions, on islands and coastal habitats around the Strait of Magellan,
Tierra del Fuego, Patagonia, and elsewhere in Antarctica. Within
recorded history, their complete migration to these permanent North Polar
breeding grounds has been scientifically noted. The complete reversal was
due to the unscrupulous decimation of the herds in the South Polar waters
by Dutch, Portuguese, English, and French sealers, who killed not only
the males for their pelts but also the females for their oil. By 1741, the
year that Alaska was discovered, there was scarcely a fur seal left in
Southern Hemisphere waters, while the herds whose scouts had discovered
and communicated their find had migrated to these islands and,
undiscovered except by a few Aleuts, had repopulated their numbers to the
millions.

The fog and the rain which we so hate have been ideal for the seals.
But had our government not permitted this ten-year rehabilitation program
since taking over from the Russians, there would have been very few fur
seals left to the world. The first Russians were more careful than later
exploiters. They set up laws based on sound biological principles that
would keep the herds perpetuated at a given number. Bad management
and greed on the part of their successors reduced the herds to a frightening
minimum, and pelagic pirating on the part of other unscrupulous sealers
very nearly finished off the rest. At the time of the Alaskan Purchase,
there were only a few seal herds left. Now the seals have prospered to a
point of saturation where, for their own health, they again must be
thinned out. The Alaska Commercial Company, since the beginning of its
lease from our Treasury Department for the sealing rights on these two
islands, has maintained strict rules for killing, so the herds should remain
at approximately the desired number for many years to come. Though I
never shall get used to the idea of killing these docile animals for fur, I
realize it has to be done or the islands could not support the seals. And
since there is nowhere else they can go, they would sicken or starve
themselves into extinction here.

The seacatchie, five years or older, haul up about May 5th or as soon
as the coastal ice breaks up. They stay close to the water's edge on the low
beaches. Each bull marks a plot of land which is to be his own kingdom
for the summer. Though he has no visible way of marking the boundaries
of his domain, he knows to within an inch what land is his and what is
another's. The site must have ample space to support from twenty to
eighty wives, his "harem."

About the second week in May, the bachelors begin to haul up. These
are the young males under five who are not yet old enough to breed.
They must pass the bulls at the edge of the water and establish themselves
on the higher ground, preferably the high plateaux known as the seals'

GOVERNMENT HOUSE, St PAUL ISLAND

parade grounds. While the bulls never go back into the water the entire summer, the bachelors go back and forth many times each day. In their constant coming and going, the bachelors wear down wide avenues past the bulls' harems and try to avoid getting into arguments with the bulls, who — because they neither eat nor drink all summer — get more and more crotchety.

The bulls, six to eight feet long and almost six feet around, weigh from four hundred to five hundred pounds when they arrive, but because they fast for more than twelve weeks, they do lose considerable weight by summer's end.

The cows (matkas) arrive a month to six weeks after the bulls and immediately drop their single pups, which they have been carrying for more than eleven months. Fortunately we arrived in time to watch the matkas haul up. I spent several afternoons on the cliff above Nah Speel watching these sleek and lovely animals come out of the water and start climbing the rocks in among the seacatchie. The old bulls were lined up like a first row at a burlesque house, watching the beautiful, slim creatures (four feet, eighty pounds) leave the surf. Suddenly one would pounce on a cow and drag her to his harem, setting her down with a pounce as much as to say, "Now you stay there!" Then he would go back to the edge of his domain and pounce on another and another until he had chosen as many as he thought he could safely handle. He does not do this all in one day. It takes about a month before all the matkas have hauled up.

The matkas have extremely soulful eyes with long lashes and many human expressions, even that of weeping real tears. They are coy and always watching for a chance to escape one harem for another. If a bull sees a wife deserting him for another seacatch, he goes after her, grabs her by the nape of the neck, and carries her back to his harem, just as a cat carries a kitten. He shakes her unmercifully and bangs her down, letting her know in no uncertain terms that he'll not stand for unfaithfulness. If, however, he meets the bull she has deserted to, he does battle. The bulls are eternally fighting over the cows all during the mating season, and their battles are vicious, sometimes even to the kill.

Within a day or two after a cow has hauled up, she gives birth to one eight-pound pup, or kotick (plural, kotickie), which she has been carrying since the mating season the summer before, a gestation period of fifty weeks! She seems devoted to the little kotick, feeding it abundantly with milk that is thicker and richer than our dairy product back home. Kotickie are just about the most adorable baby animals I ever have seen, and I cannot stay away from watching them whenever the weather permits. So far there are only a few. But later in the month, when all the matkas have hauled up, there will be thousands of them. In July and August, I shall have the fun of watching the matkas teach the youngsters to swim, a sight the natives seem to enjoy tremendously, because they already are talking about it. The natives seem to require only the simplest events for their amusement and entertainment. Even I seem not to miss *the gay social life of the Capital too much. I could do with some good music, especially that little chamber music group, and, if there were a piano here, I'd do a bit of practicing to amuse myself. Other than that, do not feel sorry for me. Life here is full and interesting, and I am learning some Russian.*

> *All my love to you and all our friends,*
> *Lib.*

JUNE 15*th*

A few days ago, Vicele announced that a few families were planning their annual expedition in their bidarrahs to Walrus Island to gather birds' eggs. The natives plan this trip for the first two weeks in June when all the nesting birds lay their eggs, which can be found in overwhelming abundance on this one tiny island six miles off Novastoshnah. The Aleuts store the eggs in their abandoned sod dugouts (a few of which still exist), where they stay fresh indefinitely. They wanted me to come along. While I am not very fond of any of the birds' eggs around here — they are all too fishy tasting for me — the chance to see Walrus Island was a temptation. I asked Vicele how long the trip would take.

"Maybe two days, maybe three," said Vicele with a shrug of the shoulder. Time means very little to these people, and counting time by days in summer, when the light lasts almost around the clock, is an uncertain quantity.

"Oh, is there a place to sleep over there?" I asked. I could see the scorn in the youngster's eyes. The Aleuts still, I'm afraid, do not think much of our beds and blankets and even the roof we think is necessary for shelter. They usually huddle together, under any shelter, for the warmth they impart to each other.

"Oh, no. Make cover with sail if rains," he said. I could just see myself huddling with several Aleut families under a sail if it rained! "Tyone says next three days nice, we go."

Vicele Mandrigan

I asked John, who is terribly busy now that the killing has begun, what he thought of my joining such an expedition, knowing he would frown on it. But I did not want to hurt the Aleuts' feelings.

"It's too risky a channel, I've heard. I don't think it's the wisest thing to do. But if you've your heart set on it, I can't stop you. Why don't you ask Mr. Morgan what he thinks?"

"It is always risky," Mr. Morgan said. "They have to sail to Northeast Point and wait there until after midnight for a favorable tide. If the winds are just right, they reach the island within a short time, usually before dawn, gather their eggs and picnic for a while, and are back before dawn of the next day. It is quite an excursion for them, requiring good sailors, but well worth the trip for the eggs they can gather."

"But would it be safe for Mrs. Beaman to go along?" John asked.

"That's another story! It would be safe enough, I think. So far, none of our men have shipwrecked on the way there or back, but occasionally they've gotten stormbound over there, and that's no fun without shelter. I've a better idea. Why don't I take both of you over myself in a company cutter? In fact we could take all the cutters and make it an island expedition."

"That would be kind, but what about the work? How can we leave it right now?"

"It can wait a day or two. We'll call a halt so that our men can go. Some will insist on their bidarrahs anyway. That way we can gather as many eggs as possible, which will help the island economy tremendously. You will find it an interesting place."

Walrus Island, I had been informed, is a small, rocky ledge of lava, flat and only slightly lifted above the sea. In fact, in a terrific storm, waves roll right over it. The most vicious storms, of course, do not come until after the walruses have vacated the place in the fall. But it is a dangerous spot for ships in fog or storm. All captains dread it except during the summer months when there is light nearly twenty-four hours. Then the danger is not as great.

Naturally the Aleuts were all excited when they learned the company cutters were going too. So instead of the usual delegation of egg hunters, the entire population of St Paul, with the exception of a few company men and the Senior Agent, migrated to Walrus Island.

The sea fortunately was not too rough once we set out on it, after an interminable wait at Northeast Point. The tide swept us along to a tricky landing in one small indentation where water was deep enough for the cutters to touch land. Masses of birds rose in black clouds at our approach, wheeled and swooped and screamed at us, then settled down on every inch of exposed rock, sand, and gravel between the walruses.

GOVERNMENT HOUSE, St PAUL ISLAND

Walruses and Walrus Island, a watercolor by Henry Wood Elliott

I never had dreamed of seeing such a sight in my life, and probably I never will see anything like this again. The island is flat — windswept flat — and in the misty, cold dawn, bleak. This desolate place teems with walruses (not a single female among them) lolling, grunting, and lumbering to and fro from the water, the ugliest beasts I've ever met face to face. The stench became so great I soon asked to go back to the cutter to wait out the egg hunt. Literally every inch of the way back to the water's edge was covered with birds' eggs lying in clutches right out on the lava rock. The Aleuts gathered more than two tons of eggs in a few hours! Fortunately the weather held, and we were back on S⁣ᵗ Paul by dawn the next day.

The Senior Agent had entered into no part of this excursion. Yet it was he who, immediately after, offered to show us Otter Island. The *S.S. Reliance* was in, a Coast Guard cutter, and Captain Baker was more than anxious to put his little vessel at our disposal. Our excursion to Otter Island was not an island project but a personal expedition among the three of us at Government House and the crew of the *Reliance*.

It was to be a little cruise. There's nothing on Otter Island to go ashore for. We planned to just sail around it and come back. The day was planned, I am sure, to cement the growing entente among the three of us, now that work is going smoothly and everything seems to be easier and less strained.

It being a Sunday, we all went to services at the church first, where, of course, I had to join the women on the women's side of the central aisle. We all had to stand during the interminably long service, which is still difficult for me to follow, though at times it is beautiful in its pageantry and music. We took noonday meal with the company, asking if anyone else wanted to come along. But Otter Island is boring to the men after they have seen it once. We went out in the little lighter, which Captain Baker likes to handle himself. The wind was not too mischievous, as he called it, so we had smooth sailing to the anchorage. He preferred sails to oars, of course.

Otter Island, though only six miles from our southernmost tip, is in an entirely different set of channels and very treacherous to visit unless the tides are right. One doesn't have to wait, however, until the heathen hour of midnight to cross over. It is called Otter Island because of the many thousands of otter pelts the Russians have taken from it. The sea otter has one of the softest, most beautiful furs in the world, requiring only a simple curing process and no plucking or dyeing. It can be used in its natural state. There are very few sea otter left anywhere, and none at all on Otter Island.

It is a tiny place, with sheer cliffs rising directly out of the sea on all sides except one which, slipping to the level of the water, reveals a strange, funnel-like crater, so recently blackened that an eruption might have happened yesterday. Yet the natives tell us that no one can remember ever having seen an eruption within his lifetime. Perhaps this is the kind of volcano that does not spew forth anything spectacular but may be active all the time, keeping the surface freshly burned out. We agreed that the layer of mist hanging over the island looked more like smoke than water vapor. But then, that could have been our imaginations.

Hundreds of bachelor seals, but no mating seals, make Otter Island a playground for the summer. We came in close enough to watch the blue and the white foxes scavenging among the seals, and thousands of birds wheeling above. In fact, it seemed incredible that such a tiny island could support so much life.

A huge Greek cross of wood stood on the shore, planted there by the Russians long ago, perhaps by Pribilof himself or in his time.

We sailed in close. No one wished to go ashore, so we idled our way around the strange little island, then headed back for St Paul. The Senior Agent seemed more relaxed, friendlier than usual. He was gallant and courteous to me and included John in all his conversations with Captain Baker, as though the two were accustomed to casual conversation at Government House. I felt an easing of the tensions that had been mounting ever since sailing from San Francisco. John, on the contrary, became quieter and quieter and less communicative than he had been lately. Whenever he grows ominously silent, I know something has gone wrong.

GOVERNMENT HOUSE, St PAUL ISLAND

But I could not believe that anything had gone wrong with this day's excursion. The weather, the sea, and the congeniality aboard the cutter contributed to a perfect little outing for which I was exceedingly grateful.

"I did not like the way the SA kept looking at you," John said when we were alone in our room.

"I noticed nothing strange," I said. "He seemed particularly human for once — a welcome change!"

"He seemed much more interested in you than in what Captain Baker was telling us."

"Good heavens!" I exploded. "Why can't a man show his pleasure when he's at ease? Must a man go about with a dour, sour face because I am here?"

"I'll not have you trying to please him!"

"But I'm not, John, and you know it. You can't be jealous! You just can't be. You've no right to be and you know it." But I'm afraid that is what has gone wrong. I do not know how to cope with jealousy, for I've never experienced it before. It can prove to be an ugly thing on these small islands.

Driving the Seals, a watercolor by Henry Wood Elliott

GOVERNMENT HOUSE, St PAUL ISLAND

June 16, 1879
Government House
St Paul Island

Dear Ones,

    *I do hope that when these letters arrive you will sort them out and read
them according to date. I write them as though I could post them to you
each day, knowing full well that they will all go in one packet sometime
in July. The reason I ended my story about the seals abruptly the other
day was because of an excursion to Walrus Island about which I shall
write you another time. I think I had better finish telling you what I
know of the seals — that is, what I have learned from discussion up here
— until I can write more authoritatively from my own observations later.*

    *Actually not all the seals are in yet, and not all the pups are born.
Last year's count, after the pups were born, was about three million seals
on St Paul and one million on St George. Of these, the company may
take seventy-five thousand here and twenty-five thousand from St George.
They may take only bachelor seals under five years of age. The company
has continued the Russian practice of hiring only Aleuts to drive the
bachelors from their parade grounds to the killing fields and to do the
actual killing. There is a large field just beyond the last row of houses
where most of the killing is done on this island. The bachelors have to be
carefully selected for their pelts and carefully driven out of the rookeries
over the wild and rugged terrain in order to preserve as near perfect pelts
as possible.*

    *If a seal is driven too fast, he "heats" and ruins his pelt, because like a
dog, he has no external sweat glands, so that all sweating is done within
the blubber layer under the skin and becomes obnoxiously odoriferous.
The pelt absorbs this odor, and even some of the fat, which makes it
rotten and stinking within a few hours. Even when carefully driven, the
seals still have to be carefully flensed, or again, their pelts are worthless.
The company men do the supervising of all this. The Aleuts do the actual
work, and the government agents have to be present to make sure that not
too many males are killed to get the quota of perfect skins. It is an ugly
business all the way around, one which disgusts John more and more each
day. I am glad that I am spared the sight of the massacre by a green rise
between the killing field and our windows, though I am not spared the
sounds or smell. I'll be glad when it is all over — in another month.*

    *The seals continue to be fascinating to watch, and I shall write much
about them. They are docile. I can walk among them, even among the
huge bulls, who only turn away or move away from me. They can be
ferocious with each other over a cow, but they are not even frightened of
man. I do not walk among them, however, because their rookeries are too
smelly and crowded. I've no real reason for going among them. They —
that is, the bachelors — and the matkas live on the abundant sea life in*

these waters. They have no defenses. Twice we've seen Orcas chase them right up against rocks in the surf and swallow them. Fortunately the natives were able to kill the second whale — an exciting episode that I also will tell you about.

After the mating season, which will last until the end of July, the harems will break up to some extent, and the bulls will go back to the water to feed and play. Then there will be even greater motion on the rookeries. Finally, when the freezing boorga blows out of Siberia about the end of August, all the seals will swim away toward the equator. No one will see them again until the following spring, when again they will come back in the same order — the bulls first, then the bachelors, then the cows, and finally the pups.

The commercial value of the fur seal depends on the quality of the fur and the size of the pelt. When taken, it is a dark reddish brown mixed with coarse black hairs having a silvery tip which extends beyond the soft fur. Almost every pelt has some damage because of the jagged rocks over which the animals swim in the water or travel on land and because of the wounds they get from predators and later as bulls fighting. It is unusual to find an absolutely unscarred pelt. Almost all the killing is done before the middle of July, because after that, the heating makes most pelts too gamey to be any good at all. The furriers of London have been able to guard the secret of properly curing and plucking the fur-seal pelts, so all pelts are taken to London and sold through there.

Here I've been talking about the pelts before I've gotten the poor animals killed! I hate to think about it. Perhaps that is why I keep putting it off. I have only John's description of what happens, and he has said several times that he hates to speak of it.

Two or three of the Americans go with a small group of Aleuts to a bachelor parade ground and carefully select those holluschickie they feel have the most perfect pelts. The Aleuts carefully prod these selected animals away from the others with large, hardwood clubs, pushing the seals always toward a path that eventually leads to the killing ground. When the men have rounded up enough to drive forward, the group sets out at the rate of about a half mile an hour. Should it be warm or particularly dry, the men drive and prod the seals at a far slower pace than this. The longest drive is about six miles, and the Aleuts have to stay with the group overnight sometimes, because the rugged inland terrain is unfamiliar ground for the seals. Often during the drives, pelts are torn or wounds are discovered that render the animal useless. These seals are left to die or find their own way back to the sea, without which they cannot live more than another day or two.

Before they are killed, they are allowed to rest and cool off for a few hours. Then the natives, who are forbidden firearms, kill the seals with a few well-directed blows on the skull. The dead seals are flensed, with a thick layer of blubber left sticking to the fur. The skins are laid out, blubber side down on the ground, for another long cooling period. Then all the blubber is scraped carefully from the skin and sent in vats to the

oil-rendering shed, while the pelts are carried to the kenching houses where they are salted and stacked until taken away by the S[t] Paul.

The kenching houses where the pelts are salted and stored.

If the animal has not heated, the meat is taken home for food. Heated seal meat is as disagreeable to the taste as the pelt is to the nose. Gamey skins, however, can be retrieved for making the bidarkas and the bidarrahs as well as other items for use outdoors. In spite of all this, a great deal of offal is left on the fields to rot. The foxes scavenge this at night, and the tabby cats by day. There are literally hundreds of tabby cats skulking in and out among the animal carcasses, fighting over every morsel, and caterwauling in the most hideous fashion half the night. They came originally on ships, but within a generation or two, they have become stub-tailed and wild, depending on dead and dying wildlife for their food. The rains, too, help clean up the mess. Perhaps the rains and the offal account for the grass of the killing grounds being the greenest of all the green grass on the islands.

I hope I've not disgusted you too much. This is the essence of our life up here, the reason we are here. I wanted you to know.

Your Lib.

GOVERNMENT HOUSE, S[t] PAUL ISLAND

JUNE 19*th*   N ext to the seal life on the island, the bird life is the
                  most noticeable. I am told that what I see here is
nothing compared to the bird life on S*t* George. Proportionally it
is nothing compared to Walrus Island. But I had no time to study
the various kinds on Walrus. The stench was too great. Even so,
the bird life is overwhelming here. There are about forty varieties
in all, but their numbers and exotic plumage deserve a whole
book of their own.

   Rap-o-loof, the red-breasted robin, was probably a passenger on a
boat or blown in by a gale, because it is not likely a native,
though now robins are plentiful. The water birds are the
fascinating ones. There are auks and auks and auks, many I do not
know by name, but every variety from the great crested *canooskie*
to the tiniest least auklet, the *choochkie,* and in between, the white-
breasted, which is most delicious to eat no matter how prepared.
Next comes *strepsilas,* the red-legged turnstone, welcomed by the
seals because they eat the flesh flies that worry the seals' open
wounds. There's *tringa,* the jacksnipe, and *charadris,* the plover;
pahtootsie, the gray-eared finch, and murres galore, called *arrie*
because of their cry; puffins with their fantastic bills, every kind;
and gulls, especially the burgomaster who soars aloft to a great
height with a crab in his bill, drops it on a stone to crack its shell,
then swoops at a terrific speed to eat the meat before some other
bird or burgomaster gets it. Gulls and gannets and puffins and all
the other birds scream and call constantly across the island, scream
and call above the snarling cough and roar of the bulls now in full
mating season, scream and call above the thunderous booming of
the surf. I sometimes think I shall go mad from the noise. At the
Lodge, the men tell me it is more likely I shall go mad from the
silence in winter, when everything, even the surf, is frozen solid
and silent under a great mass of ice, and only the wind howls out
of Siberia.

Neither the seals nor the birds would be here except for the vast quantities of fish in these waters, quantities beyond human imagination. I have been doing another little inventory, because the relationship has become more and more strained between John and the SA. This killing season is a terrible thing. It does things to the men. Even I feel affected. But I don't want to think about it. Instead I will finish this inventory.

Each seal (except for the bulls, who fast all summer) now on this island and on St George eats between fourteen and forty pounds of fish a day, or an average of about twenty-five pounds a day. There are, by count so far, more than four and a half million seals on the two islands, including about 70,000 bulls. That means that our seals eat about one-hundred million pounds of fish a day, or 50,000 tons! Beside the seals, there are thousands of hair seals, sea lions, and walruses, as well as the millions of birds that also feed on fish, which should account for the consumption of at least another ten thousand tons each day. The season here is about 120 days long, so that means about seven million tons of fish are taken from these waters annually! More, I warrant, than the whole population of the United States eats in the same length of time, and this is an area of only a few square miles! The idea is staggering.

One of the first real friendships we've made here is that of the company's doctor, Dr. Kelly, a fine looking, portly man in his late fifties, with graying hair and a gray mustache. He has been fatherly toward us without being patronizing and constantly has given us good advice about what to wear, what to eat, and how to take care of ourselves — advice gleaned from his four years here. He came originally on a two-year contract but has dedicated or, I should say, consecrated, his life to the welfare of the Aleuts. He's a good Irish Catholic with a medical missionary's zeal. He has little good to say about Father Paul, but that could be due to his Roman prejudice. He has only good to say for the rest of the Aleuts.

Even though this is his busiest time of the year because of the nasty accidents that occur during the killing season, he has been trying to get me to see what the native dugouts were like when he arrived here in '75. There are a few left where foods are stored, and two or three are still inhabited by natives who absolutely refuse to move into a company-built house. Kazan Gallanium's family insists on remaining in a barrabkie. I've just been to visit the Gallaniums with Dr. Kelly, and, in spite of a bath and the last of my little horde of eau de cologne, I feel as though every dog and tabby cat in town must be following me, drawn by the stench.

"When I came to the island, all barrabkie were like this one," Dr. Kelly said, "and the interior conditions were far worse."

"Could they possibly be?" I exclaimed, frantically searching for a handkerchief to hold to my nose. We had stooped, virtually crawled, into a low mound covered by sod. This proved to be a whole dwelling underground. The first room we entered — nearly dark except for the feeble light that followed us in — was an open space in the middle of which the cooking for the whole family was being done over a small open fire.

When our eyes grew accustomed to the dimness, we nodded toward the cross with its primitive icon, for this is the custom when entering all native houses — to cross oneself before the shrine (the Greek way, at which my escort always fusses and, I am sure, surreptitiously does his own way). Then one offers a prayer to the patron saint of the head of the house. A visitor's respects always are paid first to God, then to the patron saint, and only afterwards to the family members, who, by that time, one can begin to discern in the gloom.

Olga Gallanium, an elderly married woman called a *babba,* or *barba,* was stirring something in a pot over the fire — seal stew, probably, which is quite delicious, but which we could not smell. All fuel is seal blubber, which gives off a burnt-fish odor. The black smoke it makes has nowhere to escape except into the nooks and cracks of the earthen walls. It settles on everything, including the inhabitants, who never take a bath from the time they are born until they die, unless they have taken part in the holiday masquerade, when they have to bathe afterward to cleanse themselves of the evil spirits that might have lurked in their masque costumes. (Some few natives have developed a love for the Russian steam bath, and there is a shed for such, but not many use it.)

Olga greeted us in a friendly way, as though it were not unusual to be squatting on the floor stirring a stew. Dr. Kelly said something to her in Russian, and she replied and nodded to an opening opposite the entrance. We went in that direction and entered a middle room lighted by a seal-oil lamp. This room was half workroom and half outhouse. Here some of the older women of the family were repairing their menfolk's *tarbossa,* those heavy sealskin boots that are truly comfortable in winter, according to Dr. Kelly, who says I will be wanting a pair myself. Some were pounding dried seal meat into edible portions, pounding it right on the dirt floor!

"Well, after all; it gets boiled for a long time," Dr. Kelly said. "Though there was a time when they chewed it without cooking it, I'm sure."

Others were cleaning or sharpening hunting knives and fishing spears and harpoons, all made of walrus bone. Seal bone is very porous and has no value at all, while walrus bone is brittle and every bit as beautiful as ivory. None of their primitive implements are decorated, though by now they could have adopted Russian folk designs if they were so inclined. One old woman, called a *starooka,* was making a *kamalaika,* which is a truly remarkable, absolutely waterproof raincoat made from long strips of seal, sea lion, and walrus gut pounded to a thin transparency and sewn together so intricately that no water can get through!

In this room, too, the odors of the burning seal oil and of human excrement are intermingled, making it almost impossible to proceed to the third room, which was about ten feet by twelve feet. In that room, the entire family sleeps huddled together for the animal warmth they impart to each other during the bitterest winter weather. There is absolutely no ventilation, and one wonders how they all can breathe without using up the air of this small space.

Dr. Kelly took a look at a raw wound on the ankle of one of the young men in the family who was lying alone in the room, apathetic and uncomplaining. He was one of the crack flensers. But a seal, which had not been dead when he had begun to strip it of its pelt, woke up and bit him unmercifully, deep into the bones and tendons. He would not be able to work for several more days.

"I wanted you to see how extensive the wound is," Dr. Kelly said to me. "Yeagor, here, walked all the way from the killing field to the hospital and sat there waiting about an hour for me while I was over on this side of town helping bring a new baby into the world, and he never let out a complaint or asked anyone else to help him. He didn't even say a word when I cleaned and cauterized his wound. They are all like that — absolutely stoic when hurt. I've yet to hear a cry of pain from any of them."

"I should think that lying around in all that filth, he'd have a terrible infection," I said when we were out in fresh air again.

"It is surprising how little sickness and infection there is among the natives, in spite of the filth. Almost all mortality is at birth or within the first year. Once a child has survived the first year, he grows up sturdy and then is carried off by some natural hazard or other disaster, seldom by disease or infection."

"I should think the odors alone would finish off any one of them."

"Well, of course, Kazan prefers to live that way. We've made tremendous headway with most of the natives."

"Not entirely with odors, though. I still get sick in church or whenever they are all together in a group," I said, holding up my nose.

"That's their unholy incense," said Dr. Kelly, and I had to laugh. I wanted to rush right up here and bathe immediately after we left the Gallaniums', but the good doctor wanted me to make one more call with him on our way back.

The Ostegoffs live in a neatly painted house in the last row up the hill. We entered (one never knocks) and did our usual obeisance. Mrs. Ostegoff's family was lying about on the floor, chairs, and couch of the sitting room. They were unkempt and smelled of blubber smoke and unwashed bodies. In spite of the company's attempt at making bright and cheerful interiors for them, the blubber fuel had smoked up everything. Our hostess shooed away the children. Like so many chicks, they scattered to other roosts, lighted, and settled down again to doing absolutely nothing but staring into space or at each other. (The adult Aleuts do this too when in a group and seem to be communicating with each other silently. I believe they have a wordless means of communication we cannot understand.) Though the children have nothing to do, they never get into mischief.

"All the Aleuts just vegetate. They're the most law-abiding, passive killers of time I've ever known," Dr. Kelly once said.

In the dining room, a tarnished brass samovar was steaming away over its seal-oil flame, and tall, cracked glasses stood ready on the dirty oilcloth-covered table. They drink gallons of chia. Mrs. Ostegoff offered us chia.

"We've just had chia," we lied politely. Dr. Kelly then checked the arm of a youngster, gashed while searching for birds' eggs. The young boys are called *melchiska,* and this melchiska had cut his arm on a jagged rock. Again, in spite of the obvious filth, the wound was clean and healing beautifully.

"That's one of the less progressive families," Dr. Kelly said when we left. "They're not all that bad. The great problem we have with them is timing. They are so slow to cerebrate. You notice how slow they are in all they do. It is not laziness, but the way they are made. They took a long time to adopt Russian ways, as far as the church is concerned, and they picked up these few customs from the Russian sealers who spent only a few weeks here each summer and were not, probably, the best examples to follow. They cannot see why they have to change from one strange set of customs to another unless in some way they benefit. They are slow to recognize benefit."

"I haven't thought of it that way," I said. "We do always think our way is best."

"Well, in this case, since the Russians did so little for them, our ways probably are better for them. But that will take convincing. I hope you will help me a little in this, Mrs. Beaman. I note a tremendous improvement in Mrs. Mandrigan and Vicele since they've been around you. Some of the young women, it seems to me, are neater about their persons. I know they've been asking Mrs. Mandrigan a lot of personal questions about you. Please do encourage them about cleanliness. Good habits will spread to the men in time. But that has to start in the home with the women and children."

"I'll try," I said. "But it looks like a hopeless job."

"The greatest evil is their addiction to kvas — both men and women and even fairly young children. You've already heard us discussing it at the Lodge. It's a strong beer the early Russians taught them to make from flour and sugar. Before the Russians, the Aleut tribes never had known alcohol in any form, but they soon took to kvas. Last year, in spite of extreme vigilance, some of the natives got completely out of hand. In fact, that is about the only trouble we ever have with them. They are docile, friendly, and absolutely honest until they've had too much kvas."

"Some of the men think the agents are too strict. The company men condone the drinking, perhaps because they like to take a nip or two themselves," I said.

"They haven't had to lift dead babies away from mothers too drunk to even know they're dead. I've done it often — taken babies right from the breasts where mothers have tried to suckle them and instead have poisoned them! I like a nip or two myself. But then, I'm an Irishman, and the Irish have handled alcohol for many more hundreds of years than the Aleuts have. For the Aleuts, it is a poison and should be forbidden. Trouble is, they always have some hidden away somewhere. Then when a special celebration comes along, it is produced."

They grow especially drunk on their saints' days, which they celebrate rather than their birthdays. On their saints' days (or name days), they get dressed up in their Sunday best and go calling on all their friends. In each household, they drink a little kvas and a little more kvas, and by the time they return home to their own supply, they are really drunk. Fortunately it does not make them quarrelsome, but it does cause them to be disgustingly obscene as to their speech and provokes them to lustful crimes. Few women are safe in the presence of a drunken man, and the women, when drunk, behave with complete abandon. They are an extremely chaste people otherwise, but they show no shame when they sober up. And as there is no authority in the native government for chastising wrongdoers, the problem is a difficult one to cope with.

John says that he is writing to request greater authority to deal with the situation, which is just becoming noticeable as the killing season progresses. He thinks that if fines or some other penalty could be meted out strong enough to make an impression, there might be less drinking. The drunkenness reaches a high degree, I am told, toward the end of the killing season. Then it dies down until Christmas, when it begins again and gets worse as the winter months advance. Last winter when Mr. Moulton restricted the amount of sugar and flour the Aleuts could buy, hoping to cut

GOVERNMENT HOUSE, S' PAUL ISLAND

down the manufacture of kvas, whole families took to pooling their rations and did without in their diet. The result was an ample supply of kvas, yet not much visible malnutrition among the children. In fact, the children abet their parents by gathering berries for them in the berry season, out of which they can make a still tastier brew. "Until the weather became impossible last year, the children were playing truant from school just to pick the berries for their parents. They would look defiantly at me if I reprimanded them," Dr. Kelly said. "Finally Mr. Moulton issued orders that the children would have to go to school. But that did not end the kvas drinking."

Apart from their kvas drinking, the Aleuts' only other bad habit is gambling. Both the Russians and our soldiers are responsible for that vice, and the Aleuts are like children about it. Father Paul is the cleverest gambler and has gained most with the cards; he seems happy only if winning from his poor parishioners. His bank account with the company attests to his success.

Otherwise life is simple. The Aleuts' pleasures are simple. They like to dance and sing. Two men have concertinas and another has a fiddle to provide the gay Russian folk music to which they dance. They sing a cappella beautifully, because the Orthodox church does not have organ or piano accompaniment for its choir. When the men dress for church or festive occasions, they wear the latest fashions imported from San Francisco. The women have adopted the gayest calico prints for summer wear and, in the winter, wear woolen materials now, using skin and fur clothes only for out-of-doors. They make their own clothes, which have little style. But I notice that they have begun to take in darts at the waistline, and some of the younger girls have asked if I minded their copying my clothes.

They all seem proud if ever I come visiting. The cleaner ones are always eager to show me improvements they've made, and a few have made first overtures to me to teach them how to cook our way and have inquired about other little domestic lore for which I am poorly trained myself. I've liked going about with Dr. Kelly, because my nurse's training during the war is of some help to him. He has admitted that what the island has needed — but he didn't realize until my first tour with him — is a woman, an American woman.

"The SA doesn't think the same way," I smiled.

"He's a hard man to figure out, and not everyone has to agree with him," he said.

The Aleuts believe that they are descended from the seals! Never having seen a monkey in their lives, this belief is much more logical for them and is a part of their legend and folklore — that is, what little they have retained of a folklore from the time before the Russians. Dr. Kelly says it is a logical belief and in many ways more valid than ours, because the seal has a far larger brain box in proportion to the body than has a monkey. The seal's eyes express human emotion where a monkey's do not, and since the Aleuts always have worn seal fur, eaten seal meat, and used the skin for boats and the blubber for fuel, they are entirely identified with the seals. If they have any theology left from the old time, their god or gods were no doubt giant seals, and they themselves have been seals in other incarnations.

While they do not have too many legends for their race, they do have a few strange customs that are not Russian. The men wander about at night in a sort of a trance, not kvas-induced. Of course the nights are light, so one can see them. They are not frightening, just eerie, moving about unseeing. No one has been able to account for this, and as they never do any harm, no one has ever tried to stop the habit. It is a bit disconcerting to run into one and have him look right through you without acknowledging a greeting. The womenfolk never wander like this and don't seem to mind when the men do. Usually the next day, the man will recount ghostly encounters he has had or visions of almost mythological beasts. I've heard them pad past our windows on occasion and wondered what they could be up to. Sometimes they are actually clairvoyant when they are traipsing about in a dense fog and suddenly scream out, "Ship's light! Ship's light!" which they cannot possibly see with their physical eyes. And always, sure enough, when the fog lifts, a ship is lying offshore!

One screamed "Ship's light!" about two this morning, sending chills up and down our spines. There's a dense, dense fog, but we think the *St Paul* may be in. She's due within a few days.

GOVERNMENT HOUSE, St PAUL ISLAND

Ruppia Maritima, an
ink drawing by
Frederick A. Walpole

The St Paul was riding at anchor when the mists finally dissipated! What a welcome sight! What a truly beautiful sight! A first link with home! Letters and messages and gifts and the purchases Captain Erskine made for me. All our dear ones seem so close in the letters they have written and by the little luxuries they have sent. They hadn't received our letters that went back from Onalaska or on the St Paul. But they thoughtfully had written anyway, so letters could be brought up on this trip. I won't ever mind that startling cry in the night, "Ship's light!" again. This is a beautiful day.

Another great surprise the St Paul has brought is in the person of Henry Wood Elliott himself! He was the first Treasury Department agent sent here. During his two years here, he mapped every inch of the two islands. But because he took his drawings directly to the Government Printing Office, I did not get to see them first. Mr. Elliott found the fur seal herds so completely decimated by the Russians that, when he returned to Washington, he pushed for legislation to prohibit any killing of seals until the herds could be reestablished. Congress passed such a bill before the writing of a treaty with Japan and Russia forbidding any sealing on land or in the waters around the islands. Mr. Elliott's greatest claim to fame, in my estimation, is the fact that he married a native Pribilof Island Aleut and took her back to live in Lakewood, Ohio, his home. She has come back to stay with her family while he goes to St Matthew Island. He will spend several days with us at Government House. Fortunately the SA's room has two beds. Then he will go over to St George to await the *Reliance,* which is to take him up to St Matthew Island some five hundred miles north of here. He is still gathering material for the book he plans to write about the fur seals, and he wishes to make sure that the Pribilofs are their only breeding ground.

Mr. Elliott is also on official government business and business for the Smithsonian, so the *Reliance* has been put at his disposal. He says that he would like to visit the Commander Islands, seven hundred miles southwest of us, but he is afraid he'll never get there — the *Reliance* is not permitted in Siberian waters. The vast amount of sailing he has done in these waters is a courageous act, heretofore unheard of in the interests of accurate, scientific knowledge about our possession and the wildlife of this area. He is also a very fine artist. His watercolor sketches and pen and ink drawings easily could be compared to the Old Masters'.

I shall be spending a great deal of time with Mr. Elliott while he is here. He is quite interested in the seal book I have begun and has asked me to make specific observations for his book at times when he cannot be here. I am flattered.

I had not realized that the excellently drawn map of St Paul on the office wall is his work; there is also a map of St George on that island. I've insisted that he sign them. This one is truly a work of art, with its profile of the approach to the island as he first saw it. He has promised to sign his name if I will do a proper job of lettering. "Yours is far more accurate than mine . . . and finer," he said. I will letter the maps for him, as well as the copies he will take back with him for his book. My lettering is finer, smaller. He shades his letters so that they do not print out as precise. Thus he has set me tasks that will keep me busy all winter.

July 10, 1879
St Paul Island
The Pribilof Group

Dear Mother and Father,
   The poor dear ladies of Czar Alexander II's court must be weeping in their caviar because they no longer can have so easily the sealskin coats they loved so much and must content themselves with the lowly mink and sable. But old Alexander needed money for his impoverished treasury after the Crimean War, so he sold us Alaska, and these islands came with the purchase, as you remember — $7,200,000! I do not know how much wealth there is in Alaska, or for that matter on the long Aleutian Chain, though we did see warehouses full of fine furs there. But there is

9

more than seven million dollars' worth of sealskins breeding, barking, roaring, and climbing in and out of the waters of these two islands right now! Of course, all the seals can't be killed at one time. But I have figured that in the past ten years and in the ten years to come, these two tiny pin dots on the map will have repaid our treasury for the entire Alaska Purchase. I'm afraid Alexander was not a good businessman!

The land may be ours now, but it remains Russian through and through. Ever since I landed, I have felt that I am living in a Russian outpost rather than an American possession.

I made the mistake of sealing each letter to you and now have forgotten whether I described this village to you. It is a pretty little place on a gentle slope. There are about eighty neatly painted cottages, occupied by the natives, the company quarters, warehouses, salting sheds, a few small shops — company owned — where the natives trade, a factory for the manufacture of seal oil, a schoolhouse, a hospital, and a large Greek Orthodox church (the Greek Orthodox Church has more members in Russia than the Russian Orthodox!). The latter was erected by the natives in '75 while Mr. Elliott was the government agent here. (He is again visiting the islands, so you see it is not as remote as you may think and also has enough of a fascination to lure people back.) The natives gave the entire sum — twenty thousand dollars — for its construction out of their earnings from the Alaska Commercial Company, which hires them to do the actual sealing. The church boasts a clock in its onion-domed tower and a full set of chimes, which can be heard above the raucous cries of the birds, the constant roar of the seals, and the boom of the surf. The chimes sound very beautiful across the bleak wastes when one is out clambering over the rocky ledges and dunes of the island.

Last, of course, but not least, is Government House, on a hill overlooking the whole village. We have made it comfortable for ourselves. The St Paul has brought the window shades we needed. I have made lambrequins, which I put over the windows, and I have brightened our rooms with drapes and other decorating that softens the austere atmosphere in which the men have lived. Many of the difficulties of my presence in this man's world were ironed out aboard the St Paul while we were coming up here. I can see now why the Senior Agent was upset by my coming. For one thing, this house was not designed for a married couple desiring privacy. None such was ever anticipated. But now John and I have a pleasant bedroom and a little sitting room to ourselves, though the Senior Agent is more often with us in front of our potbellied stove than at his own. Yes, while you are sweltering in the heat of the Capital in July, we have to have a fire indoors to be comfortable, although at midday it is warm outdoors but usually raining. The hills are aflame with deep-hued blossoms. Flowers are blooming in the wildest profusion so that, as long as one stays indoors and looks out at them, it is not difficult to imagine ourselves nearer the Equator than the North Pole.

Natives do our household chores, but we dine at the company mess for the present, at the invitation of its director, Mr. Morgan. John is quite content with this arrangement, as he did not want me to have to cook for the SA, *which is what might have happened. These are little things we hadn't foreseen when we set out. But you can see how easily we have managed to settle our problems.*

For now, this is our home. It is a well-built little bungalow with papered walls and dark-stained hardwood woodwork — like any simple bungalow on the outskirts of Washington. I've been able to purchase materials at the company stores, so I did not have to send to San Francisco for very many things. All the goods have been extremely inexpensive. This seems unbelievable, considering the cost and hazard of transporting everything here. But I've been assured that the company does not want to make any money out of the natives, for whom they maintain the stores, and only wishes to encourage them to better their way of living.

I've bowlsful of the brilliant and exotic flowers everywhere, and I only wish I knew all their names. Henry Elliott has promised to help me classify some of them, since Captain Erskine could find no botanical guide helpful enough in San Francisco. Mr. Elliott says I will have to write one. But he is the trained naturalist, and I am not. I plan on taking an inventory, nevertheless, because I am grateful to the flowers for breaking the stark, hard reality of this pile of rocks.

From the living room, which serves as an office, we can see the wharfs and the main plaza of the village. From our sitting room window, which looks over to the cliff and Nah Speel, I can watch the seals, which look like tiny dots from here. In the little sketch I am enclosing, you can just see them at the water's edge. I am no good at perspective, as you remember, so while everything seems close, there is considerable distance between buildings and rookery. Also, we are higher above all this than I can make us look. Anyway you can see that construction is good, that all the ice is melted, and that we're not so primitively situated as you dreamed.

The killing grounds are on the other side of a low hill beyond our bedroom, so I do not have to witness that particularly ghastly part of our lives here. As I've written you before, I think, I plan to spend the winter writing about our lives and the seals' lives in detail so you will understand better why we have to be here. The little pups are being born daily now, and some are grown up enough to play in groups called pods. *I think I shall write about the baby seals separately, because they are so fascinating. Soon their mothers, the matkas, will give them their first swimming lessons. You see, I will have much to amuse and entertain me while the men are busy.*

The St Paul, which has brought your precious letters and packages, is loading the skins that already have been salted in the kenching houses. It will take this huge packet of letters to San Francisco. Then it will call back here in August for the last time this year, for the last time until next spring! Then, indeed, we will be cut off from the world. Once the ice closes in these waters, there is absolutely no communication with the rest

GOVERNMENT HOUSE, St PAUL ISLAND

of the world. I do dread the thought of isolation, so I try not to think of it often. Time enough when it arrives!

Both the natives and white people eat the flesh of the seal, which is very tasty, I assure you — though you can imagine with what timidity I tried my first bite. It can be prepared in many ways once it is properly butchered. Right now, of course, we can have it fresh daily, because the killing season is in full swing. Five-year-old males are a bit tough and strong, but the younger ones Cook selects are indeed good, and we are also permitted to kill some of the male pups for food. They are delicious. Sea lion is still more delicious and our preference, because it can be prepared just like good beef without the addition of bacon or other seasonings and does not need every shred of fat removed as the seal meat does. Sea-lion fat is like beef suet. Seal fat is a strong, horrible-smelling and horrible-tasting tissue which must be entirely removed. The meat is then cut in thin slices and soaked at least twelve hours in strong salt water, then fried or stewed, and served with a thick brown gravy. You see how domestic I've become in spite of not having to cook! We live on wonderful bird meat, fish, and seafood galore, and occasionally, actual beef and lamb. We are never hungry, for this is a great storehouse of nature's abundance.

Below us is the roof of the company store, with its weather vane and the signal staff where signals are run up for the St Paul or other ships on the water. None can anchor close to land. In my sketch, there is a little native bidarka with sail out on the water. You can see the natives' drying racks, called laabas, *where they begin to dry their meat and fish for winter use. It is difficult for the company to provide all the food, especially staples of flour, cereal, and sugar, so everyone often goes hungry by spring, in spite of this early start at preparation.*

A tiny bird eats crumbs I've put out for him; his nest is in the cliffs. There are many seabirds. Sometimes the air is shrill with their calls and black with their wings. So many are good to eat. The natives eat their eggs, which I find too fishy for my taste. But as food gets scarcer and scarcer in the wintertime, I may have to change my mind, I am told.

We do not miss, as I expected we might, the daily newspapers. We have no bloodcurdling murders, no robberies, no noisy carousing, no brawls, and no Chinese labor difficulties such as the West Coast was experiencing when we left. In fact, we are in the midst of peace and quiet (except for the animal sounds to which we have grown accustomed). The climate, though cold and densely foggy or actually wet, is not unhealthy. No one gets colds or pneumonia. We do not see the sun very often, but we have daylight enough to read until about 2:00 a.m. It is not difficult to get about at any time during the night. This is a blessing, since the little outhouse is some distance back of the house. Of course, we shall have a corresponding period of dark during the winter months. By then I should know my way about.

There was no celebration of the Fourth of July. The natives were too occupied with the killing and skinning. This is the busiest season, but it

GOVERNMENT HOUSE, St PAUL ISLAND

*will be ended in a few days. So the Fourth went by without notice, about
which I was a bit upset. Tomorrow the natives celebrate the name day of
St Paul Island, Emannimik as they call it — actually on their calendar,
it is St Peter and St Paul Day. This is the date on which Pribilof
discovered this island and named it St Paul. (St George, which he
discovered later, is named for his ship, the St George.)*

*The islanders love nothing better than an excuse for celebrating, and
this is their last big day until the Russian Christmas, January 6th. They
will engage in various amusements at the schoolhouse, where Russian chia
will be served as well as all kinds of sweetmeats, which they love. During
the evening, there will be fireworks, much in the fashion of our Fourth,
which we will watch from indoors because it is too cool to stand about
outside.*

*In fact, it is difficult to believe that the season is so far advanced that
— while you are perspiring in discomfort of the hot sun, wearing thin
clothes, having Sunday School picnics and firecrackers — we have to rush
to the stove to warm our fingers enough to continue writing to you.*

*I doubt that anyone has undertaken to teach these people any American
history. Most of their teachers are natives who, though trained in the
States, have reverted to the Russian language. No one has been successful
so far in arousing a desire to learn the English language or to learn very
much about us. Their tyone said he was sure I would be asked to teach
English to the children at the school. I doubt whether I could succeed
where others haven't. I can't, try as I do, understand — let alone learn
— the Russian grammar. How could I explain anything to the youngsters
unless I know their language? They will think it mighty odd that I can't
learn theirs when I want them to learn ours! When you want a pleasanter
thought of me this winter, think of me trying to get Aleut children to
change from one barbaric language to another.*

*I hope to tell you more about the natives and their customs. Many of
the older natives still speak Aleut, which I have not even tried to master.
But as a sample of what is also in store for me, I copy the number which
indicates how many months I have been away from Washington.*

*Akintinmah-tah-khansug-nahr-tah. You see, it has been a long,
long time — seven months!*

Affectionately as ever,

> *Your daughter,*
> *Lib.*

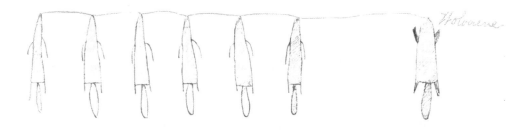

JULY 12*th*   The men have begun the final week of killing. The *S*^t
Paul has departed to deliver Mr. Elliott to St George
and to load the skins taken there. The work is at its heaviest in
order to get it all done soon, for the pelts get too gamey if not
taken early in the season. Even this is a bit late, except that the
weather has remained cool enough to prolong the work. Though I
am spared the actual sight of the slaughter, the noise is so terrible
that I am constantly aware of what is going on. It is an awful time
to live through. The whole idea upsets me, and I am in a state of
nerves that has me worried. After all, I must have visualized some
sort of slaughter to get the pelts, but I never dreamed that it all
would take place so close at hand. I probably thought, if I thought
about it at all, that there was some remote spot for, and dainty
way of, expediting the poor seals — far from any personal
experience or involvement for either of us — and that John would
have to stand at some warehouse door, after it was all over,
counting the skins that came in and billing the company for the
number of pelts in the name of the U.S. Treasury. How sadly
different!

John is sick at heart over the real job and physically sick, too,
for he hardly eats, just picks at the food on his plate. He does not
join in the conversation around the table, which is a little louder
and more boisterous than before. He is so silent, stooped, and
white that I worry about him.

"It's a messy business, Libby, ugly and contrary to anything you
or I have ever been taught. It's just no place for us. Yet what can
we do now? I feel as trapped as one of those animals — more so I
guess — because I know what's happening. Fortunately they
don't." This John said a few days ago. He hasn't said much since.

While I watch him grow more morose and disgusted with his
job, I have sensed a rising tension among the men of the company
and among the natives, too. Perhaps the men have become so
restive because of the very bestiality of the job they have to do —
selecting the animals, directing the drives to the killing grounds,
directing the flensing operations, making sure the skin is taken the
moment the animal is killed, being right on the field in the thick
of the blood and offal, coming in spattered with blood and dung,
and reeking of decaying carcasses with almost nothing but the
putrefaction of death in their eyes and minds and nostrils.

Each night, by the time we arrive for dinner at the Lodge, they
are gruff, less careful of their language, and less carefully attired.
Though I have seen none of them take a drink, I have smelled
alcohol on some breaths, and I have noted many bloodshot eyes.
The natives, always so docile and well behaved in front of me,
also are more keyed up. Neither the SA nor John can find any
kvas, but they know that the Aleuts have been drinking more
heavily. Their tyones (they also call a native foreman *tyone*) have

been warned to keep them in order or they will lose their jobs. But each day grows more difficult to get through, and I wish the whole business was over with. Naturally I could not write all this to my family, who would be shocked and worried as I am shocked and worried.

I am afraid to write, yet I must write, what happened today. I write with the hope that perhaps the whole episode will become clear. I try to understand why it happened, why I let it happen. But some things are beyond human calculation, beyond human control. I know these are difficult days. The killing season should be ended, but because we have had extremely bad weather at times, it has been prolonged. Fortunately it has been cool enough to keep the pelts from rotting, which they usually begin to do about now. The men are tired and excitable, and so are the animals, especially the bulls at the height of their mating season. They fight constantly and viciously over the matkas, and one of the favorite pastimes of the natives is to stand at the edge of the harems and bet on the fights just as men at home might bet on a cockfight or a wrestling match. Aleuts will bet on anything that presents a challenge. So they pick their favorite bulls and spur them on from the sidelines.

I've stayed away from the rookeries because I do not like the noise and heat of battle. Yet now that the baby seals are being born, I've wanted to watch them closely so I can write fully about them, which means, of course, that I have to spend some time close enough for careful observation.

Walking is not easy on this island. There are no well-worn paths anywhere except to the spring, where we get our drinking water, about a mile and a half away from here. I am tired of always walking in that direction, which is inland, because no seals are to be seen along the way. The longer walks I had once anticipated taking so far have proved to be short excursions only. Some obstacle — such as slippery rocks, deep ravines, sudden fissures, or bogs — always stand in the way of going on to the farther rookeries.

Today started out to be such a beautiful day, the clearest we've had so far. Since I couldn't stand the din from the killing grounds and knew that the men had just finished driving the seals in from Polavina across the island, I decided I would take advantage of the path the animals wore down. Mr. Elliott told me that Polavina is

JULY 13th

the most beautiful sight on the island and an interesting rookery. I wanted to see it before the rains washed away the seals' path and while the weather still permitted sketching.

John did not, as was his custom, ask what I would be doing all day. If he had, and if I had told him, he would have forbidden me to go. Instead, and with a certain amount of resentment in his voice, he announced that he had been ordered — *"Ordered, Libby,"* — to supervise the killings at Novastoshnah.

"You knew you would be sent. The log records that the assistant agent always supervises the operation at Novastoshnah."

"But it means that I must leave you alone here, alone and unprotected."

"I can manage. Do not worry." I had assumed he'd be gone for just the day, so I made my plans accordingly.

Past Kamminista's volcanic peak I climbed, seeing dead and dying seals along my path, rejected seals that had been left to find their way back to the sea or perish in this high, unfamiliar region so unlike their natural habitat. Flesh flies swarmed thick upon them, and white foxes lurked among the rocks, shy of me, but waiting to scavenge as soon as I had passed. I have no fear of the white foxes. They will not harm a living, moving creature. They are the island's sanitation corps.

I've had no real fear of meeting any Aleut. I know them all by name. They've all been friendly to me even when they've had kvas. We mumble a greeting — possibly *spasibo* for an answer — and go our separate ways. I've come upon children hunting birds' eggs. They are less silent, less secretive. I hear their laughter before I come upon them. Their elders sometimes give me quite a start. But I've known no real fear of anything so far up here on the islands. That is why I could not understand why John was so fearful for me.

But later, when I began to reconstruct the horrible day, I could understand. Three times I thought I saw a slight motion out of the corner of my eye. Something, or someone, kept disappearing behind a rock like a wraith. None of the natives would act that way. Then I suddenly remembered that Mr. Morgan had brought up a few stranger Aleuts from Attu whom the natives did not like. I dismissed the thought of them because they were all employed. I'm not sure whether I'd really have been frightened if I had met a strange Aleut face to face in that high rugged place. I breathed more freely when I came onto the open dunes. No further thought of danger crossed my mind.

How still the air was on the high dunes, away from the din and stench of the killing grounds! Then as I approached, I could hear the noise of the bachelor parade ground below me, and even that seemed wholesome. The wheeling, screaming birds had a hypnotic effect. They calmed me. I followed the recent driving

trail over the last tumbled rocks, down to a broad plateau above a seacoast shelf. This plateau extends about a half mile inland from the edge of a sheer cliff, which drops directly down several hundred feet into the sea. This bachelor parade ground teemed with hundreds and hundreds of holluschickie that had escaped the killings for another year. The herd seemed scarcely decimated, and the bachelors appeared particularly happy on their pink sand and highly polished basalt playing field.

Nah Speel Rookery — I love to watch the changing color of the dunes.

I passed between Polavina Sopka, a high conical peak, and a lovely little lake with a margin of jagged rocks on one side and great grass-covered dunes on the other. Vivid flowers dotted the grass like confetti — giant nasturtiums and great patches of deep blue gentians, early brilliant phlox such as I've never seen before, pulse with its delicate odor (when the wind was not from the rookery), and other flowers I must learn.

I sat on a ledge at the very edge of the cliff, at this point a highly polished red rock that goes straight down to steely blue-black ledges far below, where bull seals exercise full rein over their harems. Below them the surf boomed tremendously against the rock, polishing it to even greater smoothness. At first I could not figure out how the seals could get back and forth to the ledges, or how the holluschickie could get way up on the high parade grounds. Every other rookery I had seen had a slow and gradual rise for approach; this one had a forbidding perpendicular wall.

Then I saw them coming up the face of the wall using little ledge-like outjuttings for stairs. These small steps seemed to present no problem to the seals in spite of their clumsy gait, which is an inching movement. They seemed to have established some order of precedence for those going up or down. Here and there, where a few had forgotten the rules, they just climbed over each other or turned and went in the same direction. I saw not one tumble off those narrow ledges.

The cliff gentles off far to the south and as soon as I had made a rough sketch, I clambered in that direction to get nearer to the baby seals, which I wanted to sketch accurately and from close up. I came to a place where many newborn pups nursed contentedly. I decided that they are about the most adorable baby animals anyone could wish to watch.

I sat on a rock close to and slightly above a small harem, a good vantage point for working. Fortunately the wind came from behind me and blew the stench out to sea. I sat for a long time just watching, fascinated by the ways of the pups with their soulful human eyes and their bleatings like little sheep when their mothers pulled away from nursing them and left them. After a while I began to sketch.

Naturally all around me, I could hear the barking and hissing, the spitting and coughing of the bulls, some challenging others for invading the boundaries of their harems or fighting over their wayward wives. But the problems of the adult seals were remote from the objects of my concern — the little pups. I could not help noticing how beautiful the young matkas looked, sleek and docile except for a slight whimper now and then when one gave birth to a kotickie or was bumped into by a clumsy bull ten times her size. The screaming birds and the *baroom* [sound of the surf] of the sea added to the din. But in spite of the commotion, I managed a few fair sketches of several pups.

"Seal mating is no sight a lady should have to witness," is what one of the men at mess probably wanted to say to me the night before. Instead he had again warned me, "Don't go near the rookeries during the mating season, Mrs. Beaman. The bulls are somethin' fierce then and mought do ye some harm. They have no use for anyone who interferes. They'll charge ye and tear yer ta bits."

"Aye," said another. But I caught the glance between them and knew they were trying to spare me the sight of actual mating.

Well, this day so much of it had been going on around me that I had little curiosity about it. I wanted to do my sketches of the little kotickie. But suddenly the bull right below me challenged the bull of the next harem over a sleek little matka that was escaping his domain for the other's. I had to stop and watch; the drama was such a human one and so close that I felt personally involved and ready to root for the bull of the little cow's choice. The hissing and spitting and swaying of the two battling monsters became so vicious that I stepped to higher ground. I should have continued sketching the babies, but the fight was too fascinating not to watch to the bitter end. Those two bulls were out to kill each other, and they set about using their powerful shoulders and teeth in such a way that neither could come out of it whole, no matter who won.

But in the middle of the row, my attention was diverted to a third bull who had taken advantage of the fight to carry off the little seal the other two were fighting over. I hadn't realized that I was sitting on the edge of this new seacatch's harem until he brought the trim little matka to my feet and plopped her down on the very ledge I had so hastily vacated. There he gave her a most ungentle trouncing, thumping and scolding her, while I retreated to still higher ground, now more curious than ever about what the other two would do when they discovered their prize gone. But the scene so close to my feet was even more intriguing.

The matka's new lord and master, after several more thudding blows that sent her yelping against the rocks, began to caress her by rubbing his long neck along her sleek body. Immediately she wriggled and snuggled up to him, as if to acknowledge his overlordship. They nosed each other all over, especially about the face, and she did not struggle to get away or to go back to the two suitors still warring over her. Instead she slithered up and down beside him. They fondled each other more and more excitedly. The expressions in their eyes were all too human expressions of passion and desire. I could not help myself. I had to watch, with not even a scientist's impersonal interest or an artist's justification, but with frank curiosity and a sense of personal involvement.

Suddenly the little matka flattened out on the pinkish sand and let the great bull cover her. Their mating lasted a long time with frequent convulsive movements that set their whole bodies to quivering. I grew limp with my own intense absorption in the scene, my sketchbook and crayon forgotten in my hands. Slowly I began to realize the enormity of what I had stopped to watch and was ashamed of myself for succumbing to such an unladylike experience, so contrary to my careful upbringing and even my own convictions. I wanted to run from my shame. I stood up, bent on going back to the dunes and away from this mass of mating, fighting seals.

I turned to face the Senior Agent standing silent, just behind me!

"Interesting, isn't it, Elizabeth?" he asked with a thin smile on

GOVERNMENT HOUSE, S' PAUL ISLAND

his lips and mockery in his eyes. I wanted to faint into nothingness, to disappear beneath the sand and the tufa, to be anywhere but there on that spot. A blush of embarrassment and confusion spread from the roots of my hair down to my toes. I tossed my head and ran past him up the rise toward the parade ground and the little lake. But the earth was so uneven and my eyes so blinded by tears of anger and shame that I stumbled often and could not run from him with the dignity I wished to show. I lost my sketch pad and crayons clambering over a particularly difficult rock in my path. He, following more easily, picked them up and handed them to me.

"Thank you," I said coldly and turned away from him toward home, wondering if he would follow me all the five miles back just to mock me. But a sudden storm, such as come quickly and go quickly, struck violently, making of the seals' driving trail a river of mud through which I floundered. Lightning on these islands is always terrifying. The Pribilofs are noted for the most harrowing electrical storms in the world, and this morning's was the worst since I've been up here, more so because I was out in it and unprepared for it. The sheet lightning spread steely blue over us with a hiss that ended in deep thunderous rolls out over the Bering. The direct lightning hit in great, vivid darts against rocks and crevices as though intent on blasting the island into bits. Thunder cracked instantaneously with the darts. It has deafened many natives and company men in the past, and I was afraid for my own hearing with each deafening crack.

There was nowhere to take shelter on the dunes of the open plateau, nowhere until I reached Boga Slov, "Word of God," with its great boulders and ledges. But Boga Slov got its name because it attracted the lightning more than any other spot in the Arctic, and this morning was no exception. Lightning illuminated the peak, which looked like a finger of God pointing a warning to all those who would break the rules.

I kept straight on toward home, floundering in the awful mud, stumbling over the jagged basalt, drenched to the skin without my oilskin, and, most of all, angry with myself for now being vulnerable to the Senior Agent's scorn.

As I came past the mountain and onto the road that forks to the spring, I think I would have fallen but for the firm grasp he took on my arm to help me over the little flash flood between us and the final stretch of the road. He had been following me all the way! And in silence he now followed me the rest of the way. How can I ever hold up my head again or look the man in the eye?

But — he had called me Elizabeth, my first name!

GOVERNMENT HOUSE, S^T PAUL ISLAND

I could not write more at the time. I had to stop, though

I could not write more at the time. I had to stop, though the nightmare day did not end with my return to the house.

I had assumed that John would be returning in the company cutter in time for dinner. I tried to get myself well in hand before he appeared so I would not have to mention any of the day's happenings. I planned to greet him as though nothing had happened. I planned to ask him immediately about Novastoshnah so he would forget to ask me about my day. I had rescued only one soaked drawing to show for all my ill spent time at Polavina. I'm never a good liar and am always much better at keeping silent. We would then go down to the Lodge together. I would avoid, if possible, an exchange of any sort with the Senior Agent. I knew, of course, that meeting him face to face would be unavoidable, and that if I did try to avoid him entirely, John would notice. I had no greater problem on my mind all afternoon than to try to be composed and serene by the time of John's return. And how could I, with the memories of the morning constantly recurring with lightning-like clarity?

But John did not return.

I waited well past the usual hour to go to dinner. There was no cutter in the bay, nor any sign of it coming from around Southwest Point, though the waters had calmed and the winds were almost as gentle as before the storm. I heard the SA leave his room and set out for the Lodge. I waited a while longer, debating what to do. Should I stay at the house until someone came to tell me some awful news, or should I go down and learn why the company cutter was not yet in? Thinking that the men may have been blown into another landing and had to make their way across the wet island on foot, I dashed off a note:

Myriophyllum Spicatum, an ink drawing by Frederick A. Walpole

> Dear John —
> Have gone to the Lodge without you, hoping to learn why you are late. Join me there.
> Lovingly,
> Lib.

I gave the note to Mrs. Mandrigan and told her to give it to Mr. Beaman the moment he arrived.

As I stepped down the path, the Senior Agent fell in beside me without a word, having come from around the side of the house. I turned my back on him and was immediately ashamed of the gesture, so I turned around and confronted him abruptly.

"Where is Mr. Beaman?" I asked.

"Why, he's out at Novastoshnah," he replied and the look in his eyes was one of genuine surprise that I should ask. "Didn't he tell you where he was going?"

"Yes, of course he told me where he was going. But he should be back by now. There's a good wind from the northeast, calm enough water, and certainly no sign of a storm to hold them back."

"But the company cutter is not coming back tonight. It does not come back until the killing is completed at Novastoshnah — usually a four-day stint, if all goes well. Did he not tell you that?"

"Did he know?" I countered, remembering how casually John had mentioned the Novastoshnah operation in the morning before he left. I was sure he did not know. He had taken nothing with him for a prolonged stay, no dry clothes or even soap. And I was sure he would have seen to my program for so many days, our first apart since we came up here.

"Of course he knew. He knows how many seals may be taken from that rookery. He knows by now how many the men can handle, kill, and flense in one day. It's simple arithmetic."

"But you did not tell him he would have to stay."

"He was told his job at the beginning. I hope I do not have to spell out every little move. The assistant agent always has had to supervise the Novastoshnah operation. He's read the log. He knows the company maintains a barracks there."

"But you could have forewarned him about staying there," I said, and it was the first time I had used a querulous tone or accused him in any way. I knew the moment I said it that I should have bitten my tongue first. I saw him stiffen and turn to face me squarely in the path.

"I might as well say this now. I find it extremely difficult to speak with your husband at all. He seems to resent the simplest communication. I avoid all dealings with him except those that have the most direct bearing upon our work. I had no intention of reminding him to take a toothbrush. I hope you understand this, E . . . E . . . Mrs. Beaman."

"John would not have gone at all if he had thought I would be left alone at Government House. I know that."

"Alone with me, you meant to say?"

"Alone with you, perhaps I could have said. But I see no reason for adding the comment. John has no cause for thinking ill of you in that respect," I said, looking directly into his eyes. For a moment I detected a grudging gratitude. But it was as quickly extinguished.

"Mr. Beaman knew from our discussions in San Francisco that there would be many times when he would have to be away from you. He knew he could not always be at your side to protect you and to escort you. I warned you myself about this. Mr. Beaman knew also that he'd have to be away several days at a time and have to leave you among rough men from time to time. I admit I have been angry with him for not making you stay in the States.

GOVERNMENT HOUSE, S! PAUL ISLAND

122

And it has been for this reason especially."

"And you've considered him a weakling for not making me stay. Well, my husband is *not* weak, and I am at fault for insisting on coming here. I shall not explain why. You never would understand. I grant that you have been right, for not in my wildest imaginings could I have foreseen all the problems. I had no idea what this killing could do to men."

"Thank goodness you do see and do understand my position. This is no place for a decent woman."

"I take that as the compliment it was meant to be, sir. But it makes your behavior this morning still more difficult to understand." I blushed to my toes remembering.

"You will not believe me, so why should I explain?"

"I've no reason not to believe you," I said, looking directly into his eyes.

"I saw you set out alone across the island. Good heavens! You must have known that the company had imported about twenty men from Attu to help with the killings. Their bestial behavior to women when they're full of kvas has been the talk of the Lodge. Two of them due to go to Novastoshnah this morning could not be accounted for. They're loose somewhere in the hills."

"Dear Lord," I whispered hoarsely, truly ashamed.

"Frankly I did not want you to know of my presence if nothing happened. But things didn't work out that way."

"No, things didn't." I did not know what else to say. Also I did not want the company men who were passing us on their way to the Lodge to overhear our conversation.

"A man cannot always help himself, Elizabeth. You are an attractive woman, you know. You must forgive me. I think you can. But please, please, for all our sakes, do not walk alone again, anywhere, even down here. Pretend you are ill. Pretend anything. I'll see that food is sent up to you until Mr. Beaman returns. Until the rutting season is over do not appear anywhere without your husband. That is an order. I cannot be responsible for anyone's actions. You understand that after what happened today. I simply cannot be responsible. I've already sent for Mrs. Mandrigan to come and stay these few nights with you at Government House."

"You need not have done that," I said, and I would have liked to address him by first name directly since he had called me Elizabeth. But I never had, and I could not bring myself to do so even at this important moment in our relationship. I saw the look of gratitude in his eyes again. I, in turn, tried to show him mine. "You need not have done that, sir. Why did you feel that you had to? You must know by now that I trust you."

"For appearance's sake — and, too, because Mr. Beaman does not trust me. It will be best for you, Elizabeth. With Mrs. Mandrigan up there, not even the company men can talk. She will meet you here after dinner. I shall stay here at the Lodge until Mr. Beaman gets back," he concluded, and he opened the Lodge door for me.

"Oh, thank you," I said, and that was all I had time to say as we went in to mess.

JULY 15th John came back from Novastoshnah today at midday, dirty, unkempt, and so lividly angry that, had the Senior Agent been here, I think he would have gone right in and killed him. Fortunately the SA is over on St George and will not be back for a few days, during which time I hope to get John mollified.

He stormed in here expecting to find my door battered down and our marriage bed defiled. Instead he found me trying to teach Mrs. Mandrigan how to use the kerosene cook stove, of which she is extremely frightened. A stove blew up one time at the company kitchen when her husband was still alive and working as a houseman. He helped put out the blaze, but none of the islanders have had any faith in kerosene stoves since. Nor have I. But they are far less smoky than blubber fires for heating water, which she does for us out-of-doors now. When cold weather really descends, it will be far more convenient to heat water in the kitchen.

John was surprised to learn that Mrs. Mandrigan has been staying with me all the time he was away and that the SA , until going to St George in a company cutter, had been sleeping at the Lodge. He was more surprised to learn that his superior officer, not I, had made the arrangements. Finding me safe has been his greatest relief.

"I've been through hell out there worrying about you. There's no other word for it — hell," he said to me.

GOVERNMENT HOUSE, St PAUL ISLAND

July 16, 1879
Government House
St Paul Island

Dear Family,

I promised you I would write you a brief history of these islands. Naturally I had so much happening that I've had time to write only descriptions of what I've seen and done, not what I've learned.

Vitus Bering, an intrepid Danish explorer paid by the czar to investigate the Arctic waters and claim all discoveries in the name of Russia, sighted the Aleutian Chain in 1731. The official date given for the discovery of Alaska, however, is 1741, because he did not sight or claim the mainland of Alaska until that year. He was shipwrecked and killed later that same year on the island which now bears his name. Other Russian expeditions followed and continued the explorations in this area. Every inch of land they came upon they claimed in the name of the czar and Holy Mother Russia. These islands were sighted by the explorer Joan Synd (a man) in 1767 but were not landed on until July 11, 1786, by Gerasim Pribilof. He discovered the fur-seal breeding grounds; otherwise he would have reported the islands as worthless volcanic peaks sticking out of the ocean. But he recognized the valuable herds for what they were and left some of his crew here to kill and flay the animals while he went back to report his find and bring in more help. The few pelts he took with him proved to be so valuable that sealers were sent back with him to fully exploit the find.

Other expeditions, getting wind of the wealth to be had, also set out. Pirates heard of the booty and preyed upon the pelt-laden ships. In spite of the most treacherous sailing conditions in these waters, there was much traffic, considerable fighting, and many shipwrecks as witness of men's greed. In time the more responsible sealers established the best season and types of seals for killing. Their commercial centers for processing and selling were so far away and the trip so hazardous at best that they finally transferred Aleuts from the Aleutian Islands up here to do the killing, flensing, and salt curing for them. Then they stopped by only once a year, in the best sailing weather, to gather the year's yield.

There must have been considerable interbreeding of the few Aleut families, since they were so isolated that they seldom could visit each other on the two islands and never could get back to the Aleutians. There was also considerable crossbreeding with the Russian sailors, who probably have the same Mongolian origins. I was never good at drawing the human figure either from plaster casts or from life, but I have made a few sketches of Vicele, who is typical of the Pribilof Aleut.

Though the Russians visited the Pribilofs only in the summer, they left their colonizing influences early. These were enhanced by frequent colonizing visits to the Aleutians and Alaska, where they had well established villages and trading posts. (When the United States purchased

Alaska, all Russians were asked to leave the territory. All natives who had married Russians had a choice of staying or leaving. Some emigrated, others stayed. Everyone living on these islands stayed, not knowing what would happen to them next. After all, their families had been here for nearly a hundred years, and they had lost all ties with the Aleutian Aleuts.)

But while the Russians were still the owners, so many excesses were committed with the natives that the czar established a semiofficial control of his new possessions by creating the Russia-Alaska Company in 1799. This company's charter ran for twenty years and was renewed for another twenty. The first administrator was Alexander Baranoff, a wise and successful agent who did much to bring some measure of civilization and civil dealings to the natives in Alaska and the islands. In 1821, a Russian ukase [proclamation] excluded all navigation from the waters surrounding Alaska. Immediately the United States and Great Britain, who had both been dealing on a friendly basis with the company, protested through their embassies in Moscow. This prompted the United States' Monroe Doctrine, an expression of concern for this sort of thing. Diplomatic discord followed sporadically through many years until, in 1861, the Russian Commercial Company finally dissolved. Prince Maksutov was sent as Imperial Governor of the territory, which by then had many towns, fortifications, and forts as far south as San Francisco. Legend has it that he was not a good administrator. And Alexander II, needing cash after his wars, sold the entire territory, including the islands, for $7,200,000. Eduoard de Stoeckl would be shocked at my history lesson. But I dare say he did have a good deal to do with the purchase.

Postcard of The Killing Grounds, St Paul Island, by Henry Wood Elliott

Watching the pups is far more interesting than studying dead history. I shall write about the pups in my next letter.

Always affectionately,
Lib.

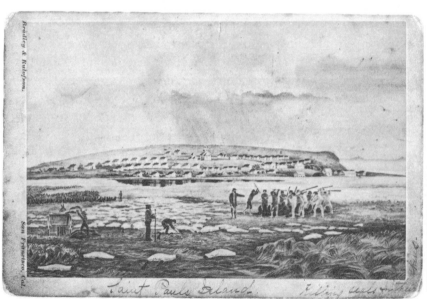

GOVERNMENT HOUSE, St PAUL ISLAND

I have copied one of John's reports to the Treasury
Department. It is factual and succinct but leads to a
discussion of his recommendations.

We arrived at Sr Paul Island, the Pribilof Group, on May 27,
1879, to find that the winter season had been unusually mild.
There had been great hardship between January and May because
so much of the natives' food supply of frozen seal meat had
spoiled. We had to approve, after the fact, of the killing of 282
young seals on May 19th and 525 more the day before our arrival.
Birds, plus an equal distribution of canned salmon provided by the
Alaska Commercial Company, had held the natives through the
difficult period until the seals appeared. Some fur seals have hung
around the island all winter, a most unusual occurrence. The male
seals began to haul up unusually early.

James Moulton, assistant special agent whom I have replaced,
had been teaching school in English with very little success.
George Butrin is teaching school in Russian, although he has been
educated in Vermont.

Killing for pelts began on June 2^d and ended July 15th. Twenty
thousand were taken from Sr George Island and eighty thousand
from here. Twenty additional laborers were sent up from Onalaska
to help with the oil making, as the natives did not have time.

The season's income to the natives for their labor was
$32,153.40; it was distributed on Sr Paul as follows (There are four
classes of native workers: skilled, not so skilled, shirkers, and sick
and part-time. Their pay is shared on that basis.):

64	First class	$410.75 each
6	Second class	$369.67 each
6	Third class	$328.60 each
2	Fourth class	$287.52 each
3	Special appropriations	
	(priest, etc.)	$650.00 each
3	Tyones	$150.00 each
Balance to church		$ 74.00

The total earnings on Sr George permitted about the same
proportionate distribution. This is exclusive of sums earned by day
work in other employment, sale of furs from trappings, etc. Their
income far exceeds their needs.

The natives tell me that the herds are diminishing due to the
new seal-oil works at the end of the island. They believe that the
odor of the steam, the offal, and the oil vapor drive the seals away.
Our count does not bear out this belief. However, if I may add my
own observations, I see no importance to our government

GOVERNMENT HOUSE, Sr PAUL ISLAND

economically from the manufacture of seal oil. Its transport is too costly.

The island is greatly in need of a water reservoir nearer to or within the village limits. At present, water is hauled more than a mile from springs located in a very muddy area. In bad weather, several days may pass under real hardship for lack of water, as at that time the road is impassable. The engineering of such a supply would be a simple matter if the authorization of sufficient funds is granted. This I urge.

John Warren Beaman
Assistant Special Agent
July 15, 1879

John sent the report with his superior's more detailed report. His engineering experience could be used to good advantage here. He already has surveyed a good part of the island and found Mr. Elliott's map to be accurate to a second. While he was doing this, he noted where improvements could be made for everyone's comfort. What is more important, he knows how to go about making these improvements. He is hoping that by making these two main suggestions this early, with reports going back on this trip of the *St Paul,* the Treasury Department will approve and tell him to go ahead with construction of an aqueduct and reservoir before the first freeze. Then fresh water will be easily available at all times. These people always have had to cart potable water from the nearest clear lake, more than a mile away. The women do all the hauling. Mrs. Mandrigan, for instance, always has hauled the water for Government House, and when I insisted that John help her, she refused to let him, saying that he would lose the respect of the village if he were seen carrying water!

John spoke of the project to the SA, explaining that it would not be too difficult or too expensive. The SA said there would have to be a government appropriation for any major expenditure or capital improvement on the island. Hence John's appended report to Washington.

I was just writing the above when Dr. Kelly dropped by, so I told him about John's idea for water to be run into the village.

"Why wait for a government appropriation? The company would benefit as much as the villagers. In fact, they've wanted water run in but haven't known how to get past some of the obstacles of basalt rock barriers. I've been wanting to condemn that filthy cistern the women use for all their wash water over there at the edge of town. But I really can't make them haul all their water that distance. As it is, it's hard enough on them to lug the drinking water."

"The rugged terrain is not the only problem," John said. "But there's really no obstacle that can't be surmounted if one puts his mind to it. I will need some of the natives to help."

"Ask Mr. Morgan to set it up as a company project. If it has to be considered as a government improvement to an island possession, I'm sure the company would, in the meantime, advance the money just to get the thing going in warm weather. As you've seen, they're not niggardly. Bring some rough sketches and an estimate of costs down to the Lodge tonight. Perhaps we can get an order off with the *S* Paul before she sails."

I went to the door to see if the little ship was still at the anchorage, for I thought she was to leave before this. But there she was, becalmed, and Captain Erskine (I know) was waiting for a spanking breeze instead of starting the engines. Nevertheless, when Dr. Kelly got back to the company office, he had someone there run up signals: "Hold ship — important" and an invitation for the captain to come ashore for dinner.

I feel particularly proud of John, after all his troubles and unhappiness, to have come up with something so vital to the well-being of the islanders and something within his own field of work. By contributing in this way to the intimate life of the village, he can feel more accepted and more a part of it. So far we have been curiosities — I especially — and all three of us up here are creatures set apart.

It is true we've tried to slip into the life of the village in little ways. We haven't wanted the natives to think of us as superior beings with lives exclusively divided between Government House and the Lodge. We've attended church services every Sunday, where I note that a few of the company men also worship. Though the service is a bit too elaborate for John's and my simple tastes, I like the pageantry and drama, and I am impressed by the natives' devout faith. This is their means of reaching the same God in whom John and I believe. I find, though, that I do have to bypass Father Shishenekoff when I try to offer my prayers to God. But the exquisite singing of the a capella choir helps lift my prayers. They are sad and earnest prayers to know what is right to do.

The natives have been pleased that we go to church with them and, in many small ways, show their pleasure. I know they will be grateful to John for bringing water to them.

Allium, a pencil
drawing by Frederick
A. Walpole

M alpha Poppoff, one of the young women of the village, knocked timidly at our door one day not so long ago and asked to see me.

"Please," said Malpha. "I should like you come to my wedding Sunday next . . . yes?"

"Why, we would be happy to come," I answered, happier still that Malpha had learned that much English. Hers was the first of many weddings coming up now that the killing season is over. We have just returned from the festivities.

When we entered the church, we had to part just as we always have to do on Sunday mornings — the men to their side of the church and the women to theirs. This has become second nature for me now, though I never shall get used to standing during a long service. There are no seats! (A few old women sit on the floor during the service, and a few young ones also sit down to suckle their young.) Everyone was in bright colored cotton with kerchiefs on their heads. The service had not yet begun, but the assistant priest, paying attention to no one, was chanting a service to the empty balcony.

In about fifteen minutes, Father Paul entered from the rear of the church in his gorgeous robes and went into the "Holy of Holies," which is separated from the main part of the altar by a partition with a central door and two side doors. Evgen Glotoff, who was to be Malpha's husband, had chosen no less than George Butrin to be his groomsman. George entered first and went up to the prayer desk, which is on the floor of the church just in front of the raised step of the chancel. There he stood on a large white sheet and took two white kerchiefs from his pocket.

Malpha, dressed simply in a full-skirted white cotton dress with a white ribbon around her head holding her lanky tresses in place neatly, stepped to one side of George and Evgen. Evgen was wearing a black broadcloth suit, recognized by everyone for its communal function as groom's garb for the entire village. It is well tailored and in the best of fashion. Evgen stepped to the other side of George, who gave each of them a kerchief and a candle trimmed with a ribbon bow.

The priest made his grand entrance through the central door, holding high a large, gold crucifix in one hand and a book of services in the other. His assistant joined him, carrying a huge candelabrum that held one large lighted candle, which he set upon the prayer desk. Then he took the candelabrum back through one of the side doors and returned with a silver salver upon which was a smaller gold tray. He gave this to the priest, who placed two gold rings on it. He placed this tray upon the altar for a blessing.

The groomsman passed the large lighted candle to the assistant, who in turn passed it to the priest. With it the priest lighted the couple's candles. All this time he chanted a service to which the choir in the balcony responded with more chanting. First the rings were placed on the couple's fingers, then incense from a censor was wafted before them and all around them three times. Next two ornate crowns were placed upon their heads. Then they had to join hands and drink wine from a ceremonial chalice. Father Paul removed the crowns, put out the candles, and spoke to the bride and groom, who each went to one side of the church. The groom prostrated himself before the icon of Christ, and Malpha prostrated herself before the icon of the Virgin and Child. They did this three times, with their foreheads touching the floor. They then returned to the prayer desk where Malpha tied on her head the kerchief George had given her. The priest departed abruptly through the central door. Evgen turned and walked out the church, with Malpha humbly following at a respectful distance. The long ceremony was over.

We were fatigued from standing so long and were slightly nauseated from so much incense, so we did not join in the general village festivities at Malpha's home. We are convinced that after these people go through such a grueling ordeal to get married, they stay married so as not to ever have to go through it again!

Just as much ceremony attends a burial as a wedding. We have had to attend a burial today because it was for the son of a tyone (one of the foremen), a tiny baby that our good doctor tried his best to save. John and I decided to watch from the balcony, as we thought there was to be no choir and we could be together. As we entered the church, the acolytes were lighting the many candles that had been placed everywhere. They used long tapers, since most of the candles seemed to be in the most difficult places possible to reach: the high candelabra, hanging lamps, a central magnificent chandelier hanging from the dome, and before all the icons. This, I am told, is not done for everyone. The son of a tyone is important. Everyone in the village, including all the company men, were present.

The plain box of the coffin, badly smeared with candle drippings, was resting in the center of the floor on two low stools. Only the white face of the dead child was visible. Around his face was a paper halo decorated with tinsel to make him resemble one of the icons. The rest of his body was covered by a blanket of soft white fur. On his breast rested the portraits of two people — I think his parents — we couldn't see. Balanced precariously on the edge of the coffin, at his head, sides, and feet, were long, yellow, lighted tapers. Russian letters were cut out of bronzed paper and attached to the sides of the coffin.

AUGUST 1^{rst}

AUGUST 1^{rst}

AUGUST 1[rst]

GOVERNMENT HOUSE, St PAUL ISLAND

GOVERNMENT HOUSE, S[t] PAUL ISLAND

After all the preliminary preparations were made, the two central doors of the inner sanctum swung open, and Father Paul entered the church and took his place at the prayer desk beside the dead boy. He read the service while the all male choir, which had quietly surrounded us, chanted the responses. Near the close of the service, a "passport," a printed sheet of paper, was folded and put in the hands of the boy. The father, mother, and sister took their final leave of the child by kissing the portraits on his breast, then his lips and his forehead, bowing and crossing themselves between each gesture. The tyone then covered the little coffin.

I saw no expression of grief or sorrow. No tears were shed, yet I had a feeling from all the simple gestures of handing the dead child over to God that great grief was involved.

AUGUST 5th

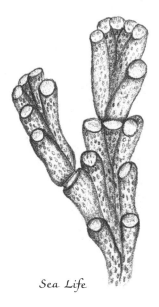

Sea Life

Where there is death, there is, inevitably, birth. Life must go on even in the remotest outposts of the world, and the church is there to bless these events in the order in which they happen. The christening of Anna Matroona's eight-day-old son, Luka, was a happy, festive occasion yesterday.

Water was being warmed over a seal-oil burner when I entered the church and climbed to the balcony, where the incense and other odors seem to be less strong. A blue wooden tub was placed in the center of the floor. The nurse and godmother, holding the baby, took their places beside it. Father Paul came through the central doors of his sanctum and approached the baby, making the sign of the cross over him and touching his face. He read the service while the choir chanted responses. After a little while, he took a small bottle from his vestments and poured something into the tub of water. He took a blunt glass probe, dipped it in the tub, and with it touched the eyes, ears, mouth, nose, hands, and feet of the baby. Taking the nude baby from the nurse, he immersed him in the water. The godmother was ready with a clean white cotton robe to receive the cold, wet infant and warm him again. Father Paul threw a tiny silver cross on a green ribbon around the baby's neck.

There was more reading of responses, then the priest touched the child at all the same points again but this time with a sponge. To conclude the ceremony, he cut a lock of hair from each side of the babe's head and formed a cross. The nurse and the godmother followed the priest around the prayer desk three times. Father Paul carried the babe to the altar and touched the child's lips to the icon of the Virgin and to another of the Child Jesus. The crucifix was brought out and put to the child's lips. The godmother made some responses to the priest, probably agreeing to be responsible for the child's spiritual care. Afterward, all marched out of the church to a feast at the parents' home.

Unless a child is christened, it goes to a netherworld which is neither heaven nor hell. These people are so faithfully attached to their church that these ceremonies are not just ceremonies they walk through, but a part of their lives. They try to practice the precepts they learn and are, on a whole, extremely good Christians. They seldom express gratitude, but they are kindly and easily managed without being servile. They never harbor a grudge. Once a matter is thrashed out, it is over with, so there are no family feuds. All live amicably with each other — they do seem to bear out the Golden Rule.

The chief tyone was correct in saying that they never covet. I have come across not one Aleut who was avaricious or desirous of possessing something his neighbor had and he had not. No one ever locks a house against thievery, for there never has been a single instance of thievery on the island. And everyone shares what he has of food, and sometimes even money, with others.

In the expenditure of money, the Aleuts are extremely extravagant because money seems to have little value for them. This is probably the fault of the company, which has provided them with homes rent free, with food and goods at cost, and which looks after the individual's welfare, paying good wages and giving free medical care. They are improvident of the future, certain that they always will be looked after. Even the widows and orphans are provided for, and those too old to work are pensioned off. It's no good arguing with them that life may not always be so utopian. The company may change hands or set up a stricter regime. They've forgotten how it was when the Russians did nothing for them except pay a pittance for their work and leave them to live like animals the rest of the year. So for the present, with the exception of the effects of kvas, the natives remain childishly simple in their faith in God, who provides everything through the company and the wealth of natural foods around them.

GOVERNMENT HOUSE, Sᵗ PAUL ISLAND

Sorbus Sambucifolia,
a pencil drawing by
Frederick A. Walpole

LEGEND

These islands never were inhabited by human beings before the Russians brought Aleuts here to do their sealing for them sometime after the mid–eighteenth century. However, among the people a legend persists about a lone woman from Onalaska who, one day many, many hundreds of years ago, went out on the ice and killed a seal. The ice she was on broke from the mainland. Winds and currents cut her off from shore, and she was driven about for several days until she was cast upon this island. Here she found plenty of sea otter, which she killed, preserving their skins. In the course of time, her brother, who had been looking for her in his bidarkah, came to this island and found her. He was unable to induce her to return to the Aleutians, so he departed with the otter pelts.

She lived alone on the island for many years. There is a deep hollow at Novastoshnah where the natives say she once lived in a big house she built for herself. She had no children, and when she died, the island was again left to its great solitude in winter and to the seals in summer, until the Russians came.

I heard a similar tale while on Onalaska. Aleuts like to believe in old wives' tales and are extremely superstitious. Some even call in Father Paul at times to exorcise the evil spirits they believe are doing them harm. The men who wander about the village so oddly at night sometimes have the weirdest of all tales to tell. But otherwise, there are few legends that one could record as belonging to a tribal or national heritage.

GOVERNMENT HOUSE, S' PAUL ISLAND

August 20, 1879
Government House
St Paul Island

Dear Ones,

The St Paul *is due in soon, and I have not yet written you about the
baby seals, who are all born by now and most of whom have been having
their first swimming lessons.*

*For many weeks after they are born, their matkas take them to a play
area on a nice sandy beach and leave them there in a huge nursery called
a pod. The pups play in these pods all day, running after each other,
rolling over each other, tossing balls of kelp to each other, or sleeping,
while their mothers are out hunting the fish that, by the time they come
inland again, are already transformed into creamy milk for the babies.*

*In the evening when the matkas come in from the water, each seeks her
own pup. She can do this because she has an individual pahknoot known
only to her own pup, and his pahknoot is known only to her. She cannot
nurse or care for a foster pup. If a pup is not claimed, he dies. Of course,
each pup squeals and bleats until he is claimed and then he goes off after
his matka, following her to the harem where he was born. There she
feeds him copiously during the rest of the night.*

*When the pups are about six weeks old, they have to begin to learn to
swim, because they must be good swimmers by the time the boorga blows
over the island and they go south to avoid the ice. Watching the mothers
teach their young is a picnic and one of the amusements for the entire
village, even for the men who have nothing else to do at this time but fish
and watch baby seals at play. The baby seals are just like children. They
positively hate the water and don't want to get wet.*

*A group of us sat for three hours at midday today on the edge of Tolstoi
Reef just doubled over laughing at the antics of the kotickie, who were
trying to avoid being made to go in the water. Their mothers shoved them
with their noses or nudged them with their shoulders, but the babies
wouldn't budge. Some mothers weren't even gentle. Several just pushed
their pups to the edge of a ledge, dropped them into the water, and let
them struggle for themselves. Such spitting and choking and squealing,
you'd think they did not know what water is. Yet they have to spend the
best part of their days in the water the rest of their lives and, when older,
are the most expert swimmers of all mammals.*

*One old seacatch, annoyed at a recalcitrant pup, picked it up by the
nape of the neck, swam way out with it, and let it go in terribly deep
water. By the time the youngster had dog-paddled back to shore, coughing
and spitting the whole way, it was so exhausted it curled up on the sand
right at the water's edge and went to sleep — but not for long. A wave
came over it, and it coughed and spit its way out again.*

*I've tried to bring abandoned pups to Government House to tame them
and bring them up. I've fed them on the richest condensed tinned milk.
But nothing works. They would be such adorable pets. Even down on the*

shore, we've picked out favorites, and we try to spot them each day and follow their progress. Their swimming lessons progress rapidly once they've overcome their fear of the water. Some are already expert swimmers and no longer play in the pods. Of course when this happens, their mothers abandon them for good, and they are on their own to hunt food. They no longer need their matkas. In a few weeks, they will be eating fish, and by the end of that time, they will start swimming away from here. The timing Nature allows for her creatures is so close, so accurate, that one cannot help but be impressed by the design and order in this world.

I've a whole packet of letters and sketches ready for you. The Reliance has put in, as have other Coast Guard ships, but none is going to a port where letters could be forwarded. So I have waited for the St Paul. When she returns to the States, it will be for the last time until next May! So do not mind some of the emotional outbursts in a few of these pages. They all have to do with thoughts of our isolation from you, even by mail, for so long. The days already are noticeably shorter. It begins to get dark about ten o'clock now, with a long twilight before. I shall have all the more time to write, study, and make notes. Somehow the time has gone swiftly, only because so much daylight makes one active. It has kept me awake much of the time. I expect to sleep a correspondingly long time during the black months. It also has grown quite cold, even before the boorga has arrived. We are forewarned that this winter should begin a five-year cycle of extremely cold weather for which the whole island is preparing. Do not worry. We are snug, and there seems to be an adequate supply of everything here. The company has seen to that. All my love goes with this. I just wish I could send a baby seal for you to play with.

As ever,
Lib.

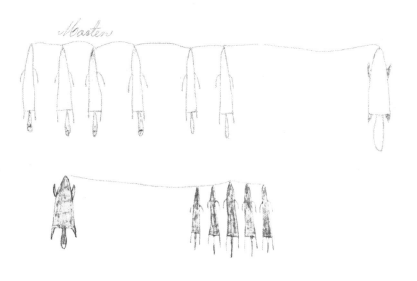

GOVERNMENT HOUSE, St PAUL ISLAND

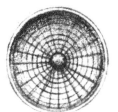

Sea Life

Today should have been such a joyous one. It started out that way. The *St Paul* moved into view early. The lighter came directly in with letters, gifts, messages, and many of the things I had ordered. Vicele came running up to the house with the first load, which contained the letters for which we had been longing — letters from John's family, from my family, from friends. They were like a treasure of gold dumped in our laps, and we spent the whole midday reading them to ourselves and to each other, John disregarding the noon meal which he always takes at the Lodge. We had difficulty hiding our emotions. The letters drew us close to our loved ones, and for a while, we were unashamedly homesick. They were, nonetheless, wonderful hours, making us feel only as far away as Nantucket or Long Island, as President Hayes once had said. We were so selfishly engrossed in our own private emotions that we had forgotten to go down to greet Captain Erskine, who had made our happiness possible.

He dropped in late in the afternoon for chia.

"Thought I'd see you at the Lodge for midday meal," he said. "It was sort of a welcoming feast."

"We've been having our own sort of feast up here, selfishly. And we have you to thank for it," I said.

"Good trip?" John asked.

"Smooth sailing the whole way. Didn't need the engines once. Pacific unusually calm for this time of year, and even the Bering is surprisingly calm. That's what has given me an idea. Thought you might like to visit St George Island before the weather closes it off until spring. I'm taking the *St Paul* over sometime past midnight. We'd arrive before breakfast, that is, if those waters are as calm as these. We might have to spend several days there, depending on the water. It's no easy task, taking on the pelts over there, as you've no doubt heard."

"How would we get back?" John asked, knowing that the *St Paul* always went straight on to the States after loading at St George.

"I'm coming back here to load after St George. That's why I thought of the excursion. Some clean sea air and a trip off this island before you dig in for the winter would be good for you two."

"Oh, it would!" I said, enthusiastically seconding his kind thought and completely forgetting what a poor sailor I'd been.

"Isn't loading over there first a radical change in routine?" John asked.

"It is that, and it sets us back a day or so on timing. But the Senior Agent had arranged it that way with the company. He said something about having to talk with Scribner again before he goes to the States."

"I didn't know Scribner planned on going to the States," John said gruffly, while I knew we'd not be taking any excursion if the sa was along.

"Not Scribner — the Senior Agent is going back with me the way he did last year."

"The devil he is!" John exploded.

"Didn't you know?"

"The Senior Agent has not been pleased to divulge his plans," John said bitterly.

"Sorry, sir, if I've let slip information I should have withheld. Naturally I thought you were informed on this matter. He has had some sort of an agreement with the Treasury Department whereby he can return to look after his business interests in the States during the winter months."

John paced the room. I could see his jaws working, a habit he has when angry. I knew he was angry because he'd had to learn this news from the captain and not directly from his superior.

"Don't apologize to me. I'd have to know sooner or later. After all, if he goes, I have to take over. He'd have to discuss that with me."

"You see, Captain, Mr. Beaman and the Senior Agent haven't gotten on too well," I explained, thinking the explanation necessary. John frowned at me in annoyance.

"That I could see aboard ship coming up. But I'd hoped the differences were settled by this trip. Your superior officer is a fine man, sir, blunt, maybe, and probably difficult when crossed. I'm sorry ye've not been able to hit it off."

"Well, we haven't," John said peremptorily, dismissing the subject he wished I had not brought up. "You can see now why we must decline your kind offer, Captain, to take us over to St George. Besides, Mrs. Beaman is not a very good sailor, as you may remember, and I'm afraid the waters between here and there will be too rough for any pleasure."

How quickly we forget our pains and physical discomforts! I had forgotten and had thought only of the chance for a little change. I thanked the captain. Perhaps we will see St George on our way home.

Our good captain expressed his disappointment. He truly wanted us aboard, though I am not sure his sailors did. An excursion away from these few square miles of rocks would be such a welcome change at this moment. John does not absolutely have to be here. After all, he was way up on Novastoshnah last time the sa went over to St George. The kvas drinking is under fair control. Boarding pirate ships — when they are driven into these waters — and seeing to it that the natives do not kill female seals for food are about the only official duties right now. But John would have no pleasure if the sa went along. And I could have no real pleasure knowing John was unhappy. I told myself that we had just postponed the trip.

As soon as we came back from dinner tonight, John motioned me to continue to our room. He opened the living room door and saw his superior gathering papers at his desk. That much I could see before John closed the door on me. I went into our sitting room and frankly eavesdropped at the sturdy partition the men had built for us between the two rooms. I had been frightened by John's mood the whole evening — sullen and silent and hurt and angry. I was afraid for both of them.

Their voices rose in anger. I wanted at times to run in and stop them before they came to blows. But I remembered the seals of Polavina, how the bulls had fought over the matkas, and I knew it was the matkas' presence that inflamed their wrath. No matter what the two men said in argument, I was behind it all, the real reason for their hatred, the matka that, by her presence, only made all matters worse.

John began by confronting the SA with his knowledge and how he had learned it.

"You haven't exactly made speaking with you easy, Mr. Beaman," I heard the SA excuse himself.

"A superior officer, no matter what he thinks personally of a subordinate, usually gives clear and concise commands or directions. I've been perfectly willing to take orders, recognizing that you *are* my superior. Instead I've had to guess at almost everything or use the log as a guide."

"You disobeyed my very first command. How could I expect you to follow any others?"

"You had no right giving that one, sir. Personal matters and matters in connection with the sealing business are two entirely different affairs. We will leave Mrs. Beaman out of this discussion. My assistantship is concerned only with the administration of the Treasury Department's affairs, not our private lives."

"Useless now to say that my first order to leave your wife at home was for your own good. I explained my reasons at the time. I was extremely frank. My reasons still hold good."

"In spite of that, there has been no reason for your constant hostility toward us, making life here even less of a pleasure. Usually a superior officer tries to inspire a certain amount of loyalty in order to get a man's best effort from him. You've gone out of your way to make loyalty an impossibility. And now this — this private arrangement you've made to look after your own affairs; wouldn't it have been a kindness to let me know that I could make such an arrangement so we would not have to spend the winters here?"

"If the Treasury Department officials wanted you to leave, they would have suggested it. Neither Moulton nor Scribner has resented my going back to the States. They served out their contracts right here. Scribner is on a second one now."

"But to what purpose? I can see by the log that there is absolutely no real reason for a resident agent once the sealing is over. I'd have done anything to save Mrs. Beaman from having to face a winter up here."

"I thought you wanted your wife left out of this discussion."

"I do. But I also want you to know exactly what I think of you as a gentleman." I heard a stir and my heart stood still. Had he risen to the challenge? Instead, it was John moving toward the door, because his voice came next from that direction. "I assume that you will be back here in a few days."

"Yes."

"Very good, then. When you return, I want specific directions as to my duties while you are in California. I want them in full. I am aware of the reports you have been sending about my incompetence. I want no such reports about my administration while you are away."

"You know that you are perfectly free to return to the States."

"And break a contract over a personal matter? No, sir, I shall stick it out here if you will leave adequate instructions."

"Very well, Beaman."

"Mister Beaman."

Oh, John, John, John, why provoke the man more? Can you understand how difficult his job has been? Can you understand that he has had to build defenses against me, just as I have had to do against all these men? No — you never can understand because you are not a complicated human.

I heard the click of the latch, so I slipped quickly into our bedroom where I would rather John find me. I heard the office door open and the roar of his superior's voice, "All right, *Mister* Beaman. Now get out!"

John slammed the door, but he did not come to our room. He has gone out into the eerie twilight. I do not know where to look for him. I would not know what to say if I found him. I do not know how to help him. My heart aches for him.

AUGUST 24*th*

John came in long after the *St Paul* weighed anchor. He was damp and cold and shivering, and he smelled of the wet sea mists. He must have been walking in the damp night. I pretended sleep, sure that he would not want to talk, would not want me to know what I do know — that he was out there struggling with himself. He crawled into bed beside me, still shivering. He held me close for warmth and reassurance and kept whispering into my hair, "Oh, Libby, Libby, Libby." We clung to each other the rest of the night. At least, we have each other.

GOVERNMENT HOUSE, St PAUL ISLAND

John has spent the entire day at his desk in the office and has shared none of his thoughts and intentions with me. Again I have ached for him, ached for the decisions and indecisions he faces. They torture him, but this time they must be his alone. Never again shall I step in to help destiny. We never can fully foresee the consequences of our acts, much as we like to think we're rational beings. I am sure John is writing his own reports and, perhaps, a request to go home next winter in exchange for a third summer in the islands. This is what I would be doing under the same circumstances. I might, under such stress, ask for the termination of the contract, go to San Francisco, and look for work on the West Coast. These things I'd be capable of in desperation.

I never have said to John, "Let's go home." If going home could solve our problems, I would be tempted to beg it. But I do not want to be the influence. This time the decision must be John's. I regret the torture.

I have been making a list of things I want my family to get for us during the winter months. They will have ample time to send things to San Francisco — think of it — eight months! Eight months without word from home! Eight months shut away up here on our island prison, icebound and isolated from all the world. Dear God, was I truly prepared for this after all?

AUGUST 25*th*

The S*t* Paul is anchored off the buoy in a stiff breeze. In spite of the wind, the lighters and the cutters have been shuttling back and forth from warehouse and salt house to ship, transferring the last of the pelts and seal-oil drums. Tonight there will be a farewell party at the Lodge. I would rather not go. But we cannot get out of it, for Mr. Morgan has asked us personally. Since he is going back to the States for this winter (a practice he set up for himself of returning every other winter), we will have to help see him off, for no one has been kinder or more paternally concerned for John and me than Mr. Morgan.

AUGUST 29*th*

The ship will sail shortly after midnight, when she will have the best tide and winds. That will be nearly dawn up here. I will take down with me my whole packet of letters, gifts and messages, notebooks, and sketches. I want as much as I have gathered to go with the S*t* Paul so that everyone will have plenty of mementos of us while the winter months drag on. The gifts are simple. There is not much I can send. The Aleuts have few crafts. They are people not of the Stone Age, but of a bone age. All their implements are made of walrus, whale, or seal bone and are purely utilitarian, not decorative works of art. I've sent Father, Charles, and Rhesa each walrus tusk knives, and Mother a raincape made of the intestines of walrus, transparent as glass and intricately sewn. It has no odor, as I expected it would, and is an ingenious garment which will cause considerable comment back home. I've wrapped each gift with loving care and have tucked in special little notes. I know that, this once, I am being silly and sentimental. But I have had moments when I feel as though I never may see any of them again. I want them to know how much I do love them.

AUGUST 30th

It is early, early morning. The *St Paul's* wake spreads out in a vast fan behind her, nearly reaching Village Cove. Soon she will drop over the rim of the world and be lost to us until next May. When she disappears, she will have severed us from all the world. I rose early just to watch her go, though I should not have. It is more difficult to bear than I dreamed. I wanted to run down to the cove, to the very edge of the water, and shout, "Take me along! Take me along!"

John is fast asleep. He's not had much sleep for a long time, wrestling with his problems, problems he will not let me share. I shall let him sleep while I watch the *St Paul* move away from here. I watch it with a haunting, gnawing sorrow. I press my head to the windowpane, then finally, I press my lips. The glass is wet with my tears.

Last night the Lodge was a festive place. Mr. Morgan and six of the company men were sent off in grand style. Five of them will not be returning. The sixth, a Mr. Squier, and Mr. Morgan will bring new sealers with them in the spring. We have entrusted all our letters to Mr. Morgan, who is most anxious to perform any services for us.

Dinner was indeed good. Cook exceeded himself. He had one of the prize steers killed a few weeks back and properly hung for the occasion. We could not have had a more wonderful roast of beef au jus at the Willard. The rest of the food was as good, with an abundance of fresh produce so recently brought up by the *St Paul*. Dinner was topped off with the delicious little berries which the Aleuts reluctantly gave up for the event.

The entertainment began with a concert. We have two concertinas and a fiddle on the island. We need a piano most of all because there is a crying need to hear good music (other than the choir) occasionally. All the performers played gay tunes, learned by ear from the Russians. Then the choir sang some lovely chants I had not heard before and some spirited folk songs, which led to some equally spirited folk dances. These were unusually active for the Aleuts, who are generally too lethargic to move swiftly or expend much energy. Because there were many Aleut girls and enough women to go around, someone suggested dancing. Dancing had not been suggested before on any occasion, so I had thought that perhaps dancing was not a custom of the island. Then I understood. By tacit agreement, the subject had been avoided until last night. The SA had had a hand in that. He wanted no man to touch me even in the formal figures of a dance!

We chose to do square dances and rounds, though the mazurka, I find, is extremely popular here. There were two mazurkas, both of which I sat out, though I dearly love the beautiful dance. I wished to preserve my dignity but felt like a prude doing so. But what alternative do I have? If I had romped through a mazurka, I would have been exhibiting an abandon that might lead to anything. The SA and I exchanged a glance. He understood why I sat out and nodded his approval, then looked the other way.

He seemed to be enjoying himself. He took great pleasure in the square dances, which he could call to perfection. It seemed inevitable that at some time in the course of the steps, I should become his partner. I found myself wanting this to happen, willing it to happen, for it would be the last chance for any exchange of words between us. I wanted him to go away with a kinder memory than of John's harsh words. I could think of nothing to say, yet knew I had to say something that would let him know I understood and was grateful for his protection. But the music always ended before a full cycle of the figures was accomplished — frustrating, like a dream or nightmare that keeps leading one on but never gets to the objective.

I was just about to give up hope when he came directly to me, bowed, and asked if I would be his partner to lead the next dance. I saw John frown his disapproval. But I smiled, rose, and willingly let him lead me onto the floor. My heart pounded the way it used to pound when, as a young debutante, I'd been asked to dance by the handsomest swain at the ball. His touch sent wildfire through my veins. I looked up at him in surprise, not believing my own sensation.

"I've asked you merely for appearance's sake," he said coldly, and the steel bars were still there in his eyes. For a moment, I had the overwhelming desire to break them down, to abolish them forever. A woman can, I know. She has subtle weapons for melting away the coldest steel. But after the steel is melted, what takes its place? Why should I try? To what end, to what good end? He was going away. He would be leaving us in peace. Why should I intrude myself upon his own peace, and where would mine be? I danced stiffly the patterns he called, and there was little time for any words. When we were well into the dance, just before we had to change partners, his hand stiffened at my waist and his other squeezed my hand slightly.

"Is there anything, anything at all, any little thing, Elizabeth, that I can bring back to make you think more kindly toward me?" Again I looked at him in surprise. This time there were no steel bars in his eyes. They were waiting for an answer.

"There's not one thing I want of you — nothing," I answered. "But thank you, sir, for asking. My thank you is for more than that. It is for everything." We did not dance again. But I felt a singing inside me and a calm peace I have not known all summer. He will be going away from here with less harsh thoughts of me and a respect I've hoped he would cherish.

The final farewells were said at the dock, under seal-oil torches, for it is actually dark now at midnight. John and I both made the rounds, for the last time, of those who were leaving. We said formal and informal farewells and shook each one's hand. Captain Erskine was impatient to weigh anchor. "You watch," he said to me. "Within a few days, the winds will come and then the storm that never ends. I want to be all the way out of the Bering by then. No boorga for me. I'll take my chances on the Pacific any day, but not on this sea when the boorga begins to blow." Mr. Morgan joined us. He bent low over my hand and again asked if there was anything he could bring back to make our lives happier on the island or more comfortable. He already had done so much for us that I couldn't bring myself to ask for the one thing I felt the island needed most, so I wished him a bon voyage and a happy reunion with his friends.

The Senior Agent, not to be outdone in public for appearance's sake, naturally had to ask the same question when he bowed over my hand.

"Why, yes," I said boldly and aloud. "The island needs a piano. Bring back a piano for us. There's plenty of money left over from that aqueduct appropriation to buy a really fine one. That would make everyone happy."

Everyone who heard laughed. There had been discussion of a piano before we arrived, I knew. But pianos took up considerable cargo space, and each trip the St Paul made, she had to carry so much essential stuff that everyone had said it would be a long, long time before the island would have its piano. John, at the fringe of the crowd talking with the captain, did not hear my request. But since I had said it on impulse and did not believe for a single moment that the SA or anyone else would think of it again, I dismissed it from my mind. "Good-bye," I called after them as they climbed into the lighter. "Good-bye, sir, and a safe journey back to your family." We had exchanged one last, long look, with all bars down, and we had found nothing in each other's eyes but candor, nothing with which ever to reprove ourselves during the black winter, nothing but understanding.

John joined me, and we climbed the hill to Government House

GOVERNMENT HOUSE, St PAUL ISLAND

for the first time without the sa's shadow over us.

"It's all ours, Libby, ours alone. Do you realize it's ours alone for the first time in our lives?"

"It is that, John," I said. "We can be happy now."

That is why John is sleeping so soundly while I watch out our window. Oh, God! The *St Paul* has dropped over the edge of the world. Our last tie is severed.

There have been times at the Lodge when I've been aware of undercurrents, aware of a certain three men who always have gathered for quiet conversation at one end of the large room whenever the sa was in deep and extremely quiet conversation with a certain two other men. I could always tell that the three were talking about the sa or his two companions because of the covert glances in their direction. I dismissed their rather hostile expressions as perhaps some resentment toward him as representing authority. Men often rebel at authority, especially in such close situations.

John and I often remarked, aloud in our room, about how graciously Mr. Morgan and, to all outward appearances, the rest of the company men seemed to tolerate the Treasury Department's presence. Of course, we've wondered why it is necessary for two agents to be here when one could so easily do the necessary accounting. True, the sa had taken on something of a governorship. John seemed to be a nonentity in the present scheme of things, even now that the sa has left him in charge. In our private discussions, we've often tried to explain to ourselves how a man of the sa's background ever could have accepted such an appointment. He couldn't possibly be as desperate as we are. Or could he? How little we've learned about him!

That is why yesterday's dinner hour stands out so vividly. While awaiting dinner to be announced, I looked over the books to select a few to bring up here. The three conspirators were in a huddle nearby. (The sa's two men had left the island with him.) Though I certainly did not mean to, I could not help overhearing snatches of their conversation. I did move farther away, but to retreat would have looked a bit strange. I tried to appear as if I were not listening, but when the sa's name came up, I wanted to hear.

One of the three apparently had commissioned friends or relatives in Sacramento to look into the sa's affairs, and he had received word from them. I gathered that the sa had some affiliation either as a shareholder of, or by some tacit agreement with, the Alaska Commercial Company, which has fur interests in Alaska and Canada as well as on the Pribilofs. He was involved in some official capacity to look after the affairs on the mainland.

"He's making a pile on the side."

"I think we'd better get in on it. There's a fortune to be made up here, and you know it."

"When he gets back, we'd better let him know what we know, then insist on a cut."

"Unh-unh. That's too much like blackmail. I'd rather keep on buying from the natives and run my own business."

"But that's only small potatoes."

"Yeah, but its legal."

"What's illegal? The ACC's a private fur company."

"The company doesn't cheat. I know. I count those pelts into that warehouse, and there's never a single pelt overage."

"The ones you never see are spirited over to the natives' fur warehouse where they store the fox and otter skins."

"Oh."

"I don't know," the first one said. "I, too, would rather run my own business. I did pretty well last year."

"You'd have done a lot better if you owned the *S*^{t} *Paul* the way he does. Nope, I'm going to join him."

"We don't know that's true."

"Oh, I'm sure it's true enough, but I'm minding my own business."

"Dinner is served."

I shall keep all this to myself. After all, it was mostly hearsay and definitely none of my business. If these men want to sell fur on the side while working for the company, that's their business. I just will have less respect for them in my heart, and considerably less for the Senior Agent, if what I heard, or only half heard, has any truth in it. I'll not tell John. He'd blow up. He's so unsuspecting, so naive. He never would understand that we've come among adventurers out to amass a fortune. I shall not let my new knowledge alter our relationships at the Lodge. We have to live out our time as best we can.

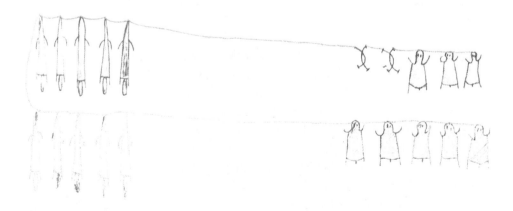

The company has tried, ever since it came to the islands, to have the natives change from the Russian language to English for many reasons, not the least of which is the hope of better communication — with them directly, rather than through their priest or interpreters. Most Americans just won't learn a foreign language. We expect everyone to speak ours. But in this case, it is best that the natives do learn English because they are now Americans. Learning our language might then encourage them to adopt more civilized customs.

With this hope in mind, the company has undertaken to send likely natives to the U.S. for an education. George Butrin was one not exactly successful experiment. There have been others, even a woman who is now on Onalaska. When they return, they all revert to their native tongues, a Russian laced with Aleut terms and endings. The company has been indulgent in this, believing that any education is better than none. School is about to open, and it is being taught in Russian.

Mr. Redpath dropped by for chia this afternoon. He found John and me trying to classify sea plants we've gathered. We do enjoy his company, for he is full of practical knowledge about everything to do with our lives here. He has a down-to-earth philosophy that makes him a refreshing conversationalist. He has helped us through many of our worst moments. At the company, he is second in command and now deputizes in Mr. Morgan's absence. His particular job is the contact with the native laborers, which not only puts him in command of them but makes him their welfare officer as well. The school is one of his many responsibilities. Since the weather has grown so vile, we expect few visitors here. But we plan to make each one so welcome he'll want to come back again. I offered Mr. Redpath chia.

"You notice I always choose teatime to drop in," he said, "because yours is especially good. I hope I am not disturbing serious work."

"Not at all," John said. "We've all winter to do this sort of thing. In fact, we are going to have to invent more things to do or lose our minds."

"Oh, now, none of the agents have ever done that!" he said in mock horror. "Those of us who have had to stay up here have survived pretty well, and we're still a fairly normal lot. I'll admit the going is tough at times. But we've managed. The idea is to develop an all-absorbing interest in something like that and pursue it so vigorously you don't have time to look out the window."

Coltsfoot, an ink drawing by Frederick A. Walpole

"That's all well and good, sir," John said. "But no matter what we do, we will be doing it with the knowledge that we might not have had to do it here — that we could have spent the winter in a milder climate. That knowledge only makes matters worse."

"Mr. Beaman is still angry with the SA for not telling him about his arrangement with the Treasury Department for going home in the winter, so we could make a similar arrangement," I said.

"The assistant special agents have always stayed here," Mr. Redpath said, rising to the SA's defense. "He probably never thought to tell you."

"But to make no mention of it until too late. That I cannot forgive. It was a cruel thing to do."

"I've noticed that the two of you have not been exactly friendly."

"John, we came here prepared to stay," I said hastily, sorry I had reopened the wound. The company men had noticed. They were aware of the disharmony here on the hill. "We will manage. Don't worry."

"I've come to ask a favor of you, Mrs. Beaman," Mr. Redpath changed the subject for me, after he had finished his first glass of tea. One never gets down to business until one has had a first glass. How easily Americans take to the ritual of chia!

"If I can grant it," I said, expecting a sewing or domestic chore such as the men had needed a few times before.

"School opens soon for the children. Twenty-nine of them are of school age. As you've already learned, we've been entirely unsuccessful at teaching them English. True, none of us came here fitted for teaching. But we've tried to train natives, and we've also offered a large salary to anyone in the States who would come here to teach. No one has had enough zeal to face these rigors — even for a fair salary. Mr. Morgan and I talked it over before he left, and we would like you to try." He had spoken swiftly for fear I would interrupt and say no before he really asked me.

"Me?" I asked, completely taken aback. "You think I could teach those youngsters anything?"

"They follow you about like puppies. They adore you. They've already learned many words from you. We think they'd do anything in the world for you — even learn English." I laughed. John frowned.

"The very first day we landed, their tyone asked me not to try."

"I know. I heard. He was afraid our government had sent you for that purpose. You've won everyone's confidence on that score. I can assure you, I will tell him it was the company that asked you to teach. I know there are a few who are willing to learn, though not too many. Vicele is one of the few, and his mother."

"Well, I've been able to spend time with them. Teaching school would be a wonderful way to help fill the long days. Perhaps there are things John could help with too. The question is, am I really well qualified? I still can't learn their alphabet, let alone their grammar. How can I explain myself to them?" I could see John's frown of disapproval. He felt the idea of teaching was too far beneath the dignity of a government official's wife for her even to consider it. But when I asked him what he thought, he said it was up to me entirely.

"The company has set aside a sum each year for the natives' education. We are not asking you to do this for nothing." He turned to John. "I hate being so indelicate. But I do know that Mrs. Beaman has been employed before."

"Oh, we can't be proud where discussion of money is concerned," John said, and there was bitterness in his voice. We both blushed with embarrassment. "We came up here penniless."

"I'd be willing to help for nothing, Mr. Redpath. But we do so want to get ahead a little."

"And not depend on Mrs. Beaman's family so much," John said even more bitterly.

"I hesitate only because I don't know how successful I could be."

"But you will at least try?"

"Yes. I can at least try."

I am writing this after school hours, though I am still at the school. I hate to go up the hill defeated. Each SEPTEMBER 20th morning I set out with high hopes for some success during the day. I walk through the icy rains that penetrate everything. I wear the same sort of oilskin raincoat the men wear. In fact, I purchased mine at the company store. It was meant for a man — a giant of a man — because in spite of the several layers of clothes I have on, it is still too big. In this raincoat, I must look like an Indian tipi being washed down the hill.

I get here early because the schoolhouse is quite warm, which means that I have to shed my layers of clothing, one by one. I don't want the children to have to watch the process. They would laugh.

They dress more sensibly, if one overlooks the odor of not too well cured skins and unwashed bodies — they do not seem to mind. Right now they have changed from cotton and woolen clothes, such as we wear at home, to suits made of sealskin shaved to just a short, soft fur. Over this they wear a kamalaika, the transparent raincoat made of walrus gut. They decorate none of their clothing with beads or quills or raffia such as the American Indians do. And though somehow they must be related, because of the color of their skin, the Aleuts seem to have been arrested in their development, while the American Indian has progressed.

Each suit is handed down to the youngster it fits, so some are extremely dirty and smelly. If the schoolroom gets too hot, the youngsters just open the front of their sealskin suits to let out the warm air that has accumulated around their bodies. Until the company insisted that they wear some sort of lightweight shirt under their suits, there was nothing between their suits and their own bronze skins.

When the rains stop in October and the icy winds howl out of Siberia, they will put aside the kamalaika and wear what they call a *parkah*. This is a greatcoat made of bear or fox fur with the hair left long; it is worn with the skin side out. It is made fairly long and has a hood attached so no cold air can get down the neck. The Russians introduced boots. The Aleuts make theirs fur lined and loose enough to tuck their trouser legs into the tops. Everything they wear is loose and oversized. They believe that anything tight — such as my clothes and especially my shoes — makes one cold. They insist I would not feel the cold half so much if I wore looser clothes.

Mrs. Mandrigan says my man should be gathering fox skins for me for a parkah. I will need a parkah for the winter. John could easily get me beautiful white or silver fox here or blue fox on St George, where he has had to go twice in the company cutter (a trip no one ever likes to take in a cutter). The company men all have native-cured parkahs and say that they are not at all smelly. Since they leave the parkahs hanging outdoors and wear them only outdoors, the winds whip the odors away. They, too, have been urging John to get us each enough skins for parkahs. We both must begin in earnest to prepare for the arctic winter ahead.

I digressed to write of what the children wear because I have a feeling that the company men did not succeed here because of their inability to stand the odor of this room. It is so nauseating that I have great difficulty putting up with it for the three full hours, through midday, that I am here. The body odors — plus the kerosene stove and the kerosene lamps — are too much to have to take. I hope I hold out until December 15, when they begin a long holiday vacation.

The Arctic night is beginning to close in on us, slowly, inexorably. Long before school is out, we will have night during the day.

SCHOOL HOUSE, St PAUL ISLAND

September 30, 1879
St Paul School
St Paul Island
The Pribilofs

Dear Ones,

I am teaching school! Just what I said I never would do. But here I am, teaching in a little white frame schoolhouse built by the company, with high hopes for the natives, some few years ago. I thought you might like to hear about my first day here.

Thirty stolid faces greeted me as I entered the room. The youngsters were of all sizes, ages, and varying degrees of cleanliness and odor. Panic seized me. How to begin? Where does one begin? Suddenly there was a stir and all the children stood up beside their desks. I thought the honor was for me, which would be most unusual because women never are honored here. They were all staring at the door behind me. I looked around and there was their tyone entering the schoolroom. He gave the youngsters a long harangue in Russian, telling them to listen to the American lady and try to learn her language. Then he said something in a commanding voice. All, with one accord, began singing "The Star-Spangled Banner" in recognizable English! They grinned at me with pride. The tyone grinned and nodded. I nodded approval. He withdrew. I faced thirty stolid faces again. But every morning, if we do nothing else, we start the day with "The Star-Spangled Banner" in good English, of which they understand not one word!

School, like everything else for them, is an adventure, now that there is an American lady to teach them. They attend only out of curiosity to see what I am wearing or what I will try to do with them. Often they stay away in little groups to go berrying or hunting. Few have any earnest desire to learn anything. Occasionally adults come instead of their children. Some come because they want to learn a little. But most come to have me write letters to the American soldiers who were stationed here and with whom they made friends or to former company personnel. Some come out of pure curiosity, like their children.

If the weather is very bad, no one shows up. If it is good, they stay away to play or go on excursions, picnics of their own devising. I had hoped to have field trips with them, thinking they would ask me the English names for things. But their lives are a constant field trip, and they can teach me more about the wildlife here than I could begin to teach them. I've tried to think up other ways to capture their attention and their interest long enough to teach them something, anything, to justify my salary and to justify the company's faith in me. Nothing works.

Forgive me this expression of frustration. I don't want you to worry for me. I just would like to help them so much.

Affectionately as ever,

Your daughter,
Lib.

SCHOOL HOUSE, St PAUL ISLAND

OCTOBER 15th   If there are nice days up here — they are so few — they
come at this time of the year. They are cold and crisp
and bright at midday. This is the two or three day season between
the rainy season and winter. Nowhere in the world are the cloud
formations so spectacular as they are westward over the Bering in
the late afternoons, with a vivid orange luminosity behind their
golden dazzling edges. Only in October and November do they
put on this magnificent display, stirred into great masses by the
frigid arctic winds hitting the breezes off the Japan Current. Soon
they will give way to frightening storm clouds, and winter will be
here in truth.

I've had very little success with the school. One day last week,
Mr. Redpath stopped in to see how classes were getting along and
found not one child in school. It was too nice a day, and they all
had stayed away! I was in tears.

"This will never do!" he said.

"I know it. I've failed entirely," I said.

"Oh, I meant your tears, not the classroom. You shouldn't be
sitting in here alone like this, feeling discouraged. It's not good for
you." I tried to smile at his friendly concern. "You've been
looking a bit peaked lately, and you hardly touch your food."

"My job has me worried. But I didn't think anyone noticed
such things."

"But of course, everyone does. Every breath you draw is subject
for conversation. It's a rare experience to have one of our own
women come to live among us."

"Even if she is a failure?"

"You're not a failure, Mrs. Beaman. We're just going to have to
find some way to convert these children from Russian Aleuts to
American Aleuts. We don't have the answer yet, but it will come."

"Meantime, I want something else to do to justify my salary."

"Please don't worry about that. Good heavens, you are doing a
tremendous amount of good by influence alone. That's one
method of teaching."

"Can't I help in the general store? I noticed it's short staffed at
times."

"You mean wait on people? Wait on natives?"

"Yes. Why not? I think I could learn more of their language that
way, and they ours."

"It's a thought. But would Mr. Beaman let you do it?"

"I think I could persuade him."

Almost the next day, it seemed, I was at the general store. I
spend a few hours there each day, doing the books and
occasionally waiting on people. Keeping books in Aleut land is
nothing like keeping books anywhere else. The natives cannot
read or write. They buy everything on credit until they are paid at
the end of the killing season, when all accounts are settled and any

surplus money is banked in the company bank maintained just for them. They also barter with trapped animals. So their accounts are quite complicated and often have to be explained to them. The only thing they understand is a graphic representation of every transaction. I have copied a few pages of my ledger to show how accounts are kept. I myself find these hieroglyphics much more understandable than the Cyrillic alphabet.

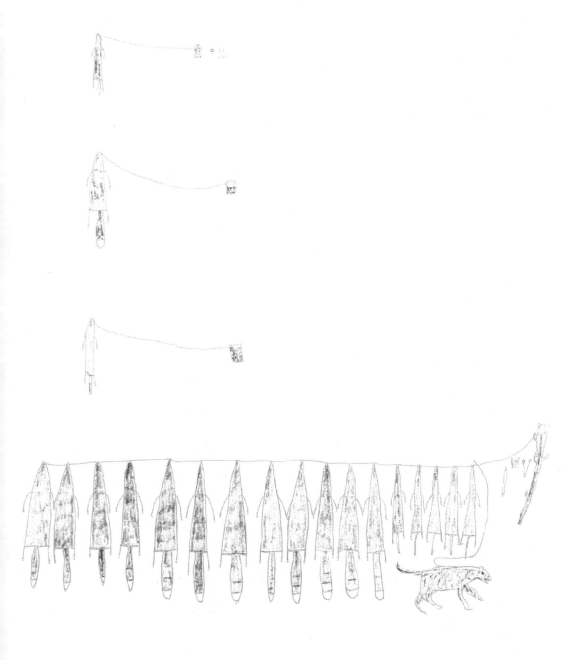

HEADQUARTERS, GOVERNMENT HOUSE,
SAINT PAUL'S ISLAND,
(Pribylor Group of Fur Seal Islands, Behring Sea, Alaska,)

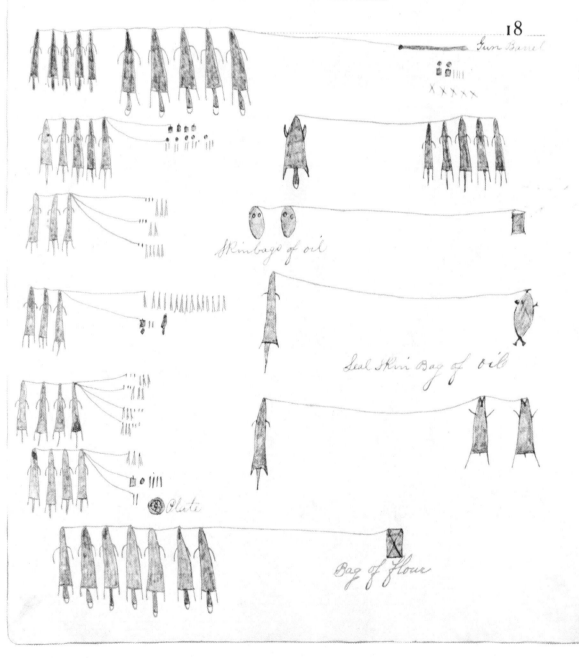

Gun Barrel

Skin bags of oil

Seal Skin Bag of oil

Plate

Bag of Flour

HEADQUARTERS, GOVERNMENT HOUSE,
SAINT PAUL'S ISLAND,
(Pribylov Group of Fur Seal Islands, Behring Sea, Alaska,)

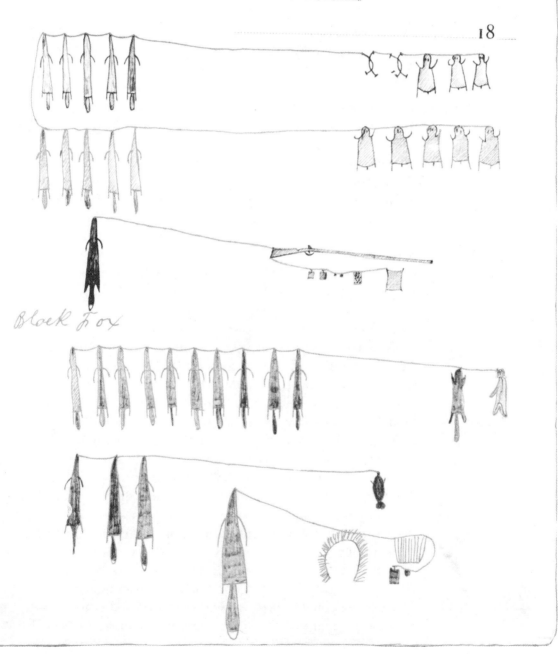

Black Fox

JANUARY 7, 1880   John and I celebrated a very quiet Christmas Day, December 25th, with the men at the company, who kept repeating, "Just wait until Russian Christmas. That's the day!" So we did wait until Russian Christmas, which was celebrated on our Feast of the Epiphany, January 6th, yesterday.

After the many services all day long at the church, large, lighted stars — something like our Fourth of July pinwheels — were brought out about 7:30 P.M. They were set to whirling in front of the church. While they were in motion, many Christmas hymns were beautifully sung with great animation. The natives' voices were particularly lovely in the night air and were very stirring at times. The star bearers took up their stars, and numbers of people fell in behind each bearer to form small groups that wended their ways in different directions all through the village. As I watched from our high windows, the lighted star processions moved like constellations in the inky bowl of night beneath us, traveling from house to house, stopping to sing and exchange greetings at each. The scene beneath us was a moving one, earnestly entered into.

Antoin Molevidoff and Kassian Nickolai, both star bearers, stopped with their groups at our house. Antoin's star was made of glass, about four feet in diameter, decorated with flowers painted on the surface. In the center was a chamber where candles burned. It was so made that it could be whirled to appear like our pinwheels. This required a second person to help, and it is an honor that every young melchiska seeks, to help whirl the Christmas stars. The decorating had been done by Heerman Antimonoff, son of the first tyone, a monk who occasionally assists Father Paul and who never has had any art training. We have struck up quite a friendship through our art.

The second star to stop at our house belonged to James Butrin, George's brother, who let Kassian carry it. This one had a transparency in the center upon which was drawn the U.S. flag, the eagle, and the thirteen stars arranged in a semicircle above its head. The group that followed it was mostly the young boys and girls whom I had been trying to teach at the school. We invited them in for chia and sweets — rather slim Christmas fare, but the best we could do because of the bad weather that preceded these two fair days. This is the only feast at which the women and girls may join in the singing, which makes it a gay and delightful occasion. I felt rewarded because each one spoke only English while in our house — not much and brokenly, but understandable. They are trying, and they are pleased because I complimented them. When they left, they stood outside our door and repeated many of the songs. Then whirling their stars and chanting softly, they disappeared into the night. Russian Christmas — Aleut style!

Just as Russian Christmas is late, so is New Year —
January 13th on our calendar, New Year's Day on theirs!
Like the Chinese, they celebrate it with fireworks, bombs,
cannons, and singing in front of the church. Seven-foot
transparencies have been erected on the plaza in front of the
company quarters. The first one has two Russian eagles with their
talons on a drum and cannon. There are crowns on their heads.
Another transparency has our eagle with the thirteen stars above
its head. Under it are two crossed American flags. Above each is a
banner with the words *St Paul*. Behind the glass, in a chamber,
lighted candles are placed to illuminate them. A smaller
transparency below each bears the legend *1880* and, below the
date, *Temperature − 20*. Each bears the Russian Old Style date as
well as the American New Style date.

The dancing and festivities have been going on ever since
Christmas. The first night after Christmas, the school hall was
thrown open for a masquerade dance. There was little originality
in costume except for the company men, who took pains with
theirs and entered into the spirit of the fun. Dr. Kelly borrowed
one of my dresses and went as the lady friend of an elegant
colored gent. The pair furnished much of the amusement that
evening. The natives did all the most beautiful Russian folk
dances, which they have learned to execute to perfection. There
seems to be no end to the variety of dances or to the stories they
depict. The Aleuts love to do the dances and we love to watch.

As the week passed, more and more clever maskers appeared in
the streets and at the evening dances. Most, in their quiet way,
seemed to be enjoying themselves. Many, of course, by now have
gotten themselves ugly drunk on kvas, which spoils the fun for
the majority, who behave themselves exceedingly well. Last night,
a few of the maskers stopped at the house. They came with the
two concertina players and the fiddler and danced for about fifteen
minutes for us, then went elsewhere. So well were they disguised
that we could not recognize a single one of them. One was a bear,
his costume so well devised that he looked like a real bear.
Another had a polar-bear body and a white fox head. One was
dressed like the Arctic hunter in *Canulickie* with his basket hat,
tarbossas, and gun. He carried a bundle of real skins (worth a
fortune back home) to keep in character. There was a fat man,
well padded in white tights and a swallowtail coat, a mendicant

with a broom and empty basket, a dark swell with patched parti-colored trousers, and others who have gathered an odd assortment of all kinds of clothes from rare visitors to these islands.

At the end of this gay season, everyone who participated has to cleanse himself by a plunge into the sea wherever there is a crack in the ice or a hole made for the purpose. This is to rid themselves of the evil spirits that might have been lurking in the costumes. The custom is dying out with the younger generation, who are not nearly so superstitious as their elders and who also do not relish the idea of a cold bath at this time of the year. The old people, who still cling to the idea of purification from festivities and of starting the New Year cleansed, are more often taking steam baths at the bathhouse than plunging through the ice, which in the past has caused a few deaths.

We have been fortunate in having stormless days for these holidays. But both John and I will be glad when the holidays are over and the island settles down again.

FEBRUARY 1ʳˢᵗ   The night and the cold have closed in about us. It seems odd to have to go about our ordinary business of daily living in absolute darkness. It has come on gradually, and we should have grown accustomed to it. But neither of us is accustomed to it. I hate feeling my way down to the schoolhouse at what seems to be midnight. It is bitterly cold, with a boorga blowing constantly. There have been many snowstorms, but the wind blows so fiercely that it blows the snow right off the rocks and out to sea. The wind veers every few hours and blows in a different direction, changing the drifts and the contour of the surroundings so that it is easy to get lost right within the village limits. I often have done so.

Worse than the snowstorms are the ice storms, not rain that freezes — it is far too cold for rain — but fine ice spicules, blown by the gales, that pile up into mountainous drifts that pack solid within an hour. The force of the wind makes of the spicules a biting blast that is impossible to walk through. We've watched it eat a coat of paint right off the side of the house. Often we've had to stay up here two and three days at a time until a storm subsides.

The sea is frozen for miles. The ice holds the surf in bondage so that there is no longer the boom and wash of waves breaking below us. The silence, except for the keening of the winds, is ominous. It is the silence of death; this is no poetic metaphor. The wind instantly kills everything living. Today is a warm day, eighteen below! There have been, and there will be, many days with far lower temperatures than that before a weak and shadowy sun moves northward to warm these islands a little.

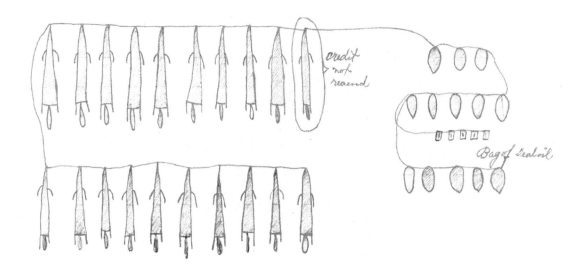

credit not received

Bag of seal oil

J ohn has been trying to get out long enough to go to the village for more supplies. But twice his nose has been frostbitten within minutes of leaving the house. Both times he has had to turn back. I doubt he can get down there anyway. There are mountainous drifts between here and the Lodge. Each hour they increase. If the wind blasts them away at one point, it piles them up at another. It is black out and we see no lights moving below us. I am sure that no one is about. Last week a few of the parents came to me and asked me to dismiss school until better weather, not only for the children's sakes but for my own. We had all been crawling on all fours against the winds. Now we cannot even do that, for our breath freezes in our lungs.

This is only the beginning of the worst weather. Mr. Elliott said that March is always the worst month. I can't imagine anything worse than this! According to the log, last winter was fairly mild and open compared to this. But Mr. Elliott records in the log that 1874 was the worst winter ever on record. Already we have surpassed his record, and it is not yet March.

Fortunately at everyone's insistence, I laid in a goodly supply of staple foods against such times as these when we cannot get out. We have a large supply of cereals, some cocoa, plenty of tea, some sugar, some flour, a few tins of milk, a few tins of salmon. The sugar and salmon were in such short supply by the end of the holidays that I had to ration it, and therefore could not rightly take more for myself than I allowed for each islander. The supply of dried and tinned fruits was entirely exhausted early. The Aleuts gorge themselves on the apricots and peaches, which to them are more delicious than anything in the world. Next to that they love our candies and sweet bisquits, which they learned to like from the Russians and which never had been a part of their original diet. I never have seen so much sugar in various forms consumed by individuals than by the *deetiah* [children] and the old people on this island. Yet it never makes them sick, and they have wonderful teeth. The day we cleared out the stores, I managed to ration about a pound of dried prunes per person and two pounds of dried apples to each family, as well as the last of the root vegetables and many cabbages.

Outdoors in the cold shed, I have a good supply of seal meat — quick-frozen the day the boorga first blew in — a few cuts of beef, lamb, bacon, and two huge hams. We also have a supply of smoked fish; that is, I tried smoking it the way Mrs. Mandrigan showed me. It looks so awful we're afraid to eat it. Carefully packed away are dozens of birds' eggs that I shall have to learn to eat if we stay frozen in too long.

On one of the days when John did get down to the stores, he managed to drag up another huge drum of kerosene, because our supply looked pitifully low and our little heap of coal outside had been so completely frozen over we could not get at it. It would not have lasted long anyway, and most of our stoves are built for oil consumption. This island uses six hundred drums of kerosene imported from the States, along with all the blubber and a great deal of seal oil produced here. Water, of course, is frozen solid all along the lines laid down in the fall. That was to be expected, until lines can be laid deep enough to avoid freezing. That will require blasting next year. Water in winter is no real problem. One reaches outside one's door, shovels up a container of snow, and boils it. We have just used a pickax on the nearest drift and have brought in our water in one huge chunk. We've closed off the living room and, of course, the SA's room, and therefore have fewer rooms to keep warm. Our wash water freezes overnight in its pitcher unless we set it near the stove, which heats only a diminishing radius of our room. In the kitchen, I have to remelt the water for tea every morning. Soon we'll give up using the sitting room. The hallway is too cold to cross to get there, although we do have much work laid out there that will crowd us here. In spite of all this, we feel snug indoors, shut away from the elements.

MARCH 2^d It is now three weeks since we dismissed school because of the weather. Not even Mrs. Mandrigan has been able to get up here, nor has anyone from the Lodge. As the days pass in such blackness outside that it is difficult to note their passing, the temperature keeps dropping (today, twenty-eight below), and the ice-laden gales continue to rage around us at more than eighty miles an hour (seldom less than forty). We look at each other and wonder how we ever got ourselves into this situation. It looks as though we are going to be housebound a long, long time. We hadn't counted on such complete isolation.

We've closed off the sitting room and have moved a small cook stove (the one that was here when we came and which had been stored in a cupboard) into our bedroom. This is the only room we now try to keep warm, because fuel is going down rapidly and the storm has not given any signs of abating. We eat, sleep, and live here in this one small room. We still have books to read to each other, including the family Bible we brought with us. We can even concentrate on the Russian language, though I do not know what good Russian will do us if we do not get out of here alive. Every once in a while we suddenly recognize a word we've heard spoken, and the strange alphabet suddenly takes on meaning. We feel so triumphant that we allow ourselves an extra prune with our cereal! I miss most the contact with others. A piano would help, though how we could get it into this room along with the many supplies we've had to move in here would be a problem now. Good music, good books, and each other — that would make life perfect. We wouldn't mind the cereal at all.

"The one thing I do miss," John said last night, "is your playing. I haven't realized what was missing." Though I never played often or well while at home, I was glad he opened the subject, because I have thought all along that I should let him know I had asked for a piano before I realized how much more the shipping space was needed for fuel oil and food. These terrible days have shown me that. "You didn't!" he exploded. "Who in the world would indulge a whim like that?" He was annoyed and not pleased, and so I let the matter drop. I'm sure I'll not have a piano anyway. It was a whim, the kind soon forgotten.

This is the fifth week we've not set foot outside our door, and scarcely outside our bedroom door. Impossible to believe! There's been no break in the weather. It is forty below today. It has been colder. We have only cereal, plenty of that, and tea left, but no sugar. I wish now I had listened to Mr. Redpath, who kept insisting, "Take more. Take more." I couldn't rightly take things for which he would not let me pay, when I had so carefully rationed things in short supply so everyone would share equally. But now the monotony makes me selfish. I do not miss the meat as much as I miss fruits and vegetables. I've developed a craving for prunes, of all things! I always turned my nose up at prunes when Tissie served them. More than a week ago, we finished our supply of birds' eggs, actually relishing their fishy taste. They were a Lucullan feast toward the end, the last fresh food we had.

The Aleuts go into a state of semihibernation at this time of year and require very little food for subsistence. They sleep most of the day, huddled together for body warmth. John and I are going to have to do the same. But we are not lethargic like the Aleuts. Our brains insist on working. The lack of food — that is, the lack of proper food — is causing us to be restless. We do not sleep well and we are extremely irritable at times. John grows angry every time he thinks of what we might be doing instead. He is furious that we are senselessly being subjected to such an ordeal.

"Senselessly!" he says. "What earthly good am I doing up here? What can an agent accomplish by being here? There isn't a thing in the world that the company couldn't handle. The island runs itself, except for the few months of actual sealing."

We thought we had enough fuel and food to last weeks. Now we can count on only enough to hold us for another week or so. Nowhere in the log is there a record of six whole weeks of unremitting weather. We are not the only ones snowbound. Everyone else is also, or someone would come to us. John often has tried to signal with the lamp. He gets no response. Anything can have happened down below, too — tragedy there as well as here. We are all in God's hands.

We are indeed in God's hands. We put ourselves there. Whenever we waver and get too frightened, we hold hands side by side at the window and look out over this blue-black sky and endless snow horizon while we pray. We feel warmer and reassured. Last night before going to bed, we stood thus at the window when suddenly the aurora borealis sprang up from the far waters of the Bering like a rainbow of promise. According to everyone who has seen the northern lights from Alaska or Canada, our northern lights are not very spectacular. We don't often have them. But they have always been beautiful to me. This time, the aurora was a tremendous display, fascinating, awe inspiring, and a little frightening. Great diaphanous curtains of colored light opened and closed the proscenium arch of the heavens. Whole ballets of darting, leaping, flying light fairies danced across the stage, back and forth, changing colors, changing shape, merging with the vast curtains, then scurrying away like quicksilver, an endless variation of themes and rhythms. We could not leave the window, though we grew numb with cold. It was as though the hand of God were improvising on an organ of light and giving us a sign of His presence. Or was He trying to show us how beautiful heaven is?

Dearest Ones,

The deep black night of winter has been with us a long time. Unless one lives in it, one cannot even imagine the few hours of half-light we now begin to see. Of course, there is no sun yet. The rest of the time it is very dark, indeed, except for an occasional fearful display of the northern lights, so overwhelmingly beautiful that one is afraid to look at them. Never in the recorded history of the island has there been such a severe winter. Following last winter's mild weather, this comes as something of a shock. Last year the natives suffered from the mild weather. This year we all suffer from the extreme cold. We suffer many hardships because all our meat is in the cold shed, under tons of ice which we cannot budge.

Fortunately, early in the fall before the snows came, we laid in ample supplies of everything we might need in case we could not get down to the Lodge. The bad weather set in early. But it abated at Christmastime and continued fairly mild into January. My idea of mild and yours are far different. Our idea of mild means bearable. After the holidays, about which I've written you, I resumed teaching school and thought the worst of the winter was over. But Mr. Redpath insisted that we lay in more supplies against another storm. Thank goodness we did, although there was not much to choose from. Our diet now has been reduced to tea and starchy foods.

This week has been the worst of all weeks, more than six weeks of being housebound! We have rationed ourselves to our few remaining stocks of food. I think when one is denied something, that is what one wants most. Right now I crave dried prunes! Can you imagine it? As I write this, they seem the ultimate of the unobtainable. In fact, we'll not see a dried prune until May, when the St Paul gets here. I am glad that by the time you read this our ordeal will be past. A ship will have brought us the supplies we need. They will seem like the greatest luxuries.

I am glad we can spend this trying period alone here. A third person in this small house would have led to inevitable trouble. We all would have been at each other's throats by now. John is angry because the Senior Agent did not suggest that we make the same arrangement with the Treasury Department that he had made: to go back to the States for the winter months. While I feel that is the more sensible arrangement, since it is obvious no government agent is needed up here these eight long months, I do not share John's personal anger against his senior officer. We came here prepared to stay two years. We had a specific reason for doing so, the saving of living expenses for these two years. I've tried to show John that we would have to try to find work in California in order to live there, and we would have to make this trip for four summers! I know I never could do it. Here we are — and we have to make the best of it, though John is doing it ungraciously because the work is not for him. It is not an engineer's job, nor has it any semblance of dignity about it. He hates being paid for idleness — some of it, such as now, enforced, of course. Altogether he is unhappy about the situation, and I am unhappy for him.

The greatest compensation for me is to be alone with John for the first time since our marriage. The experience is a rich, full understanding of each other, and a maturing we never might have experienced elsewhere. These days of being completely housebound have been revealing days, difficult to get through from the outward physical point of view, but wonderfully complete in our love of each other.

We read to one another. We write. We keep the log meticulously. We keep our watches wound so that we know the passing of the days. We mark the calendar, both the Russian and our own. We record the temperature and the weather picture. There is little more that we can record. Anything could be happening in the rest of the world. Anything could be happening in those houses right under us, and we never would know. Our isolation is that complete. Only a thaw can liberate us now. We could do with crawling into our lairs and sleeping until the spring like the Aleuts do. This is the month of thaw. We pray that it will begin soon.

But — dear ones — if we should not survive, someone will find this letter to you and all our other things. They will send them on, I know. You must know my love for you. I never should rest in some far yonder if I have caused you any sorrow by my willfulness. When I came away with John, it was to be able to live with him as his wife. I have had my happiness and no regrets because I did so. If that is selfish, please forgive me. You will know that I died happy. It has been a good marriage. Again, forgive your loving daughter,

Lib.

MARCH 27th We look at each other with a deeper fear in our eyes. We've still plenty of cereal and tea to keep our bodies fed. But the fuel oil is running so low that we have rationed its use to a minimum amount of warmth and for boiling water. For that reason we stay huddled in bed most of the time, even though we are now beginning to get some daylight during the middle of the day when we should be up and about. I do all my writing while the water is boiling because I can benefit from the warmth to keep my fingers from going numb. They are not only stiff from the cold, but cracked and blackened from the soot and oil. John's, too, are cracked and blackened. Our faces are streaked and dirty. In spite of his meticulous care of the flue — for fear we will suffocate or have a fire — our room is smoky and sooty and we no longer try to wash often. The effort of getting water in is reserved only for cooking water for our porridge and our tea. We have begun to doubt that we can survive. Though the temperature has been going up steadily for the past few days (it is ten above today), it will take ages to melt the packed ice under which our world is buried.

Someday, someone will find us, find my letters home, my notes, and my sketches. I hope they send them on to my family. May! June! Perhaps not until July or August even will our families know! Dear God, is this really the way we have to end our young lives? This diary will be destroyed before anyone finds it. It is to provide a last few minutes of warmth after all our fuel is gone. I have promised myself to burn it if I am capable, and if I am not, John has promised to burn it without reading it. I can trust my husband even in this.

Even though a thaw has set in there is no way of getting out. John has tried with pickaxes and mallet to make his way through the pack ice, since he cannot get up over it. The thaw has not yet softened the mass more than an inch or two in depth. We have to wait, and the waiting is a terrible thing. The cold is a bitter, damp cold now, penetrating. We have to spend more of our time in bed. Our fuel is so low now that we have only our bodily heat to keep each other warm. That and our love.

MARCH 28th

We enter a seventh week of this! Thaw one day, freeze another; it is disheartening. John is determined to break out of here. He's been hacking away at a great mound in front of our door with superhuman strength, but he gets nowhere. Neither of us can see any signs of activity in the village. Now that we can see that far in the light, we believe the whole place is buried under deeper snow than we have here on our more exposed hill. We figure that if we can get over the first biggest mound, we can slide down on boards. Our problem would be to get back up. There's no long rope to tie to the house with which we could pull ourselves back. We would have to have something to hold onto because of the wind and the slippery surface. Perhaps we could stay down there. But if conditions are worse there than here? We keep weighing every possibility. Better to perish here in each other's arms.

MARCH 29th

APRIL 15th I can only remember waking up out of a black, black, abysmal, dreamless sleep to light coming through a window not ours; an eerie half-light, rather blue. Mrs. Mandrigan and Malpha — big with child — both wearing white coveralls, were standing beside my bed jabbering in Russian. A basin was beside my cheek. Nausea overwhelmed me, and I half remembered I had felt that way before. A little while before? Or many times? Nausea became a part of a bad dream. I opened my eyes. I was not in my own room. Another wave of nausea swept over me. But there was nothing in me. The noise brought Mrs. Mandrigan to me instantly. She said something hurriedly to Malpha, who disappeared.

"You wake?" she said to me. I nodded weakly. I was too weak to speak. My head pounded, felt like a huge melon, and whenever I opened my mouth, the cold air striking my teeth made them ache. The calves of my legs also ached unmercifully. I am ashamed of myself now. I heard myself whimper like a baby, frightened because I did not know what was wrong and because I could remember nothing beyond the black sleep. The next time I opened my eyes after a bout of futile retching, Dr. Kelly was standing beside me, feeling my pulse.

"You're going to be alright, Mrs. Beaman. All you need is some good, nourishing food." Food! I retched again.

"Chia — chia," Mrs. Mandrigan said as though she had been arguing about this with Dr. Kelly. "Give strong chia."

"With sugar in it, Mrs. Mandrigan," he said. "You may be right. Anyway, it's worth trying." John's dear face hovered into view, disembodied over me. He bent and kissed me and in the kiss lingered a faint last wonderful memory.

"It's alright, Libby," he said. "The men got to us just in time." Later, when I was better, he told me with what difficulty they reached us. "You've got scurvy from all that cereal. As soon as you can eat some fresh foods, you'll be better."

"I guess I tried forcing the limewater too hard," Dr. Kelly said. "It's the only thing I know of for scurvy, and you had me frightened there for a while. We'll try to get your stomach settled first before I try forcing any more down."

Malpha came with a cup of strong, hot tea, and John fed it to me slowly, sip by sip, with a spoon. It stayed down and seemed to warm me wonderfully, though the heat of it made my teeth ache. I slid down among the covers and dozed for a little while. Mrs. Mandrigan gave me more hot tea. And because she was so pleased about her success, I dared not tell her that it made my teeth hurt terribly. After that I rested and sipped tea more often. The next time John came to me, I tried words.

"You?" I asked.

"I'm alright, Libby. I've had one good meal. Everyone is trying to eat as much of the meat as possible before it spoils. The warm air will spoil it soon. You've got to get well so you can help eat it up." Later Dr. Kelly told me that John had lost several meals before one stayed down. Our stomachs seem to have shrunk so and had grown so accustomed to only oatmeal gruel that they've revolted at all the good things. I say all the good things, but there isn't much, really. The whole island has suffered extreme privation during the seven weeks of endless storm and these weeks since, until they could get to the meat. Actually both John and I had been without food for nearly three days, because I had gotten sick and could not even prepare the simple gruel. Apparently John had not tried, deciding to starve with me. But during the third day, the roar of ice breaking up had roused him to action. When he looked out the window, he saw Dr. Kelly trying to make his way up the hill to us. John dressed warmly, clambered over the great slushy heaps of melting snow, and ran to meet the good doctor halfway. He collapsed in Dr. Kelly's arms, saying something about me. These things he hadn't dared tell me until a few days ago. I can vaguely recall his going for help. I was too weak to protest, and my legs already had given out.

"Your husband recovered faster, that is all," Dr. Kelly explained.

"Proving that men are stronger than women after all," I tried a weak joke.

"Did you ever doubt it?" he asked. There in the hospital, we had been having many long discussions while I grew stronger and better on his hideous-tasting limewater. I was his only patient, in spite of the hardship everyone had suffered. The little hospital next to the Lodge scarcely ever had sick patients, only wounded ones who superstitiously were afraid to stay there.

"No," I said frankly, where I might have hesitated to say so only a short while back.

"Everyone is slightly weakened because of the long ordeal, and I've no doubt a good many have actually a slight touch of scurvy, though at the Lodge I carefully rationed the fruits and vegetables to hold out until the S*t* Paul gets here. In the meantime, I'm pouring limewater down everyone until the supply gives out. We usually use a few gallons of it at this time of the year. The Aleuts make a medicinal tea of certain grasses which they say does the same work. I don't know if it really is efficacious. It tastes awful. But as our supply of tea is running low, we may have to come to it."

"Mrs. Mandrigan says it is good medicine. Witness — the Aleuts are seldom sick."

"I never argue with them about their three medicines because I've never known them to do any harm."

Some of the thawed meat was salvaged by smoking it. Some

HOSPITAL, S*t* PAUL ISLAND

can be stored a while longer in cold sheds supplied with blocks of ice cut from the sea. This has been a bit treacherous, so I hear, because the sea ice is breaking up with terrific explosions that buckle it into huge piles — with rocks included. I can hear the thunderous roars of the sea ice breaking. I should like to watch the drama. But my legs still will not carry me.

The thermometer hovers between freezing and slightly above each day. There can be uncomfortably cold weather before the St Paul gets here with more fuel. Everyone has to watch his supply carefully. Soon the coal that has been congealed into the solid ice beds will be liberated and can be used. Soon too, the hills, now running Niagaras of water, all will be melted off, except the high peaks and the gullies which retain their snow for a long time. Soon we can think — or pretend — it is spring.

The melchiska take advantage of the daylight to go as far out on the sea ice as they dare to scout for the first birds or the first seals and to fish through the ice or between the cracks. The sea ice is a treacherous place to be, and there have been many accidents, even deaths, in the past. No one knows whether he is above land, above shallow water, or above deep water. Often a great floe will break from the mainland and move far out where the youngsters, all unaware of what has happened until they turn toward home, cannot leap the intervening space. Then, unless a brave Aleut dares launch a bidarkah in the treacherous waters between, the floe carries the children to their deaths. Often no rescue can be made, for the cutters and small boats are frozen in solid. Everyone holds his breath until the melchiska are safely back on dry land after their scouting expeditions.

I have been in the hospital several weeks! Not in bed all the time. Because I needed care, and no one could get up the hill to look after me, Dr. Kelly thought this was best. He has been sorry that he and Mr. Redpath didn't insist that we live in the hospital during the winter. But then, no one anticipated such a winter. My legs still will not carry me. They ache just as my teeth still ache, horribly. My teeth ache when they come in contact with the air because the scurvy has caused the gums to recede so far that the sensitive part of each tooth is exposed. It is a dreadful disease — a dreadful sounding disease — that one thinks of as happening only to the starving hordes in India. Yet here I am with a good case of it, the first time I have ever been sick in my life!

John has grown angry and moody again over this senseless nightmare we've been forced to live through — angriest when he realizes that it nearly took me from him, as he puts it. Nor are we sure of the outcome yet. At first I had trouble even keeping down all the tea with sugar. I tried hard because inadvertently I discovered that the sugar was a last tiny horde several Aleut families had given up just for me! There are still so many things I cannot keep down. In fact, the sight or thought of food sickens me. One only has to mention limewater and I am lost. I have everyone worried.

I am back at Government House at last. I came back yesterday. Although we still live in our one room to save fuel, Cook sends food up to me with John, tempting me to eat. Mrs. Mandrigan has been trying to get the room cleaned up around me. She spent several days here, before John brought me back, getting the room ready for us again. But until yesterday, it did look as though I might never get back.

Dr. Kelly came to the hospital with John after midday meal yesterday. They brought me a fine piece of fresh seal meat just caught the day before, a first seal that had hauled up unsuspectingly at Reef Point only to be immediately spotted by Vicele, who had been watching for days on the bluff. The meat was beautifully prepared, and Dr. Kelly and John were proud of the gift. All I could do was push it aside. I wept because I hurt them so.

"But, Libby," John said, "you'll not regain your strength this way." He looked helplessly to Dr. Kelly and asked what he should do to tempt me to eat something, or whether he should force me.

"Would you give me a little while alone with Mrs. Beaman?" Dr. Kelly asked. John consented, said he'd take the steak back to Cook. Someone, no doubt, would eat it. When he left, Dr. Kelly looked searchingly at me. "You know that your symptoms are those of a bad scurvy, Mrs. Beaman," he said quite seriously and looking directly at me. "But they are also the symptoms of something else we may have been overlooking all this time because of the malnourishment. You could be pregnant."

I looked at him a long time uncomprehendingly. What he said seemed not to have sunk in at all. Then suddenly, overwhelmingly, the sure knowledge of how right he was swept over me. Oh, dear God, there are two of us needing food — two of us needing the right food!

"But of course!" I cried excitedly. "But of course! Why didn't I know? Why didn't I guess? The weeks have passed. I haven't kept track of them. It has taken you to tell me what I should have known."

"Not so fast. We can't be sure. This may be only extreme malnourishment. It may be other things. I'd wait until we are really sure before saying anything to anyone. Don't look so stricken."

"But it has to be a baby!"

The rookery at Ketavie, Sᵗ Paul Island.

"If that is what you want, I hope we are right. I sent your husband away so we could talk about this. I've been suspecting it for several days. You should have rallied from the scurvy sooner. I figured something else was complicating your recovery, tuberculosis perhaps. But this isn't like tuberculosis, and since there's none on the island, you'd have had to bring it with you. In that case, I think I'd have known it before this."

"Consumption! How horrible! Oh, I'm sure I've not brought that here."

"Well, if it is a baby, you must arrange to leave the islands in plenty of time to have it in the States. You could never bring forth a live baby up here."

I was so excited that I could not think clearly; in fact, I am still excited and still cannot think clearly. But I did do a hasty calculation from the night of the aurora, that first night the gates of heaven opened to us.

"November," I said. "Sometime in November."

"We'll get you home for that."

"But John's contract isn't up until the following May. I can't ruin John's career. Why can't I bear a live baby up here?"

"I don't advise trying. There is no way to help you should you get into difficulties. I'm not equipped to take care of anything more complicated than a simple delivery. And should the baby be a simple delivery, and alive, it could not survive. Infant mortality within the first year is sixty percent. You must go home, even if your husband has to stay here."

"Yes, I see that I must," I sighed. "I want a live baby more than anything else in the world. There probably never would be another winter such as this, but I guess I wouldn't want to subject an infant to an Aleut winter no matter how husky he would be."

He stood and smiled at me. "Here we are crossing bridges before we get to them. We could be all wrong."

"Oh, no," I said. "Oh, no. I know you're right. I know what is happening to me."

"We'd better wait a little while longer and make sure," he said, and he left without saying a word about my trying to eat. But I was suddenly ravenous, and I have been ever since. John thinks Dr. Kelly hypnotized me into wanting to eat. I know better. There are two of us to feed. There are two of us to make up for lost time, and though the going is a bit hard, I think I'll manage. I insisted on walking over the threshold into this house and into our room. I know Dr. Kelly has warned me to wait until I am sure — medically sure, that is. But in my heart of hearts, I am sure. And I thank Thee, Lord, for the Arctic night and the cold and the aurora.

I 've copied what I wrote at the hospital into this diary. MAY 24ᵗʰ
One of the first things I worried about, when I began to think again, was the fate of this book. Had I had strength enough to destroy it before I became too ill? Had John destroyed it for that last warmth we expected of it? Had he let curiosity overcome him and read it? I was afraid to speak to him about it — afraid to know the truth. But it was here, locked and waiting for me, a lesson in many ways. I'll not be so careless of my resolutions again.

The days drag — in spite of my new knowledge — because my legs limit my activity. I do get about some, now that the ice and snow are gone, but oh, so slowly and so painfully. I have to lean heavily on John's arm, and my legs ache whenever I sit down. Walking out has had its rewards, however. I stood above Nah Speel to watch the great, dramatic scene of hundreds of bull seals hauling up out of the sea and over the rocks to the small rookery beneath us. I have made sketches that cannot do the scene justice. Nor can words, though I have set it all down in *The Seal Book* just as it happened. (I've spent more time writing in *The Seal Book* than I have in this, because Mr. Elliott may come back, and we did get far behind during all those months when we had planned to write and didn't.) The bachelor seals now are hauling up to higher ground beyond the bulls. That, too, is a dramatic scene. I

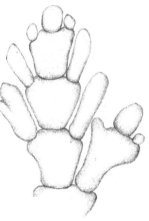

Sea Life

wish I felt strong enough to go with John to watch the hauling up on the great rookeries, where they come in by the thousands instead of the hundreds.

Today I enjoyed the excitement of watching the bulls challenge the bachelors as they crossed through their harems to get to the parade ground. The bulls challenged the bachelors every inch of the way. It is bedlam all around us, for the birds, bless them, are also back. We welcome the bedlam. The noise and excitement are part of living. The ice and the silence were a part of death. We prefer to be alive.

Everyone grows impatient for a sight of the St Paul. Today, according to the log, is the earliest date that the little ship has ever reached the island. There is no sign of her in the direction from which she should appear, and a nasty fog is closing in. It folds itself over like layers of soft white flannel, smothering us and hiding everything from view. No navigator could get in through this. The villagers have gone to church to pray, and an air of hopelessness and discouragement has descended over the island with the fog.

I have just told John about the baby. I could not keep the secret from him any longer. In fact, as soon as Dr. Kelly left the house a little while ago, I told John. I want him to savor every moment of the same pleasure I am having, anticipating a little one. Instead, he seems to be filled with deep concern for me and has gone down the hill to find the doctor and talk with him about it. The calmest passage is during August. I have promised him that I will go home in August to have our son.

Son?

John wants a son.

MAY 25th A whole year on this island, and I've been waiting to hear old Barlashkin's weird cry. Last night, just after midnight, the whole village awoke to the spine-tingling cry of one of its strange nocturnal wanderers. "Ship's light! Ship's light!" he screamed in English and in Russian. But though we searched the fog in every direction, we saw no light anywhere. Yet when the fog lifted today, there — hanging like a mirage against the horizon — floated the S.S. St Paul, a beautiful sight. More beautiful still was the sight of a little lighter skimming in to us under full sail. The whole village ran down to the wharf to welcome our saviors, and I was reminded of our own arrival last year.

It has been a busy, active day, with cutters and lighters and bidarrahs shuttling back and forth from ship to shore, the warehouse ringing with shouts and commands, everyone gorging himself on tinned peaches, raspberry jam, sweet bisquits, candy — all the good things we have not tasted for a long time.

There was a service of thanksgiving at the church later.

Captain Erskine joined us here for chia after the excitement died down. "Pure luck again," he said in answer to John's compliment about his navigation. "That's all it is, pure luck. We've been way out in the Bering four days because of storms and fog banks, or I could have made it sooner and broken the record. Getting in this early was pure luck."

"And fine navigating," John insisted. "We're certainly beholden to you for risking it. We've been in dire need of everything."

"I feel as though I should be down at the stores checking things in," I said. "I've become storekeeper since you were here last."

"Let the men do it, Mrs. Beaman. I hear you've been mighty sick."

"I'm ashamed of being the weak one," I said and smiled.

"I shook my head over you many a time this past winter, and told Mrs. Erskine I was wondering how you were faring up here. I've my doubts that any of our women can make it through a whole winter. I really do, Mrs. Beaman."

"Well, the men were nearly as badly off," I answered in self defense. "We all are more than grateful you've brought us the things we need." John and the captain went back to the wharf, where the activity of unloading the Sr Paul continued for a long while. I had not asked Captain Erskine whether the Senior Agent was aboard. I wondered when he would appear.

I was in the living room at John's desk when the SA came up the steep path, alone. I would have hastened to meet him on the path but thought better of the impulse. I know I was glad to see him, like a good friend and familiar face returned — sensing also all the trouble his physical presence again would create. I opened the front door to him. The gesture seemed to surprise and touch him, taking him off guard completely. He looked at me a bit flustered and obviously pleased that someone stood at the door to welcome him over the threshold. But he did not know quite what to say. So he turned to Vicele and one of the other youths who had come up behind him with his baggage and motioned them to go through to his room.

"Elizabeth, I am sorrier than I know how to say it that you've had to go through this," he said, hat in hand as though a visitor. I held up my hand to silence him.

"Say nothing. Do not apologize for anything. I've had to accept what's happened to me. It's one of the hazards of my being here against everyone's will. I hold nothing against you. You do know that. So welcome home to the Pribilofs!"

"You are generous. I expected recriminations."

"John hasn't already quarreled with you?"

"No."

"He is angry still, terribly angry. I'm afraid he'll pick a quarrel again. What must I do or say that can help?"

"I do not know, Elizabeth. I do not know. I have thought about the ridiculous situation a good deal this winter. I could find no solution."

"Because I am still here. I remain the problem."

"We, at least, understand each other."

"I wish you could like us a little better. Can't there be friendship?"

"That's a large order, my dear. If you weren't so . . . so attractive, it would be easier."

"Me? This gaunt bag of bones? No one will look twice at me this summer. You need not worry." I nearly blurted out the truth about myself, but decided the first moment of his return was not the right moment. After all, since it was a secret between John, Dr. Kelly, and myself, why should I let this hostile individual share it? I could see from his eyes that he still did not like me or the idea of my continued presence in this house. "I wish you could make your self-imposed discipline easier. I am sorry that I am the one who makes your life so hard for you," I said.

"I appreciate your frankness. I am happy, too, that you at least recognize what the problem is, though I still wish you could have foreseen it and not come here. And now, my dear, we are going to have to get you well again. Scurvy is not incurable. We've arrived early with the fresh foods you need."

"I am sure that is all I need. And again I promise, as I did last year, that I will stay out of your way as best I can."

"I'm afraid that may be impossible, Elizabeth. I see visitors coming up the hill." I turned around and looked down the path. I could not believe what I saw.

"I can't believe it!" I exclaimed. Several men were hauling a spinet piano up the steep hill to Government House, and half the village was trailing behind! "I can't believe it!" I turned toward him impulsively. "You remembered, you remembered! How can I thank you?" But I'm sure he could read the gratitude in my eyes.

"By playing for me."

I was about to answer that I was an indifferent pianist with only an indifferent training, when the men pounded on the door and we went to let them in.

What confusion and excitement this new toy has created! Everyone wanted to see it, touch it, touch the keys to hear them make a note. They all filed past it in awe and immediately called it, in Aleut, the-great-big-concertina-one-sits-down-to-play, a not

GOVERNMENT HOUSE, S⟨sup⟩t⟨/sup⟩ PAUL ISLAND

unmusical sounding word as they pronounced it. Everyone who jammed into the living room — the only place large enough to accommodate the piano — wanted to hear music made by it. So, cracked and stiff as my fingers are, I sat down to play for them. Because my heart was full, I played for them a Bach hymn of thanksgiving, which was only a beginning. The village would have had me play on and on, but I reminded them that the real thanksgiving for all our blessings was scheduled at the church. We all went there together.

I am no great musician, and I know few things by heart, or well, except hymns we sang at church and Sunday School back home. I never felt a true vocation for the piano, though when John was courting, he used to like to listen to me play. What pleases me most now, of course, is that I can at least try to play from the books which the SA thoughtfully brought with the piano, so we can have some of the wonderful music out of our own pasts and not always have to resort to the Russian liturgical or folk music to satisfy our needs.

In my heart of hearts I have the feeling that perhaps the music under our roof will ease the tensions that exist there. This afternoon when I played, I noticed that John relaxed and that the steel bars in the SA's eyes came down. I am glad now that I dared ask for the piano.

Village of St George, a watercolor by Henry Wood Elliott

GOVERNMENT HOUSE, St PAUL ISLAND

175

JUNE 15th

Sea Life

<big>B</big>anished! We are banished to St George Island! There is no other word for it.

The piano has been directly or indirectly the cause, I think, though I cannot rightly know. I am still so upset over this hasty move to this bleak and barren mass of rocks that I cannot yet write about the events that led up to our exile here, though I know that I shall have to set it all down as I have in the past.

Here we are, living at Government House on the other Pribilof. It is a smaller edition of the one on St Paul, as is the whole village around us a smaller edition of the one we left. There are only twenty-two Aleut families living in twenty-two white frame bungalows on a single curved street that faces onto a plaza where five or six company buildings, a little school, and a little green and gold onion-domed Orthodox church are grouped like a toy setting for a Russian fairy tale.

St George is only thirty-eight miles from St Paul, but it might as well be a hundred and thirty-eight, for it is almost inaccessible by any small craft. There is no landing and only bad anchorage for larger craft. Even the sturdy little company cutters seldom ply between the two islands, so communication is tenuous. The whole time we were on St Paul, we were scarcely conscious that this island existed, except occasionally when it was mentioned. Because of certain strange Arctic currents that pass near it between the two islands, the waters are too turbulent to navigate. The island's isolation is made more complete by its almost impregnable approach. But for a few dips to narrow beaches, it presents a solid rock wall (in some places as high as 950 feet) that falls into masses of mammoth rocks or directly into the sea which, with the surf, pounds and undercuts it. The cliffs are mostly highly polished black basalt which, together with the vicious baroom, permit no beaching for any craft.

This little village, situated in a break in the wall, is on the north shore, as are the few rookeries. The *St Paul* has had to wait far out at the anchorage as many as two, and sometimes even three, weeks before being able to send a lighter in. She cannot get closer herself because the winds would smash her against the seawalls. She dares not navigate these waters in a fog for the same reason. The currents and the winds are the most treacherous in the world. It was not the *St Paul,* however, that brought us here. The Coast Guard cutter *Reliance* brought us and is standing by waiting for calm waters so its little lighter can get back to it. Mr. Scribner, who has been here for three years, is to go back to St Paul and take John's place there. When he leaves, we will have this house to ourselves.

Dr. Kelly was sent over to exchange places with Dr. McIntyre so he can continue to look after me. That was Mr. Morgan's idea, not ours. But it does ease the situation of coming to an entirely

strange community, to have one good friend to turn to. We can see how reluctant the villagers are to part with Mr. Scribner and Dr. McIntyre, who seem to be held in great esteem. They, too, having heard of their transfer only yesterday when we arrived, seem unhappy at the thought of parting with the Aleut friends they've made. "We've enjoyed our work here," Dr. McIntyre informed me. "In fact, we've so enjoyed our work here that we renewed our two-year contracts, Mr. Scribner with the Treasury Department and I with the company. You know, of course, that I came up here originally to visit my brother who was a Treasury Department agent. He suggested the trip. He left. I stayed."

Again I feel guilty because, directly or indirectly, I am the cause of disrupting their lives. "It's only for a little while that you'll have to be away from Sᵗ George," I told the good doctor. "I am going home at the end of August. Then the islands can get back to normal."

Sᵗ George looked bleak and forbidding yesterday as we approached it. Fortunately the weather was clear, so we could come right in, a rough ride in the little lighter. The narrow cove gave us our first glimpse of the town. Grim black and purple-black highly polished basalt cliffs rose directly out of the water two and three hundred feet, throwing a sharp, hard outline high against the sky. The soft greens and vivid colors of flowers are nowhere to be seen. There's no soil on Sᵗ George in which a plant can put down roots, and if there were, the ever-present ferocious

Postcard of Village of Sᵗ George by Henry Wood Elliott

GOVERNMENT HOUSE, Sᵗ GEORGE ISLAND

winds would blow it right off. The winds accompany the strange, contrary sea currents, change direction every few hours, and are as violent as the sea or, perhaps, make the sea so violent. The winds have a keening sound. They are responsible for the clean-swept, polished barrenness of the place.

What gives the island a strangely haunting beauty all its own — a beauty which John cannot see at all, but which I can see — are its many waterfalls. We live within the sound of three which drop over perpendicular escarpments, one from the island's only little stream and the other two from clear little mountain pools. They drop — in long, thin, diaphanous veils blown out by the winds — into the sea below.

More fog lies over this island than over St Paul. Mr. Scribner says they have not yet seen the sun over here, though there are brief periods at midday when it is warm enough for people to be outdoors a while and clear enough to get about. Walking is impossible. No one walks anywhere on this island. Everywhere are deep and sudden fissures, slippery ravines, and jagged crags. The village is on the one rounded hill with a gentle slope that spills toward the sea between the high bluffs of the island's north wall. The only other break anywhere near in this formidable wall is at Garden Cove, where a huge herd of sea lions lives. They will be our meat for the summer, since there is no pasturage over here for cattle. Unless a company cutter visits occasionally with fresh meat from St Paul, we will live on bacon, smoked meats, seal, birds, fish, and sea lion — not a bad prospect.

Everywhere, in every chink, cranny, ledge, overhang, or tiny cave, live not thousands but millions of birds. Nowhere else in the world is there anything comparable to the numbers of birds to be found on St George Island. It is fantastic! I've tried to take a hasty inventory of just those birds I can see as I look up from this page — impossible to list them all because I do not yet know them all by name. But among those on the cliff which drops from under my window and on the rocky shelf just under, I count thousands

of Pacific kittiwakes and red-legged kittiwakes; hundreds of the most beautiful and different kinds of ducks the Aleuts call *ootkies;* hundreds of jägers; thousands of gulls, all kinds, called *gooverooskies;* and puffins beyond number and description — *tawporkie,* the tufted puffins, and *epatka,* the horned puffins; *oreel,* the red-faced cormorant and another cormorant I do not recognize; hundreds and hundreds of short-tailed albatrosses; Rodger's fulmars, called *lupus* here; millions of the delicious *bailliebruskie* or the parroquet auk; all the other birds I've listed for S*ᵗ* Paul; plus snowbirds, snow geese, a little brown owl, the magnificent Arctic owl, many familiar red-breasted robins, and hundreds of tiny gaily singing house wrens, for which the Aleuts have the most picturesque name of all, *limmershin,* which translated literally means *a chew of tobacco.* That is just about what they look like.

There are only five fur-seal rookeries over here, with a population of about two hundred thousand seals. Not all the matkas have come in, which means that not all the pups have been dropped. There may be as many as fifty thousand more seals before long. But, of course, the killing season has begun, and about twenty to thirty thousand bachelors may be taken from here. There are not enough low beaches to support more fur seals for their summer breeding cycle, and the beaches the island does have — Zapadnie, Starry Ateel, and the others — are small compared to those on S*ᵗ* Paul. Zapadnie is the only rookery across the island on the south shore, and the skins are taken directly from there at great hazard to the cutters that risk going in to pick them up.

There are many herds of sea lions scattered around the island, more than at S*ᵗ* Paul, and more hair seals also. They do not need the beaches for their breeding. Apparently they mate in the sea. They enjoy the hazardous baroom and the rocky coast for play. Above them, in lairs in the cliffs, dwell the scavenging white foxes and the rarest of all foxes, the blue, which are found nowhere else

except on this island. Unfortunately, because of so much trapping, they are becoming extinct. On St George — and St George only in all this vast Bering area — breed hordes and hordes of lemmings, whose mysterious life cycle not even Mr. Elliott has been able to trace.

We have one house mouse, brought in, no doubt, with supplies from a ship. It will not last long, because there are more tabby cats on this island than on St Paul, in varying stages of growing wild again. Their caterwauling is as great here and as hideous. Though we are more remote from the noise of the rookeries, the pounding of the surf, the shrill calling of the birds, and the howl of the wind all combine to make this a noisier place to dwell.

Poachers at work on St George Island, a watercolor by Henry Wood Elliott

GOVERNMENT HOUSE, St GEORGE ISLAND

O ur days on the island are numbered. I begin to count them and exult in my heart. I am going home . . . I am going home! But though this place is bleak, it is not banishment as I had at first thought. John and I live a beautiful idyll, too beautiful to last. We live here, perched on a high cliff 350 feet directly above the sea, alone, all alone, in a little house. No winter shuts us into a solitary room, and no other inhabitant spoils our privacy.

It is true that John is exhausted when he comes in from the killing field. It is a purely physical exhaustion though, without the tensions of last summer. He bathes in leisurely fashion when he comes in and dresses, while I — with the help of our two Aleut girls, Loobov and Maria — prepare and serve dinner. I still am a poor cook, though I am trying to improve before we go home, because I shall have Tissie's help for such a short while.

Sea Life

The killing, which started just before we arrived, has been going on now for three weeks. On this island, the driving is extremely difficult because of the terrain. Yet the rookeries are so inaccessible by boat that all seals have to be driven over this tortured earth to a central killing ground right under the windows of the last house in the village. The seals are far more remarkable than the men in getting over the rough ground. They take about eight hours of motion, broken by long and frequent rests for cooling, so each drive lasts for about twenty-four to forty-eight hours, depending on the distance. The men cannot stand the grueling climbs into and out of the ravines for long, so they work in relays to relieve each other. Naturally the seals have to be driven slowly and carefully, so as not to destroy or overheat their pelts. Several times, John — who occasionally has accompanied the drivers just to see the rookeries — has had to send back word that he was camping out for the night since it was impossible to return until he had rested and slept. He's been carrying a waterproof pack in case of such need. But when he is home, he is human and relaxed and more like the John I married.

We have guests occasionally — Dr. Kelly, the other company men, officers of the navy cutters the *Rush* and the *Reliance,* when they can get in on their patrols of these waters. Often for chia, we have the tyone and his wife and other natives who drop in. We've made friends quite readily with the islanders. Loobov and Maria have helped in this. They are two young girls who have been doing all the chores at Government House for the last two years. They are gay, chatty, intelligent, and speak English beautifully. They dress in the latest fashions brought to them from San Francisco. The company is planning to send them to the States in another year or two, when they are eighteen, to have them educated to teach here. They cannot wait and already are excited at the prospect, especially now that they have talked with me.

GOVERNMENT HOUSE, St GEORGE ISLAND

Looking at the cliffs outside our west window, Gov't House, Sᵗ George.

When I asked them if they will separate, one to teach on Sᵗ George and one to teach on Sᵗ Paul where I failed, they shouted, "Oh, no! We belong to Sᵗ George." I've come to understand that though the Pribilof Aleuts originally came from the same families in the Aleutians, the Sᵗ Paul Aleuts and the Sᵗ George Aleuts, during their hundred years of isolation from each other, consider themselves entirely different tribes.

It is pleasant having young ladies chattering around the house all day. They've been extremely curious about every little feminine article of clothing, jewelry, toilet articles — in fact, everything I possess. I miss Mrs. Mandrigan's unselfish devotion, which is an unusual trait in the Aleuts. But she was a stolid, uncurious person compared to these two young girls, who act more like young Americans than anyone we've met so far. Young people such as Loobov, Maria, and Vicele are the hope of these islands. There are a few others, of course, awakening from their long, bone-age hibernation. But most are slow, and others do not want to be waked.

GOVERNMENT HOUSE, Sᵗ GEORGE ISLAND

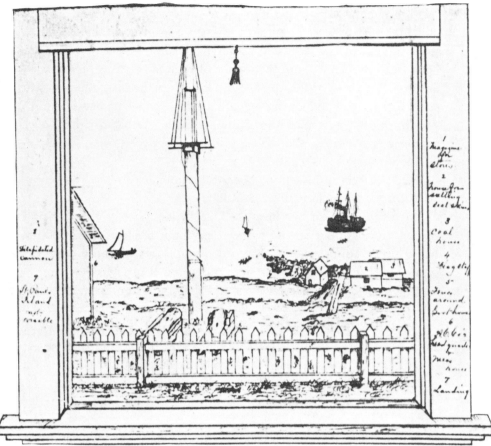

This is the view from our sitting room window.

Tyone Ustigoff and his wife paid a formal call yesterday and we had tea. He is more progressive than Phillip Volkov. Both he and his wife speak good English. They told us what a fine influence Mr. Scribner and Dr. McIntyre had on the island. They admitted that — perhaps because they were a smaller group to work with and because they were so extremely isolated — they had been easier to teach. The tyone even admitted that the two Americans had been stern disciplinarians at first and had insisted on all the natives learning English now that they are Americans. They had insisted on cleanliness and other healthful changes. Mr. Scribner did not seem to have the difficulties I had teaching English. These people speak it, because if they did not learn, they were denied some sweet or other privilege they desired. All in all, the tyone corroborated our impression that St George, for all its bleakness, is a happier place to live.

Even the kvas drinking, which grows excessive at this time, seems to be kept under some kind of control. We've heard of none of the beastly treatment of young girls and the savage coercion of the women such as happened to a fantastic degree by the end of the killing season on St Paul. There is some drinking, but it is not evident.

JULY 10th

GOVERNMENT HOUSE, St GEORGE ISLAND

Loobov and Maria came into the sitting room and joined us at chia like guests, which amused us. They chatted with the tyone's wife in Russian and in English interchangeably and were polite enough to use only English if either of us was listening. John was amused. Every relationship is so different here because the people seem different. The fact that we are leaving soon helps color the relationships. The tyone wanted me to teach school now that Mr. Scribner is gone.

"In summer?" I asked.

"We have school in summer because winter is too bad. We close school in bad weather."

"Mrs. Beaman has not been well," John hastened to say to help me out. He will not let me work at anything for fear of losing the baby, but of course we do not want the villagers to know why. "I cannot let her teach until her strength comes back. Mr. Scribner will be back here in a few weeks. Let the youngsters have a holiday until then."

The tyone seemed disappointed, so I added that perhaps now, since I had come to the islands, other wives might, and then he would have a lady teacher — maybe too many of them!

"We wish you come back," he said, and that was one of the most heartwarming things that anyone has said for a long, long time.

"I wish I could. But there will be too much water between us. I do not like the water."

"Someday big snow goose bring you back."

"I'd like that better," I laughed, pleased with this show of imagination. But Loobov tells me there is a legend they have about a snow goose that brought their ancestors to the islands.

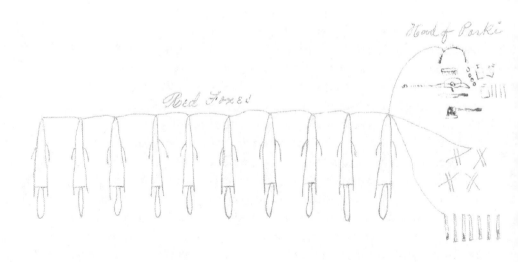

July 15, 1880
Government House
St George Island
Pribilof Group

Dearest Ones,

I am coming home — Home — Home!

I am coming home because I shall be presenting you with a grandchild in November! If all goes well, I shall be in Washington by the end of October, only shortly after you receive this packet of letters.

I had decided not to tell you what was happening to me, if I stayed up here, until after the baby was safely born. Too many things could go amiss, and I did not want you to be worrying about me needlessly. You see, you would not even know you had a grandchild at all until it was toddling, for it would be born after any letters could be sent to you. In fact, we ourselves would be on our way home when you could get the first news of us. But now all that is changed, and we are leaving before John's term is up. And now that our departure is so near, I thought I'd better prepare you so perhaps you can help prepare for me. I haven't a thing up here suitable for the little one except some soft furs to wrap him in.

Dr. Kelly has taken such good care of me that I have completely recovered from the scurvy, and he believes the baby has not been harmed by the early deprivations. He has insisted that this is no fit place to have a child. I had half hoped that I could produce America's first "snow baby," but John says I'd better be sensible and produce a live baby. And John is right.

I write this from our new home, our very own, since there is no one here with whom we have to share it. I had believed at first that to have to change places with Mr. Scribner would be a terrible comedown. Instead, I honestly can say I like this little island. It is smaller and rockier, but in a way more beautiful, though John says I'm mad to think so. He can see no beauty anywhere. I insist that the black, highly polished rocks with their more intense shadows and stark outlines against the luminously misty sky and the sea beneath us, windwhipped and opalescent like mother-of-pearl boiling in a cauldron, have their own beauty. I think I will miss the simplicity and grandeur of the ever-changing scene when I get home.

The village is a miniature duplicate of St Paul, set in the basin of an extinct volcano. The rim of the crater is extremely steep and rugged with jagged peaks that, on the outer side, plunge steeply down into a booming, churning sea — some of them plunge more than 1,000 feet. The cliff we live on drops only 350 feet and is at the edge of the rounded hill on which the rest of the village is built. Great mountains of ice and icy currents sweep down from the North Pole to meet the Japan Current right at our front door. The clash of warm air and ice makes a fog blanket that lies over this island more often even than over St Paul. But it is the fog that the fur seals love and have to have to breed. And we are here because there are fur seals here.

I have been intensely happy in our new home — perhaps because it is only a temporary home, and I know that I shall be going to my real home with you. I have been longing to see all of you again. I will be seeing you so soon that I shall not write any more letters but concentrate instead on my journal and the seal notes and all the things I've wanted to record before we leave.

And — please, dear parents — do not be too excited. With all my firsts, this will not be the first grandchild ever to be presented to the world. This letter goes with the next sailing of the St Paul and with all our love.

Your daughter,
Libby.

JULY 20th We will be leaving these islands soon — never, I am sure, to come back. These have not been entirely lost months of our lives. We have learned much of human nature along with all we've learned about a strange part of the world. We've been humbled by our banishment here, of which I must write before I close the pages of this book upon our Arctic adventure.

If I have learned anything of great worth to take with me out of this cold and miserable ice-locked world, it is that I would not have done otherwise but go through all the hardship, terror, and unhappiness again to have had this much time to know my husband. I no longer shall be so rebellious against the everyday strictures placed about my sex. We can throw them off only gradually and not all at once, as I should have liked to do. They become insignificant before the great truth that we were created first to bear children, and only after that do we take our places in the affairs of the world. It is worth rebelling occasionally, perhaps, to learn this truth.

GOVERNMENT HOUSE, St GEORGE ISLAND

Perhaps now that the *S.S. St Paul* has left with my messages home and the *Reliance* is due back soon to take us off St George, I can write in detail and with less passion of what happened between the Senior Agent and John. How can I begin? Where does one begin? Like everything else, there is no real beginning, only a continuous chain of events — the piano, one link in it.

Ever since the piano's arrival, life at Government House had changed, at first barely perceptibly, then bit by bit more noticeably. For one thing, more and more villagers stopped by on the flimsiest pretexts. They would always linger near the-great-concertina-one-sits-down-to-play. It intrigued them. Also Vicele — much too old to be under his mother's feet — instead of snaring birds with the other melchiska, hung around the instrument all the time until one day he worked up enough courage to finger it. He actually picked out a recognizable tune and looked up at me in something like fear, surprise, and pleasure. I could see he had an aptitude for playing and needed my humble help. Two of the concertina players had asked me to teach them how to play, and one of the company men, who had played at home, asked if he could limber his fingers on the piano occasionally. I agreed to help them all. But because the piano was in the office living room, I had always to arrange for times when the agents did not need the place. Even then, there had been considerable confusion of changed schedules. Finally after a few weeks of being in the way and arranging for lessons at the wrong times, I suggested that the piano be moved to the schoolhouse where it would be accessible to everyone and not bother the SA especially.

"Bother!" the SA thundered. "I brought that piano all the way up here to this godforsaken island for our own pleasure, not the village's. I looked forward to evenings spent listening to good music after all the ugly work is over. That piano is government property. It belongs in Government House. I'll not have it down at the company's schoolhouse where we'd have to traipse to hear it."

"I wanted only to save you the noise and confusion in the office. When I asked you for it, I had no idea of the furor it would cause."

"You don't have to bother with the villagers. Let them send for their own piano."

"Mr. Morgan has. He's rather jealous that you beat him to it. The *St Paul* is to bring one up on its next trip, if there is room. In the meantime, Vicele and the others show so much talent, I've wanted to help them as much as I can while I am still here." I caught myself about to reveal the fact that I would be leaving the islands in August.

"I brought that piano to listen to you play, Elizabeth, you and no one else," he said in no uncertain terms, as if issuing an order. I saw the steely determination in his eyes. "You know, my wife plays beautifully. Her playing has been the one thing I've missed most during my long summers away from home — her playing." His admission showed me a side of him he'd never revealed before, an intimate side of his life. I think he never would have revealed that much except that he felt so strongly about the piano.

"Very well," I said, and I let the matter drop. After that, we had music only in the evenings. I did not tell John of the conversation. He could not deny me the pleasure of playing, nor did he wish to, for he also enjoyed the music. Thus, for once, the three of us sat together in the living room, congenially bound by music. I was just about to thank the piano for drawing us together in a semblance of friendship when John confronted me one night in our room after a particularly relaxing evening of quiet, melodious old favorites.

"Libby," he fumed, "I'll not have you making eyes at that man from across the keys. I'll not have it, I tell you!" I could think of no single instance that could have given John such an idea.

"What do you mean?"

"Tonight — other nights, too — you looked up while you played. You looked up and exchanged meaningful glances, as though you had some secret understanding."

"Oh, John," I tried to laugh it off lightly. "I looked up only to see if he approved of how I play. You see, his wife is an accomplished pianist. I'm afraid that sometimes my poor playing must be torture to him. I just wanted to see whether he approved."

"I've watched him nod and smile to you."

"Of course, if he approved. How else could he let me know?" But I knew that ugly thing called jealousy had attacked my husband. There is nothing one can do or say that alters the disease once it's taken hold. "You know my love for you. How could you question it? And if you don't want me to look up, why, I'll not look up again."

John said no more. But of all times to be jealous again! He knows he has nothing to be jealous of. Jealousy is an evil thing for which I know no remedy. I just hoped that, like everything else, it would wear itself out. The piano wasn't solving our situation after all.

A few days later, I could hear the two arguing in the office over some small detail. Their voices were raised in anger. John came into our room and flung himself down in a chair, exasperated.

"He's such a boor. I hate having any dealings with him," he said loudly, so that if the SA had gone to his room, he could have heard.

"Oh, no, John. He's not that. He's in a difficult situation. That is all."

"There you go, defending *him* again. If anyone's in a difficult situation, I am, and he has put me there."

"What was the argument about this time?" I asked, sighing. There had been so many.

"Novastoshnah again. He's sending me there early in July."

"You knew you'd have to go. The assistant agent always does."

"I know. But I begged him to let me stay here this time, because the men already are getting into an ugly mood, and I felt that you were not safe with them."

"John, you didn't? Why? I'm safe here with Mrs. Mandrigan. Nothing happened last year, as you well know."

"What I really meant was that I don't want to be where I can't get to you immediately. I couldn't tell him why."

"You sound frightened. Has Dr. Kelly been telling you old wives' tales? I know I'll be all right. This isn't the first baby ever to be born."

"It's our first, and I mean to have a well one. I just will not be away from you like I was last year — a whole week without being able to communicate."

"But did you have to raise your voices over the issue?"

"One thing always leads to another when I am with him. Neither of us can keep our tempers down."

No — neither of you can, I thought. *The old animosity is there, lurking just under the surface, waiting to be provoked into open battle — I, the matka provocateur.* Other incidents happened oftener and oftener, warning me. I played less in the evenings, usually alone. Both men left their doors open to listen but, like little boys, tacitly refused to sit in the same room to enjoy the music. Not only the killing season was under full swing, but the breeding season had begun causing a more palpable tension throughout the village, sometimes ominous.

I was sure the SA had prepared reports on John's insubordination. Yet I knew John would not hide behind my pregnancy as an excuse. I felt terrible because, again, I was the cause of the friction. The Novastoshnah supervision was not being solved. I was sure the SA would not give in and do it himself without an overwhelmingly valid reason. I knew John would remain equally adamant. Matters were at this impasse, and the two men virtually growling at each other, when the *Reliance* put in one clear day. I was sitting on the bluff above Nah Speel — sketching the rookeries at a safe distance so I would not be exposed to the sordid scene of animals mating — when the lighter sailed in and Captain Baker walked directly to Government House with several thick envelopes in his hand. As soon as I had finished my sketch, I went in. As I passed the office door, the Senior Agent came to it and handed me the envelopes, all addressed to

John. His lips were tight-pressed, and the steel bars were more than ever firmly fixed in his eyes. I had no opportunity to greet the captain.

I took the dispatches to our room. Each one was official and marked *urgent*. I wondered if I should brave the stench and the sights of the killing ground to take them to John, but I decided against that for fear I would have another period of nausea. So I waited, toying with each envelope in great curiosity. One was from the Treasury Department, one was from the General Land Office — but not from my father's office — and one was from General Allen of the Army Engineering Corps. General Allen was an old, old friend from whom we had not heard in several years.

John saw the letters in my hand when he came in, as usual spattered and reeking of offal. He reached for them avidly and tore each open with trembling hands. I waited silently while he read. He read them in silence and with no expression on his face to give me a clue to their content. Then he jumped up and grabbed me to him, hugging me tight. I could feel the trembling of excitement through his body, a quivering excitement that made him hold me as in a vise.

"We're going home, Libby. We're going home together," he said. "We're going home for good!"

"Oh, John, you haven't broken your contract because of me?"

"No, Libby, no. Here — you can read them for yourself. The Treasury Department is releasing me from my contract, not at my request, but at General Allen's request. The land office also has collaborated, as the work will be coordinated with theirs. Both say they are aware that I might like to be released. This much they gathered from my request to be permitted to go back to Washington with you and serve out my contract time by spending a third summer here."

"I suspected that you had written something of your unhappiness here, but I'd never have thought of the third summer idea. Oh, John, John!"

"I did not mention my unhappiness. Anyone in Washington could gather that from the Senior Agent's reports, I'm sure."

"I'm too excited to read. What is the big job General Allen wants you to do?" Actually tears prevented me from reading the letters John had thrust into my hands.

"An engineering job after my own heart, Libby. I'm to work on the plans for the flood control dams on the Missouri and Red rivers. What pleases me more than anything that has happened these last few years is that General Allen sought *me* for the job. You cannot know what that means to me. He says that he had a bit of a shock when he went calling at Q Street to find me at the other end of the earth."

"Q Street," I said. "Q Street!" I wept openly.

GOVERNMENT HOUSE, St GEORGE ISLAND

"But you shouldn't cry, now that we'll soon be there. General Allen has set things in motion to get me back as soon as possible. The *Reliance* is to put back in here as soon as the killing season is over. It will take us both off the island sooner than you expected to go alone."

"The *Reliance!* That little cutter all the way to San Francisco? We sail back home in that?" I felt nauseated even at the thought.

"It's almost as big as a packet, and I'll warrant it cuts the water better."

"A river packet!" (I began right then to have a tremendous dread of the trip back to the States. The dread lasted only until the *Reliance* brought us here. I'll never question her seaworthiness again, and I am all set to go home aboard the little cutter.) "Do you suppose the Senior Agent knows?"

"He must have received communications in the same pouch. Captain Baker is still with him. They're probably discussing this latest news." But the fact that the Senior Agent had received not one single word, nor even guessed what was in the dispatches, precipitated the whole nightmarish affair.

He and the captain had gone to the Lodge while John bathed and dressed for dinner. The captain had wanted a drink before dinner. Navy men may not have liquor aboard their ships and have to wait until they come ashore to imbibe. I do not believe the Senior Agent has ever taken a drink of an alcoholic beverage while stationed here. I think we'd know. But the genial way in which he departed with the captain, as though he planned to join him, made me think that perhaps for this occasion he might indulge. It is his own business, of course, but it would lower him in our estimation. Sorting through all that happened, I could believe that he did join the captain in a drink or two. The rest of the company men have not always been so moderate. Mr. Morgan has said often that I've been a restraining agent, or matters by this time would be worse. On this particular night, the men had been drinking heavily out of disgust for their work, and they were itching for excitement.

I had a presentiment as we set out for the Lodge that John and his superior would have an altercation over the news. I did not want it to be a public one. For appearance's sake, the two had confined their quarreling to the office or out of earshot of others in the field. They had not wished the company men to know of their animosity, and they always put on a civil front in the men's presence. *Just postpone your anger, dear SA.* But in my heart of hearts, I knew it would be inevitable.

I steeled myself and went in. The cigar smoke and alcohol assailed me, very nearly made me lose my resolve and turn back. I had to swallow hard several times. I said to John under my breath before he released my arm, "Please, please, for my sake, if the

GOVERNMENT HOUSE, St GEORGE ISLAND

Senior Agent starts something, turn away. Don't let an argument get started." John pressed my arm reassuringly. We were met by the announcement that something had gone wrong in the kitchen and dinner would be about a half hour late.

Whenever this happened — not often — I would go to the library end of the hall and find a book to peruse while John joined the men in earnest discussion. I did this not out of snobbishness, but because I felt I had disrupted their lives enough. I tried to be as unobtrusive as possible. So on this occasion, too, I spent some time selecting a book, then sat in the little lounge nook to look it over. I could not help looking up from time to time to see if any fireworks had begun. The SA stood in a group at a little improvised bar at the far end of the room, while John had joined a small group not far from me.

I think, from the way he gestured and the way the other men listened, that he was telling them about the letters he had received. It just happened that one of the men of his group drifted over to the SA's group and, in the course of conversation, must have mentioned what John had just recounted. I saw a look of utter surprise on the SA's face, then a sudden flush of anger. He had indeed been taken unawares. He bellowed across the room to Captain Baker, "Why the hell didn't you tell me Beaman was running out on the Novastoshnah job?"

Captain Baker, midroom, looked equally surprised. Still in the dark, he walked over to the SA and, in a coldly offended voice, asked him what the hell he was talking about. The entire assemblage became suddenly silent, deadly still.

"Beaman's deserting before he's finished his job up here." I could see John turn a gray-white, then red as he swung around to face the SA across the room.

"Sir, I demand that you take that back. This is no place to discuss the orders I've received. I would have discussed them with you and the captain, but you left the office before I could speak to you. As you must know, General Allen issued the orders."

"I'm sure you manipulated your release," the SA sneered.

"I assure you I have never asked to be relieved of the post. Didn't General Allen notify you regarding this matter? The letters are here for you to read." John reached for an inner pocket of his jacket. I could see the SA fuming. He looked as though he would charge John like a mad bull. Others had the same impression, for they moved in close to the two antagonists. Mr. Redpath had rushed to my side.

"The ninny! The pip-squeak — crying to be relieved of Novastoshnah so he can stay here and protect his lady — always more concerned for her than for the job the Treasury Department wants him to do. Well, gentlemen, you all know that I protected her last year, and no harm came to her while he was away." But the way he said it had an innuendo that embarrassed me. Where could such an argument lead but to fisticuffs? I could see the men all ready to restrain the two. John's ire became visible.

"You leave my wife out of this." The two glared at each other over the men's shoulders, then suddenly and at the same moment, both broke from their captors and rushed at each other, fists at the ready and such hatred in their eyes I thought they intended to kill each other.

Just as suddenly I stepped between them.

"Please, please, gentlemen," I stammered. I could think of nothing else to say. I turned to the SA. "John knows why he wanted to stay at Government House instead of Novastoshnah, and it is, indeed, because of me. You see, sir, I am with child, and I will be leaving the islands soon. He wanted to be here to see me off, for it will be a long time before we will see each other again."

I had not meant to give our secret away. I could see John wince at my frankness. I am sure no woman ever had spoken to a man not her husband as I had spoken. I do not know exactly what happened immediately after, for I ran to the door and out into the cool night air. In my swift retreat, I caught only a glimpse of the SA's face — grim and unyielding. How could we ever go on living under the same roof, even for the few weeks left to me? How could I ever leave the island with John alone in that house with the SA?

I felt a strong arm lift under my right arm and support me as I staggered toward Government House.

"Let me walk you home," Dr. Kelly said. "I'm sorry you had to be there. The men will keep the two apart now. I'm sure they'll know how to handle the situation," he added as he left me at the door. John came in some time later. I thought from his silence that he was angry with me for making such a scene about something so sacred to ourselves.

"No, Libby, I am angry with myself for causing you to do what you did. I bless you, dear, for saving us from a fistfight. I do not want to beat the SA, my superior, and I would have, for I am bigger, younger, and stronger. I fear for what I might have done to him." He leaned over and kissed me on the forehead. "Perhaps it is best that everyone knows about us now. They'd have had to know why you would be leaving the islands ahead of me if the letters had not come."

"None of what I did solves your problem with your superior."

"I know. I know." he sighed. "I don't see how the two of us can live under the same roof after tonight."

We were interrupted by a knock on the door. Mr. Morgan and Mr. Redpath wanted to speak with John. They had prevailed upon the SA to stay at the Lodge for the night. He had agreed, and he also had agreed to a solution to the problem here. "We're here to discuss it with you," Mr. Redpath said.

"Gentlemen," said John, "I apologize for that scene down there. It's been brewing for a long time."

"So we've noticed. We're powerless to prevent further trouble. You might as well know that here and now. The SA is a large shareholder in the company. We are working for him, in a sense, just as you are. So you see, our hands are tied."

"I might have known!" said John. He must have suspected something of the sort for a long time, though he never had mentioned his suspicions to me. "I've tried not to precipitate an argument. But there's always been an argument boiling under the surface. I can't see any way to solve the problem as long as we are here."

"Well," Mr. Morgan cleared his throat, "would you and Mrs. Beaman be willing to leave here tomorrow for St George? We can keep the SA at the Lodge that long. It was he who suggested sending you over to St George and bringing Mr. Scribner back here to do the Novastoshnah supervision. He admitted that he can't always keep his temper under control. We knew you regretted your insubordination and told him so. We thought that best."

"You've been more than kind to take our part," said John. "St George is a good idea. It solves the Novastoshnah problem. Yes, St George seems like the very best solution."

John looked to me with a question in his eyes. Did I agree?

"It won't be for long, Libby."

"No. It won't be for long. How do we get there? I dread a company cutter, even on calm waters."

"Captain Baker has offered to stand by to take you there tomorrow. He can take you more comfortably and more safely than in a company cutter. He says he'll just postpone his northern inspection a day or two. Get some rest tonight, Mrs. Beaman. Let Mrs. Mandrigan help you with the packing. Don't rush. Don't get excited. We'll all help however we can. We all have enjoyed your presence among us and will be saying farewell only a few weeks sooner."

I felt infinitely hollow after the men left. I looked at John with a stunned sense of helplessness. So much of our lives had been decided for us in a few short hours. We had no wills of our own, we who should have been strong. John's eyes showed his relief.

Only while I packed the next day did I begin to realize how much of a wrench leaving St Paul actually would be. Not because we might seem to be leaving in disgrace, but because we had, in spite of ourselves, grown into the island, into Government House, and into the lives of these primitive people. I'd almost forgotten the horrors of the seven-week storm in the happiness of approaching motherhood. I'd almost forgotten the echoes of all those altercations in the office in the happiness of having a

GOVERNMENT HOUSE, St GEORGE ISLAND

husband come in from work each day for more than a year. I went about the house, tenderly touching even the most prosaic objects of use during this year. John would have called this foolish sentimentality, but he was not there to see. He had gone to the killing field, knowing his superior was not there. He wanted to say good-bye to the company men and the Aleuts. He had learned to like the men, though he always had hated the place. He will continue to hate the place. Sr Paul Island, Government House, and the Lodge always will represent humiliations he'll want to forget. There are other things about our lives here I never shall forget.

Early the next evening, I had everything packed and carried to the wharf. John walked down the hill beside me for the last time with his head held high, silent. There really wasn't much we could say. I think he was wishing that we could have been spirited aboard the *Reliance* without having to face the village. But the whole village was there. Everyone had been given leave from the killing field in order to say good-bye. We were deeply touched by their little expressions of affection and their small tokens of gratitude, a trait Aleuts seldom show.

Malpha presented me with a baby blanket — which she had stitched so carefully — of alternate diamond-shaped patches of pure white and dark belly fur from seal pups. Around it she had sown a wide border of the rare white fur, truly a beautiful gift and worthy of a czarevitch. I wept over it and hastened to search out several of the little wool things I had been knitting. Malpha would need them soon. We could look into each other's eyes, this primitive girl and I, and understand each other. Each of us is about to become a mother.

Mrs. Mandrigan and Vicele wanted to come with us into our exile. But Tyone Volkov would not let them leave Sr Paul. They belong to Sr Paul. It would upset the balance of things. Until this parting, I hadn't realized how deeply attached I'd become to these simple people and how much a part of our lives they had become. There were the children I had tried to teach, the young people I had tried to help, my old friend George Butrin — who spent hours with me after school perfecting his English — and a host of others. I found myself suddenly wishing a strange wish — that I did not have to leave them.

The company men, sobered by the near fight, shook hands with us and wished us well. Some ventured that they might even look us up in the States. Mr. Morgan said I'd been a good influence on his men. They had cleaned up and dressed each night for dinner. Their manners and their language had improved. They'd all miss having me among them. I smiled at this, knowing how much my presence had disrupted their lives. I'd envisioned the sigh of relief when I left.

I thanked Mr. Morgan and the company for making our lives so

GOVERNMENT HOUSE, Sr GEORGE ISLAND

much more comfortable than I ever had anticipated. I thanked him too for the friendship he had extended and expressed in so many ways, right from the day of our arrival, and for his paternal care of me.

We were just about to step into the little dory Captain Baker had sent for us when Father Paul, in gorgeous robes, came majestically down the wooden pier to its very edge and held a golden cross high over us, pronouncing the Russian blessing on those who are about to depart upon uncertain seas. For all his worldliness and unorthodox ways, he, too, has been very much a part of our lives. We never will forget Father Paul Shishenekoff — never.

One person alone stayed away from the pier. Only one person on the whole island.

For all my anger at his treatment of John and at his duplicity, I can't help admiring the SA, even now. I suspect that his attraction to me — with which he struggled and which he held in check — was as much the source of our problems here as John's independent attitude. And, I must admit, there were times when I was attracted to him as well.

No, my dear SA, there is no way ever to communicate my real thoughts with you now. You never will know what is in my heart as I leave the islands where you did not want me to be. But if you ever should lift the lid of our piano, you will find there a little note addressed to you. It says, quite simply,

Forgive — Elizabeth.

This morning, we came aboard the *Reliance* just after the sun came up. The sun, on one of its eight days of appearance, seemed to want to give us a proper send-off. The waters were so calm they made no thunderous boom against the cliffs. Even the birds were less raucous, as though they were sad that we were leaving the islands.

The motion of the ship as it gently rocks on broad, low swells has not made me seasick. Probably, at last, I've gained my sea legs. I wish our entire passage could be this calm. I was able to stand at the rail aft for a long, long time while the sails filled and began to carry us away from land.

John left me at the rail to go to the bridge. He wants to learn to navigate a sailing vessel. Captain Baker said it is really too late. I detected a nostalgic sadness in his voice. He said that the navy will have installed engines in all its sailing vessels before the year is up and that soon there will be no more sails upon the seven seas. I may have had many firsts to my credit, but now I must record that perhaps I am journeying aboard our very last sailing vessel.

The *Reliance,* though much smaller than the St *Paul* since it does not have to carry cargo, is a trim little vessel with an ample guest stateroom and a wide deck for promenading. The galley and dining saloon are a bit snug for extra passengers such as ourselves. It seems impossible that any ship as small as this can weather — has weathered — the terrific Arctic storms we've experienced while it patrols our possessions in the Bering Sea.

The morning sun I wrote of set the black escarpments into sharp relief, shadow upon darker shadow, as they drifted farther and farther away from us. John, before he left for the bridge, looked long and hard at the polished, perpendicular monoliths. "Libby, how did we ever survive them?"

John is relieved that we are leaving, and I understand perfectly why he feels that way. Oddly enough, I am very sad to be leaving, even though life on these islands has not been easy. I have not forgotten that we nearly died. I have not forgotten the tensions inside Government House. And yet . . . I wish we could stay.

I wish our child could be born amid the stark beauty of these islands and, at least for a while, run through the abundance of flowers whose colors and fragrances seem more precious here than anywhere I have ever been. I wish he could watch the seals, learn the cycle of their lives, perhaps even become their friend. I would spare him the experience of the brutal slaughter, which, even today, I cannot reconcile within myself.

Finally, I wish our child could be exposed to ways of life far removed from Q Street. Life on the Pribilofs is so different — the customs, the languages, the food and clothing. Even though it took some getting used to, I feel honored to have been exposed to this other way of life, to have seen merit in other ways of being, to have been accepted by people so different from me.

This morning, St George loomed like a misty silhouette floating on an opalescent horizon. Then, all too quickly, the island fell over the edge of the world, sliding away in the sunlight. And we were left alone in the vast sea, between ports, between the chapters of our lives.

It is beginning to grow dark — even though it is only August, the Arctic night has begun to creep upon the Bering Sea. No one has come to light the whale-oil lantern. Fortunately we will go ever southward into more and more sun, into more and more light.

What else lies ahead is unknown. We are returning to a familiar way of life, yet who knows how things may have changed at home while we were away. We, most certainly, are not the same.

E.G. 13.

Libby Beaman and Betty John on Q Street.

EPILOGUE

Libby's father died about the time she wrote the last letter home (July 15, 1880). She did not hear of his death until she reached San Francisco where word was waiting to be taken back to her by the *St. Paul*.

The almost "snow baby" was born November 26, 1880, on Q Street in Washington, D.C., a healthy, husky boy. He was my father, Charles Worcester Beaman, who later became Cincinnati's first pediatrician after World War I.

Libby Beaman often spoke of her Pribilof experiences to me as I was growing up. She showed me some of the sketches in her journal, but never allowed me to read the journal itself.

Henry Wood Elliott published *The Fur Seals of the Pribilofs* in 1885. He gave no credit to Libby for her work, mentioning that on his return to St. Paul, he found so many natives, so many company men, two government men, and "one white female." Today a set of his watercolors graces the walls of the rare books library of the Cleveland Museum of Natural History. These watercolors were published in *National Geographic Magazine* in the early 1930s.

The SA, Harrison Gray Otis, returned to California where he became a civic and business leader in Los Angeles. In 1882, he bought a fledgling newspaper, the *Los Angeles Daily Times,* which later became the *Los Angeles Times.*

Libby died in 1932 at the age of 88. What was left of her journal and sketches — torn pages without the red leather cover — came to me after her death. Those pages have been the basis for this book.

Betty John

BETTY JOHN is the author of three children's books, *Hummingbirds, El Capitano Pelicano Cafe,* and *Seloe,* which is based on Libby's notes about the seals' life cycle. She served as a war correspondent during World War II, and her experiences gave rise to her book *Flak Bait.* In addition, she has written plays, magazine articles, and an internationally syndicated medical column.

Betty John is perhaps best known as the founder, with her late husband Dr. Henry J. John, of the first camp for diabetic children. As a designer-craftsman, she has also won international awards for her liturgical enamels. She currently lives in Albuquerque, New Mexico.

LIBBY

Editorial

ANN E. WEISMAN
SALLY DENNISON
HAZEL ROWENA MILLS
MICHAEL HIGHTOWER
PAULETTE MILLICHAP

Picture Research

SALLY DENNISON
ANN E. WEISMAN

Design and Typography

CAROL HARALSON

Production Management

COMAN AND ASSOCIATES

Production

KAREN SLANKARD

Maps

KAREN SLANKARD

Typesetting and Manuscript Preparation

ANN E. WEISMAN
SUSAN COMAN, COMAN AND ASSOCIATES
DONNA SMITH
JUDY CARR
CAROL HARALSON
CLELIA KRIECKHAUS

Special Thanks to
Lenders
of Objects for Illustration

COLONIAL ANTIQUES, JEAN MARIE DENNISON,
CAROL HARALSON, RON MEADOWS,
SCHMIDT'S ANTIQUES, AL "SLIM" STATUM,
RUSSELL STUDEBAKER

Illustrations

FROM THE COLLECTION OF BETTY JOHN:

DRAWINGS BY LIBBY BEAMAN:
13, 54, 62, 63, 67, 70, 81, 83,
92, 99, 117, 132, 137, 170,
171, 176, 181, 182

POSTCARDS OF WATERCOLORS
BY HENRY WOOD ELLIOTT:
51, 126, 177

OTHER: 2, 47–50, 51, 55, 57, 66, 69,
101, 107, 109, 113, 115, 124, 129, 133,
136, 146, 153–155, 157, 159, 184, 186
187, 198, 201

•

FROM THE COLLECTION OF BONNIE WHITE
(LIBBY'S GREAT GRANDDAUGHTER):

DRAWING BY LIBBY BEAMAN:
183

•

FROM THE STEAMSHIP HISTORICAL SOCIETY COLLECTION,
UNIVERSITY OF BALTIMORE LIBRARY,
BALTIMORE, MARYLAND:
11

•

FROM THE COLLECTION OF
THE RUTHERFORD B. HAYES PRESIDENTIAL CENTER,
FREMONT, OHIO:
36, 37

•

FROM THE ALASKA ARTS AND ILLUSTRATIONS COLLECTION,
ALASKA STATE LIBRARY,
JUNEAU, ALASKA:

HENRY WOOD ELLIOTT WATERCOLORS:
55, 64, 65, 86,
94, 96, 175, 180

WORKS BY FREDERICK A. WALPOLE
ON INDEFINITE LOAN FROM THE
SMITHSONIAN INSTITUTION TO THE HUNT INSTITUTE
FOR BOTANICAL DOCUMENTATION,
CARNEGIE–MELLON UNIVERSITY,
PITTSBURGH, PENNSYLVANIA:
84, 108, 121, 130, 134, 147

PHOTOGRAPHIC REPRODUCTION OF LIBBY'S SKETCHES,
HISTORICAL PHOTOGRAPHS, AND DOCUMENTS
BY DAVID BLUST

AIRBRUSHING BY JOHN E. CRUNCLETON JR.

PHOTOGRAPHS BY DON WHEELER, INC.:
13, 14, 17, 20, 21, 23, 29,
39, 46, 48–49, 53, 78, 100,
142, 162, 178–179, 196, COVER

LIBBY IS TYPESET IN BEMBO,
AND PRINTED ON SIXTY-POUND
MOHAWK SATIN, CREAM WHITE TEXT,
WITH TWO INKS.

TYPE IS FROM TYPO PHOTO GRAPHICS, INC.,
TULSA, OKLAHOMA.

PRINTING IS BY WALSWORTH PRESS, INC.
IN MARCELINE, MISSOURI.